Troubling Play

Troubling Play

Meaning and Entity in Plato's *Parmenides*

Kelsey Wood

State University of New York Press

Published by
State University of New York Press, Albany

For information, address State University of New York Press,
194 Washington Avenue, Suite 305, Albany, NY 12210-2384

Production by Judith Block
Marketing by Susan Petrie

Library of Congress Cataloging-in-Publication Data

Wood, Kelsey, 1960–
    Troubling play : meaning and entity in Plato's Parmenides / Kelsey Wood.
        p. cm.
    Includes bibliographical references and index.
    ISBN 0-7914-6519-5 (hardcover : alk. paper)
    1. Plato. Parmenides.   2. Ontology.   3. Dialectic.   I. Title.

B378.W66 2005
184–dc22

2004027304

10 9 8 7 6 5 4 3 2 1

This book is dedicated to the memory of J.N. Findlay

Contents

Prologue

"As things are I can, for example, invent a game that is never played by anyone.—But would the following be possible too: mankind has never played any games; once, however, someone invented a game—which no one ever played?"
        —Ludwig Wittgenstein, *Philosophical Investigations*

The Unity of Logos

The *Parmenides* seems to lend support to Heidegger's claim that Platonism is the beginning of a tradition of forgetting the question of being and privileging a 'metaphysics of presence.'[1] For the dialogue shows the *eidos* to be the one in many that that makes experience intelligible. However, Plato's figure of Parmenides just as decisively undercuts the notion of ideal presence by making it clear that form is not in itself knowable; for if the *eidē* allow assimilation of particulars in complete synthesis, this formal universality would strip, not only sensible particulars but also the form of its singularity.

In this pivotal Platonic dialogue, Parmenides makes time (*chronos*) thematic in order to show young Socrates how the notion of participatory being is decisively not to be understood: as if *eidos* occupies a distinct locus (*chōra*) apart from worldly entity.[2] The key issue in this dialogue is time, for it is primarily by way of interrogating the being of time that Parmenides reduces to absurdity Socrates' initial conception of the forms (which would have played into Heidegger's critique), and develops paradoxes that effectively invalidate the notion of form as ideal presence.

This recurring Platonic theme—that being cannot be thought—explains why the pivot of the *Parmenides* (155e–157b) is a demonstration for young Socrates that there can be no instant of univocity: we cannot intelligibly claim that a singular moment (*exaiphnēs*) of time exists. A close look at Parmenides' dialectical game (137c–166c) reveals its profoundly negative character, and shows how the failures of conceptual discourse—

1

especially in relation to time—ultimately justify Socrates' analogical approaches to being and the good.

At the outset, a young and enthusiastic Socrates attempts to resolve Zeno's paradoxes by claiming that there exists an *eidos* in itself (*kath' hauto*) of likeness, and another of unlikeness. *Auto kath' hauto* (128e9) means "itself, according to itself." Socrates distinguishes the form apart from the entity that instantiates it, and urges that real entities derive their being from these ideal entities.

Socrates argues that he himself is many, insofar as his right side and his left side are different (*hetera*). He is one, however, insofar as he is one among seven persons in the room (129c–d). Since Socrates' own identity and divisibility seem to him so obviously compatible, he is not overly impressed by Zeno's paradoxes. Socrates insists that the intelligible form (*eidos*) of the entity is not subject to such minglings and divisions, although he believes that all the many other things (*ta alla*)—things other than the form—do manifest opposing characters (128e7–130a3). Socrates initially attempts to defend (at 129a–134e) a theory of ideas similar to that which was later criticized by Aristotle (the philosopher). It is this misguided effort—Socrates' attempt to ground being and knowing in the positive existence of the form—that is the impetus for Parmenides' remedial dialectical game. Parmenides' demonstration will show that Socrates' conception of the separate existence of the intelligible implies a hypostatization, or reification of the idea. In what follows, Parmenides successfully reduces to absurdity the notion that an *eidos* exists separately as the original of which the phenomenon is a likeness.

Parmenides' troubling performance is intended to show Socrates the impasses implicit to the dichotomy between intelligible meaning and entity. He leads Socrates to the insight that although existence implies analogical correlation, nevertheless, for intelligibility, such correlation is simply incoherent. And though Parmenides shows that intelligibility involves universal forms or types that disclose the inconsistency of analogical indications of existence, he also demonstrates that intelligibility itself implies a moment of pure particularity or singularity that cannot be thought according to universals. Parmenides names this singular moment of nonconsistency *to exaiphnēs*, "the instant" (155e–157b).

Moreover, in Parmenides' dialectical game, meaning is produced by relations of difference; his demonstration exhibits a negative logic, the goal of which is the silencing of reason in a moment of paradox. This silencing is indicated both dramatically and argumentatively in the dialogue. Socrates' last lines are at 136d—followed by thirty pages of dialogue in which he is silently but actively engaged—for the purpose of Parmenides' game is the training of Socrates.

Parmenides accomplishes this by leading the silently attentive Socrates into the problematic ambiguities between the singularity and universality of form. If unification is lived as analogical correlation, nevertheless, empirical hypotheses and the syntheses of imagination (*eikasia*) they imply are—for thinking—simply unintelligible juxtapositions. But more significantly, intelligibility, in itself, implies this unintelligibility: for if the notion of logical identity requires the nontemporal instant, still this odd nonpresence simply cannot be made intelligible. In this way, the *Parmenides*, like the central analogies of the *Republic*, indicates that the conditions of possibility of intelligibility are not in themselves intelligible.

The *Parmenides* shows that what is still commonly referred to as Plato's theory of forms can be rescued only if it is a descriptive account that indicates the nature of logos to be dialogical, not monological. Parmenides demonstrates modes of logos that imply both the universality of form as well as the particularity of a present manifestation, and then discloses a paradoxical moment of dialectical reflexivity, or intercontextuality. His troubling game indicates that if unity is (137c-160b), then problematic ambiguities of universality and singularity infuse both logical and empirical disclosure. But if the one is not (cf. 160b-166c), disclosure without conceptual unification still prefigures the way up and the way down of reflexive intercontextualization. If one is not, the many are still organized into apparent unities by the imagination (164b-165a). But if such analogical correlations can occur apart from intelligible unifications, does this imply that indications of existence are more fundamental than expressions of identity?

Parmenides demonstrates for Socrates that although these modes of disclosure may apparently be unproblematically distinguished, this distinction may neither be simply eliminated nor completely developed. Paradoxically, the forms that reduce particularity to universality, or sameness, also allow recognition of irreducible difference (*to heteron*). And when it is rigorously interrogated, the distinction between the timeless meaning of propositions and the temporal course of statements is undermined (155e-157b). Both the *Parmenides* and the central analogies in the *Republic* indicate that modes of logos and being ultimately elude categorial analysis, for being is inherently ambiguous. The manifestation of being in and through logos is simultaneously a movement in the *psuchē* (life, soul) and in the entity that is disclosed; furthermore, such participatory being is inherently finite.

The *Parmenides* not only develops the notion of movement in the *psuchē*—the transfiguration of the whole that is the goal of ironic dialectic—the dialogue, if read attentively, produces this movement.[3] Platonic dialogue acknowledges the limits of *alētheia* (truth, disclosure) offering the occasional glimpse at the origins of being through the limit and veil of logos, not through direct manifestation. If the dialogue that is philosophy discloses many senses of being, then its discourse must be as slippery as water, as evanescent as an instant of time. In the *Parmenides*, Eleatic negative dialectic (e.g., reduction to absurdity) discloses the ambiguity of existence and thereby indicates the necessity of analogical discourse.

Although he is critical of Socrates' untrained analogies at the outset (e.g., 131b-c, 132b-c, 132d-133a), Parmenides himself initiates the denouement of his dialectical game by illustrating the fundamental role played by preconceptual syntheses of the imagination. His game indicates, on the one hand, that analogical unifications can occur even when conceptual unification does not; on the other hand, conceptual unification does not occur entirely apart from—but only in opposition to—analogical unifications. Significantly, this precognitive potentiality of disclosure is evoked by means of analogical references to painting and dreaming (see 164d and 165c).

Parmenides' invokes, for Socrates, a strange juxtaposition; he shows that the intelligibility of what exists intimately involves what does not exist; intelligibility is curiously permeated by unintelligibility. The dialogue indicates that the ratio, which is rationality, is not to be understood as a harmonious and univocal synthesis. Instead, the proportion that is the participation of idea and thing, of meaning and entity, is shown to be ruptured throughout by *chōrismos* (separation). The *Parmenides* demonstrates that the ideal substitution of *metalambanein* simply cannot be understood as assimilation in complete synthesis, for participatory being involves an odd bartering, or exchange.[4] This trafficking produces unintelligibility even as it allows intelligibility. Parmenides repeatedly demonstrates that the "otherwise than" (*chōris*) of the form makes it unknowable in itself.

Although the dialogue expresses this oddity through logical argumentation—primarily the reduction to absurdity—more importantly, the *Parmenides* indicates the transcendence of the form poetically, insofar as the form of the dialogue itself eludes schematism. The text is illuminated by a unity of theme and structure that is remarkably clear and beautiful, but this omnipresent unifying form is never really present; for Parmenides initiates Socrates into philosophy by miming sophistry and therefore indicating the being (*to on*) of philosophy only by contrast, in a negative way.

The true nature of philosophy is shown to reside in, not unambiguous, universal method, but rather in an ironic and indirect *meta hodos*, or "passage beyond." The *Parmenides* shows that the being of philosophy absolutely transcends *mimēsis*, or representation: this being informs the whole text, and yet it is indicated negatively, by contrast. None of Parmenides' ironic repetitions of reasoning (*logismos*) in the dialogue adequately express the being of philosophy, for disclosure of being in logos implies not only repetition (*dierchomai*) but also the paradoxical discontinuity of *chōris*. Philosophy is shown to be the way beyond schematism to a negative dimension of existence that eludes conceptualization.

In the introductory passages of the dialogue (127e–136d), a very young Socrates seeks to learn about the relation between, on the one hand, beings (*ta onta*) and, on the other, the forms of conceptual thought (*noēsis*) and arguments (*tōn logōn*). In what follows, Parmenides demonstrates a highly unusual form of exercise, a troublesome play[5] intended to help Socrates avoid misunderstanding the role of the ideas. This demonstration of philosophy as a provocative dialectical game is the main body of the dialogue (137c–166c). But it is the pervasive—though often neglected—mood of irony that enables Parmenides' troubling play to open the doubtful questions as to what the role of the ideas might be in our interactions with actual entities.

Is it the case, for example, that logos (reason, account, or word) is determined by our encounters with beings? Or is it rather that the inflections of logos circumscribe and condition our grasp of the world? Alternatively, are mind, language, and world reciprocally informed in the effort to achieve commensuration? It is apparent at the outset that questions about how language refers to entities cannot be resolved without also considering how humans interact with each other and with other beings.

It may seem reasonable to believe, as the young Socrates initially does, that nontemporal intelligible meanings are foundational in human interactions with temporal entities (129a–130a). However, if we follow up this assertion with an inquiry into discourse itself (as the Platonic Parmenides does), we learn that even the effort to focus the inquiry on logos leads inevitably to questions about existence and time. But if questions about time and being are related in a fundamental way to questions about how language facilitates knowing, then it cannot simply be the case that linguistic signs determine our grasp of the world. Parmenides shows Socrates that the role of the intelligible form is not foundational in experience insofar as visible objects simply cannot be understood as the images of ideal originals that exist separately. Is the *eidos* the universal? Parmenides' troubling game indicates a sense in which it neither is nor is not.

This surprising result not only implies that for Plato, logos is derivative and being is more fundamental; moreover, Parmenides' game shows Socrates that although existence and language are unified in some way, the ideal substitution that is *metalambanein* implies an irreducible incommensurability (*to mē metechon*). Consequently, Plato's *Parmenides* forces the apparently un-Platonic conclusion that being is not reducible to the forms (*eidē*).[6] Parmenides begins by assuming a distinction between meaning and entity, but his demonstration is an undermining and an overcoming of this very distinction. But Parmenides does not simply reduce meaning to entity or vice versa, but instead indicates something more fundamental that both meaning and entity share.

We begin to get a sense of the strangeness of this metaphor of sharing (*metechein*) by considering that, if language—taken as an interconnected system of signs that refer to signs—determines our interrelations with entities, then the presence of entities would be derivative, and differences in the interrelations of signs would be more originary. The being of entities, on this view, would be a result of the activity of differentiation inherent to signification itself. This would imply that we do not confirm meaning in ongoing interactions with entities by means of their presence to sensibility. Plato's *Parmenides* initially seems to support this construal, insofar as pure identity, or self-presence in an instant (*exaiphnēs*), is shown to imply an irreducible *heteron*, or heterogeneity (143b–157b).

But if otherness or difference is implicit to any disclosure, then there can be no signification pure and simple. Why should the possibility of representation in speech (logos) or writing (*gramma*) belong intrinsically to physical presence? Can things be conceived apart from the signs that represent them? But language involves references to its own system, as well as to the nonexistent past and future. If no instant of pure identity is possible, and meaning is a function of differences between signs, then there are no positive terms, and no self-identical presence (*ousia*). If repetition implies discontinuity, then no form has intelligible presence. But how could general terms possibly refer to objects if there are no self-identical forms? This seems to imply that intelligibility cannot be or be intelligible. Significantly, Parmenides eliminates this inference at the outset, suggesting to Socrates that it would be like using discourse to deny the possibility of discourse (135b–c). Still, we seem to be faced with a choice between an implicitly contradictory account of intelligibility and a paradoxical assertion of unintelligibility.

Plato's *Parmenides* indicates a third possibility, a third way beyond this dilemma. Put simply, the *chōris* (differently from, otherwise than) of the *eidos* in itself does not mean that it has no mode of truth whatsoever. Nor does it mean that the *ideai* exist separately somewhere. Parmenides shows Socrates that true relations of ideas are not sufficient for meaning: expression of identity can never disambiguate itself. But if the idea does not admit of unequivocal definition, this is because logos and existence are interpenetrations.

The *Parmenides* shows that very general oppositions transcend definition precisely because they are fundamental to the process of discursive definition itself. The troubling play Parmenides demonstrates for Socrates indicates that these pairs of opposed *archai* (beginnings, origins) are signposts of the bounds of being. But an *archē* may not be thought: the fundamental oppositionality with which thought begins may be given various names, but each of these singular terms is defined (ambiguously) in opposition to its other, by way of differences of function within an ideal nexus.

Moreover, the ideal matrices themselves share in this indefinable heterogeneity. The form has singular meaning in dialectical differentiation from more fundamental *archai* oppositions, in differentiation from other forms, and by contrast with its own various instantiations; for the disclosure of any particular meaning occurs only within the context of human orientations toward entities in the world.[7] The upshot is that a complete matrix of ideas—an ideal whole—cannot be thought, not even by a god.[8] Furthermore, we do not know the *archai*, but live them; we cannot think fundamental oppositionality, but we cannot think without it. In the Platonic dialogues, the good is Socrates' name for this precognitive ontological vectoring. Because the good as *telos* (goal) informs all disclosure from beyond presence, existence itself is teleological: a single moment (*nun*) implies reference to the future and to the past.

If it is a matrix of ideas in the context of goal-oriented existence that yields intelligibility, then being is participatory; for as sensed, the form of being involves more than its present perception. *Eidos* is the intelligible meaning that exceeds present perceptions. And yet there is no perception without meaning. Participatory being is the one in many that unifies present perceptions but necessarily implies more than what is present. This exceeding of presence is the transcendence of existence in Socratic accounts of the good. Transcendence refers to the odd circumstance that, although to be is to be an idea, still what the idea signifies is, in itself, nothing to us: Parmenides repeatedly emphasizes that apart from all extensional correlations, the intensional space of the *eidos* is empty of intelligibility and being.

But this empty nothingness signifies significance itself: the disclosure (*alētheia*) of being manifests itself as a tension-laden opening of perimetry and *apeiron*.

It is thus not only pure unity and pure plurality that the *Parmenides* shows to be ultimately indefinable. The implication is that no *eidos* is knowable, taken as something single; it is an entire nexus of *eidē* within participatory, temporal being that allows knowing. What is pure negativity—or dialectical differentiation—for thought is analogical correlation for precognitive existence. But because preconceptual differentiations—ontological vectorings—are conditions of possibility for thought, even if a god could grasp all relations of ideas this would still not be *epistēmē* (134d–e). Modes of temporal manifestation vary depending on the being that one encounters; nevertheless, Parmenides' reductions to absurdity leave open the possibility that time is not the grounding principle of being and intelligibility. If there can be no instant of univocity—no unmixed presence—then it is the finite manifestations of participatory being that structure *chronos* and *chōra* (place), and allows disclosure in logos.

Because Parmenides' dialectical game reveals the forms to be defined by their differences in relation to one another, this dialogue parallels, in many ways, recent efforts to overcome metaphysics. It is therefore no accident that critiques of Platonism are unable to incorporate the *Parmenides*: an ironic dialogue that articulates a logos of logos by way of negative dialectic proves formidably resistant to deconstruction. The mood of playful irony that predominates and is made manifest by the provocative suggestion of sophistry prohibits taking Parmenides' conclusions at face value. But more significantly, the third beginning (155e–157b), if it is a distinct beginning in its own right, undermines the organization of the eightfold hypothetical inquiry outlined by Parmenides at 136a–c. A further complication arises from the fact that the coherence of the method is internally violated, in that the two ostensibly distinct modes of disclosure that articulate its structure interpenetrate one another. The fact that Parmenides is unable to keep these two orientations separate (*chōris*) indicates that Socrates' initial distinction may neither be dispensed with nor rigorously developed and maintained. The third beginning on the instant shows precisely why this distinction may not be completely developed.

But the eightfold hypothetical method Parmenides uses to test Socrates' untrained distinction is violated from the outset. Therefore, to understand the import of Parmenides' game, we must acknowledge that the troublesome play contains more returns to the beginnings than the eight called for by the manner of training briefly outlined at 135d–136c.

Not only does the third beginning (155e–157b) exceed this eightfold hypothetical method, but, in addition to the central inquiry into the instant there is also another reorientation, beginning at 143a5, that has never been satisfactorily incorporated in any previous interpretation of Parmenides' allegedly systematic reasoning. If this reorientation as well as the instant are named beginnings and enumerated, this would make ten returns to the *archai*, rather than the eight called for by Parmenides' initial projection. And, strictly speaking, because the two thematic modes of disclosure interpenetrate in every section, there are indefinitely many returns. Why does Parmenides exceed his own projected schema? It is primarily because the instant cannot be assimilated in any intelligible way that the form of the dialogue as a whole, eludes representation.

The only method consistently employed in this dialogue, and the only form of discourse that survives the test of irony, is the incessant and provocative exposure, by means of philosophical reflection, of the limited legitimacy of all forms of logos. The most methodical aspect of Plato's questioning of being is the repeated evocation of the incompleteness of various modes of logos, including finally the dialectical mode. It is important to remember that our fragmentary understanding of the Parmenides poem is very different from the "father Parmenides"[9] that Plato knew. But because Plato's figure of Parmenides demonstrates a negative Zenonian dialectic, does this imply that Platonic dialectic is also negative in that discloses the limitations of positive dialectic? The interpretation of the dialogue's central inquiry into time holds the answer to this question; for the impossibility of any univocal account of the instant shows that all repetition implies discontinuity. This result indicates that for Plato, the question of being is evoked by a dialectic that is *apophatic*, or negative insofar as it clears the way for its own supplement: philosophical *poiēsis*.

Parmenides initiates Socrates into a rigorous and imaginative ontological play, an effort to meditate on the incomprehensible nonpresence that accompanies the inevitable privileging of the present now (*nun*).[10] The dialogue evokes conceptual systems repeatedly, but only to playfully show their inadequacies. The *Parmenides* is an exuberant but dangerous gymnastics for the mind that leads beyond the *eidē* to nonrepresentable dimensions of time and being.

If, in earlier dialogues, word and deed are positively correlated, nevertheless Parmenides' inquiry into *chronos* (time) shows that, for thinking, the unfolding of truth must be said to happen in a negative way. Positive correlations are thrown into question insofar as the notion of pure presence in an instant undermines the intelligibility it purports to explain. But if a dialectical approach to being proves to be inadequate, then even Parmenides' negatively dialectical strategy must be supplemented; for it only clears the way for a moment of insight that simply cannot be put into words.

The Sign Language of Philosophy

In the play *The Miracle Worker* about Helen Keller and her gifted and determined teacher, Anne Sullivan, the most memorable scene depicts the moment of insight when Helen grasps the connection between the gestures her teacher makes in the palm of her hand and the previously unnamable world.

Helen Keller was almost nineteen months old when she was left blind and deaf by a prolonged fever. But before then she had been a precocious infant and had learned to say several words, among them "water." All the subsequent years of her childhood were spent in the darkness and silence of a world without language and therefore without community. It was only when her teacher took Helen to the water pump that the doors of recollection swung open. She put one of the girl's hands under the flowing water and repeatedly pressed the signs for water into Helen's other hand. In a moment, the child's whole life changed, and the painful and frustrating mystery of her existence blessed her with the promise of understanding. It was at this point that Helen Keller's furious tantrums ceased: she developed a lasting friendship with her teacher, and eventually became an extraordinarily gifted teacher herself.

Unless the child relates the gesture to an experience, she has no insight into the unity or identity of any sign; there is no sign and no communication without this reference to lived context. But this always evolving context involves a nexus of significant interrelations.[11] Furthermore, it implies fundamentally different modes of temporality based in different modes of being: for what is abstracted from the indefinitely repeatable sign, when it is considered in itself, is precisely the lived temporal context, or interconnected matrix of signification, that allows gesture to be present as sign. In this sense, learning a language is acquiring both a self and a world.[12] Before the dramatic moment of insight depicted in the play, Anne Sullivan formed gestures in the palm of the child's hand and Helen mimicked bits of the sequences. But such merely mimetic unifications do not grasp the form; initially, for example, the end of one set of gestures might be grafted onto the beginning of another.

And even when regularity is recognized and correctly mimicked, there remains the problem of isolating the significance of the repetition. We acquire a familiarity with instances where the sign is expected and in fact occurs, as well as cases where it might be expected to occur though it does not. Language use is analogous to the performance of music in that repetition in a context allows differentiation of the scale (*Philebus* 17d). But recognizing cases where the repetition is not expected is an implicit part of this process as well. Revisions of understanding also occur by way of the dead ends of communication: the impasse (*aporia*) indicates the inadequacies of anticipations of possibility. Learning involves transcendence—the exceeding of presence—insofar as the idea exceeds its present instantiation; meaning implies a productive ambiguity or excess that transforms the whole. This transcendence, this possibility of further disclosure, is not explained by conceiving it as either "presence here" or "absence here but presence somewhere else." Intelligibility implies an odd nonpresence that is neither simply presence nor the absence of nonconsciousness.

This moment of formative insight at the water pump is evocative of the dialectical method of collection and division as employed in the *Sophist* and the *Statesman*; for behind the ironic examples of *diaeresis* (division, reckoning) given in these dialogues, a genuine hermeneutical strategy is indicated. Learning seems to involve this type of sorting procedure: as Aristotle reminds us, we are educated when we recognize the forms implicit in the phenomena. One might generate examples endlessly of correspondences like these, for the single most fundamental theme in Plato's dialogues is formative insight: learning itself. And yet Platonic dialogue is *erotic* insofar as the pursuit of wisdom involves an attraction toward something that withholds itself, something that exceeds intelligibility. The most fundamental questions do not admit of unequivocal answers.

The *Parmenides*, which this essay examines in some detail, is an example, not so much of Plato's late ontology, but of that reforming of the *psuchē* which is the goal of philosophical education as indicated in the *Republic*.[13] But because Plato's Socratic Parmenides playfully exceeds the limitations of logos in order to evoke the inexpressible, this reforming might be expressed as the conversion away from the stability and reliability of intelligible form and toward the groundlessness of time. The transformative moment of insight facilitated by Socratic dialogue is disclosed, not as an acquiring of new facts, but rather as a reformative remembering of what was somehow always already implicit. The fact that the dialogues in general, and the *Parmenides* in particular, apparently end in failure, or inconclusively, or even in contradiction, indicates the difficulties in achieving and teaching this transformative insight. But the greatest difficulty, according to Parmenides, is the fact that the "otherwise than" (chōris) of eidē would appear to make them unknowable (133b).

Because Parmenides (like Socrates in the *Republic*), highlights the "otherwise" of being, existence for Plato is not reducible to a system of interrelated eidē: for example, the *archai* oppositions that negative dialectic discloses are not themselves forms. The *Parmenides* articulates a logos of logos, but in a primarily negative way: Parmenides reduces to absurdity the notion that any one may be thought apart from the many.

Formative insight occurred for Helen Keller by means of a developing dialogue with her teacher, repeated in a multitude of situations and shifting contexts that were unified by the goal of learning. This learning was for the good both of teacher and student, as well as Helen's concerned family. Helen Keller's life-changing insight did not occur until one of the unified gesture sequences—the term intended to signify water—latched onto her present experience.

Her teacher's gestures—that had been meaningless intrusions— became a voice and spoke to her, confinement opened onto a whole world of organically interrelated meanings, and existence changed utterly in a moment. In a new openness to the other, she gained a self and a world. Existence prior to such insight is not a world that we can remember or imagine. In a sense we are not even alone before initiation and training in language—we are inexpressibly neither there nor somewhere else—an incommunicable and unfree way of existing, something like what Plato's Socrates evokes in the familiar parable of the prisoners in the cave. But when her teacher's gestures became a voice and drew her out, genius spoke through Helen Keller's hands.

Plato's *Parmenides* evokes the paradoxical moment of insight in which a particular is recognized and known. The only way the individual moment can signify is in relation to a whole of signification, but this whole can never be repeated or made present all at once, in an instant. Parmenides paradox of the instant (to exaiphnēs) shows why any particular—if it exists and can be known—is also a whole that is never present.

Can we believe in that which transcends our understanding? And yet somehow the discourse of philosophy, like the life-changing insight communicated at the water pump, discloses what-is to rational investigation. But if discourse is to open up the nature of disclosure itself then it must be as slippery as water, as evanescent as an instant. For the changing entities in nature flow away from us, and we too flow away: our names are writ in water. Yet in order for us to know these things about time, and about ourselves, in order for us to know anything at all, something must abide.[14] Philosophy, as Socrates indicates in the closing lines of the *Cratylus*, is the inspired, frustrating, and relentless search for what abides. Remembering speechlessly, the philosopher seeks the forgotten language, the abiding key to the mysteries of time and death, of love and community.

Community and Catastrophe

In Attic tragedy during Plato's lifetime, the Dorian dances of the chorus suggested a unified mode of existence. Accompanied by the *aulos* (flute) of Dionysus, rather than the lyre of Apollo, chorus sings and thinks and moves together, *in unison*; even the noun is singular. The tragic flaw that leads to destruction of the individual and of the polis is the forgetting of this organic interconnectedness that is whole as well as part; this is the occasion when pride misses the mark on the side of excess. Opposition between individuals—the erotic striving for personal success, honor, and excellence—within the unifying wholeness of social and political practice, enhances the well being of the polis.[15] Would the public dramatic festivals have occurred without the rich citizen, the *chorēgos*, who defrayed the great costs of bringing out the chorus? This was an honorable and personally enriching way of paying one's taxes, and the prize in the fierce rivalry in bringing out choruses (*chorēgikos*), was the greatest of all prizes, the prize we pay to the gods: the esteem of the polis.

Irony in *Oedipus the Tyrant* hinges on the fact that the audience, the polis, shares an insight that the arrogant and independently-minded individual is incapable of perceiving. The blindness of hubris is remedied when the proud egoism of the atomic consciousness pays the penalty and is merged back into the whole. In this twilight, boundary moment of ego-dissolution, Dionysus emerges, is remembered, and honored. Tragedy is in this way emblematic of the fullness of disclosure that is *alētheia*. But the gestalt signified by chorus and the Dorian dance suggests an archaic interlinkage of human action, a mode of coexistence; and Dionysian ecstasy signifies pure active engagement: an existential unification in opposition that precedes the individuation of conscious thought. The moment of *poiēsis* from which philosophy arises already indicates the sign function of human praxis, prior to expressions of logical identity.[16]

But if the unity of actual mind involves logical identity, and this arises in opposition to potential mind—as interlinkage of action—then the god's retributive ego-destruction is isomorphic with the transcendence facilitated by philosophical dialogue. For like the tragedy, the Platonic dialogue also demonstrates the consequences of forgetting this unified—but oddly mixed—wholeness that exceeds the sum of its individual parts. The implicit absurdities of conceptual thought are overcome by reflection on the question of being: insight into what-is involves seeing through the limitations of discursive reasoning.

Such learning involves remembering the interrelational nexus that is one dimension of human being. In Greek tragedy, self-transcendence and the overcoming of arrogance are shown to be impossible without proper regard for the being of other individuals, the laws of the *polis*, and of the gods. Similarly, such reflective consideration of the other allows the self-critique and development of soul that is the Socratic life. We remember the organic interconnectedness of being through dialogue because transcendence is initiated by philosophical encounter with that which is utterly otherwise. Because learning involves this moment of self-transcendence, Socratic piety is distinguished from both an unthinking conformity and an arrogant egoism.

The tragic dilemma is that whatever the individual chooses as individual is wrong: Agamemnon chooses whether to relinquish his command or sacrifice his own daughter; Orestes interprets Apollo's oracle to mean that piety requires him to murder his own mother. And Oedipus privileges himself above all others and single mindedly persists in detecting the murderer of Laios because his power as *turannos* is based on the fact that only he was able to save Thebes from the Sphinx. But the unified being of the chorus is opposed to the individual existences of the protagonist and the antagonist. Moreover, one of the ways these latter are differentiated from each other consists in their different ways of relating (or failing to relate) to the chorus. These contrasts between opposed ways of to be (or not be) develop and alter as the tragedy unfolds. Insofar as it implies the juxtaposition of opposed modes of being, Greek drama evokes an ontological dimension.

The peculiar power of tragedy, which gives it its fateful character, lies in its disclosure of paradoxical modes of existence, practices and situations in which ego-enhancement inevitably brings ego-destruction. Like Aeschylus and Sophocles, Plato demonstrates consequences of the forgetting of the oddly juxtaposed mixture of the wholeness that is human being. The singularity of hubristic praxis arises in opposition to the shapes and relations of a whole that exceeds representation. The dialogues indicate, in a variety of ways, that the simple conceptual opposition between individual self-interest and the interest of the group is itself formed and transformed by the striving toward the good. Because the good, like justice, proves to be not only immanent, but also transcendent, the inadequacies of definitions and the dilemmas that Socrates evokes in the dialogues are reductions to absurdity. But the irony hinges on giving the priority to conceptual thought rather than to being, for both the relativism of the sophists and the materialism of the atomists implicitly assume this priority of epistemology.[17]

Consequently, the *aporia* (impasse) revealed by way of Socratic refutation is overcome by remembering the whole that is more than the sum of its parts: the interrelated and teleological, or goal-oriented nature of being toward the good. Problems of existence and knowing that appear to be simply irresolvable to certain later philosophers are staged, illuminated, and transformed in the Platonic dialogues against this scene of individual action (*ergon*) within a whole socio-political and axio-ontological context.

Synopsis

The following are some of the questions that guide this inquiry. How does the theme of time relate to the distinct employments of logos that articulate Parmenides' ironic and playful performance? What is the precise function of the dialogue's third beginning, the discourse on the instant (155e–157b)? What is the role of irony in the dialogue, and why are so many of Parmenides' arguments equivocal—is it not possible to avoid both contradiction and ambiguity? If, as the *Phaedrus* indicates, participation in living dialogue is the way to actively engage the learner, why does Plato portray Socrates as silent during Parmenides' demonstration? In other words, if logos is the mediator between the world of the sign in itself and the factual contextuality of human existence, what role could a purely individual dimension of existence play in this process? And is there a relationship between the implications of the discussion of the one in this dialogue and the discussion of the unity of the *psuchē* and the social *ethos* (custom, habit) in the *Republic*? If so, how did Plato conceive the link between the axiological[18] and the ontological?

The dialogue indicates that this provocative encounter with a great philosopher stimulates one of the young interlocutors to develop into another great philosopher. We are not to forget, however, that the other young man turns away from philosophy and becomes a *turannos*. The young Aristotle, future member of the Thirty Tyrants, dutifully accepts the suggested protocol and does not dispute the utterances of the revered Parmenides, no matter how apparently contradictory or equivocal these provocations are.[19] But equivocation cannot have been the entire story. We are informed by Plutarch that Parmenides—who is presented by Plato as fabricating this provocative web of paradox—organized his native Elea by the best laws, so that each year the citizens required the officials to swear that they would abide by Parmenides' laws.[20] Based on this clue, what may we reasonably infer regarding Socrates' affirmation in the *Republic* of the relation between philosophical inquiry and political responsibility?

In the *Republic* a mature Socrates offers (after a show of reluctance) the familiar but elaborate likenesses in which well-formed habit (*hexis*) is compared to the sun that illumines and sustains all beneficial disclosure of ideas (509a). But what remains implicit is that this origin of intelligibility is not itself accessible by the very modes of logos that it informs. Socrates says he cannot speak of the good in reference to itself, for we have no knowledge of this (505a6–7). But he will speak of its useful and true offspring (506e4 ff.). And yet these offspring seem to be both good and bad (505c9-d1). This ambiguity of the offspring of the good was already indicated (e.g., at 408d ff.) in Socrates' remarks that familiarity with what is good for humans is gained also by experience of what is bad for them. If we have no knowledge of the good itself and dialogue involves *poiēsis* and imagery, still these are images made philosophical by the process of discursive reflection in which they arise.

But it is not initially apparent how the troublesome play of the *Parmenides* might be related to the philosophical education described in the *Republic*.[21] Parmenides' dialectical game will show that this training (*gumnasia*) cannot be conceived as a univocal curriculum. If geometry is one of its prerequisites, the game (*paidia*) nonetheless involves a sustained effort to disclose the arbitrariness of the starting points of all nonphilosophical discourses. In this respect, Parmenides' game parallels Socrates' efforts in the *Republic* (e.g., at 510b–511d), to disclose the power of dialogue: *tē tou dialegesthai dunamei* (511b4). Philosophy discloses the beginnings (*archai*), the assumptions (*tōn hupotheseōn*), and the privileging in other modes of disclosure.[22] But more significantly, Parmenides' game develops beyond its own allegedly hypothetical method; in this way his negative version of dialectic ultimately throws open to critique philosophical rationality itself. The implication is that it is by means of irony and other performances of nonliteral discourse that we discern the way of philosophy, the way beyond the limitations of logos. Philosophy is the way of *alētheia* (truth, disclosure); it is not in spite of, but by means of the irony of the dialogue that we achieve insight.

Chapter 1 initiates the development of the theme of the juxtaposition of modes of disclosure by noting some general features of philosophical reflection as manifested in the *Republic* and the *Parmenides*. The

discussion in chapter 2 indicates in what sense the philosophical education is a reforming of *psuchē* rather than training in any particular *technē*
(art, skill). The nature of philosophical disclosure as opposed to other
modes of disclosure is articulated by consideration of some implications
of the introductory section of the *Parmenides* (especially 130a–137c). The
difficulties inherent in the young Socrates' initial distinction between
eidetic and phenomenal disclosure are cast in terms of two especially productive topics for philosophical inquiry as conceived by Plato, namely
chronos, and the implicit *chōrismos* between the intelligible as such and the
beings that are made accessible by means of intelligible form.

Chapter 3 initiates the investigation into the dialectical game, dealing with the first beginning (137c–142a). However, we will see that from
the outset Parmenides' game undermines its own rules (the allegedly eightfold hypothetical method) and thus ironically reconfigures Socrates' distinction upon which it is based. Chapter 4 deals with the second beginning
(142b–155e), and chapter 5 with the third, the central account of *to exaiphnēs*, the instant (155e–157b).

This section of the dialogue is usually viewed by commentators as
part of the second beginning, but the fact that Plato did not intend it as
a simple addendum or digression is indicated by the fact that Parmenides
explicitly refers to it as a third discourse (155e4). None of the other beginnings is explicitly enumerated in this way. Difficulties relating to time are
central to Parmenides' demonstration both in location and thematically.
Reflection on time shows why the allegedly eightfold hypothetical method
actually turns out to involve diverse juxtapositions of 'in relation to itself'
and 'in relation to another' discourses. This means that they imply not
eight but indefinitely many returns to the beginnings (*archai*). Consequently, the pivotal nonhypothesis of the instant is much more than just
an ironic parody of schematism.

The account of time and *to exaiphnēs* is shown to be central to the
discussion not only in location but also insofar as it develops the themes
already indicated; for the irreducible ambiguity of the notion of the instant
constitutes a reduction to absurdity of axiomatic systems and, by implication, an elicitation of the radical incompleteness of conceptual dialectic
and logos itself. The instant is an antinomic axiom, therefore although
Parmenides ironically purports in the third beginning to explain *chronos*,
he in fact reveals the kinds of *aporiai* or impasses implicit to the application of any formal system to existence. The third beginning simply cannot
be incorporated into the hypothetical method Parmenides outlines at
135d–136c.

Chapter 6 examines the fourth beginning (157b–159b), and the fifth (159b–160b). Chapter 7 deals with the sixth (160b–163b), the seventh (163b–164b), the eighth (164b–165e), and the ninth (165e–166c). A brief Epilogue brings into focus the Platonic theme of forms of time, logos, and being in the dialogue. This discussion indicates that the sense in which the *Parmenides* embodies an implicit ontology cannot be separated from the pedagogical intent and negatively dialectical form of the work.

The *Parmenides* is typical of Platonic dialogue in that it indicates the proportionality (*emmetria*) of intelligibility: ironic dialogue is not nomadic dialectical wandering, but neither is it a monologic theory of being, or any other form of sophistry, despite appearances to the contrary. The pedagogic irony of Parmenides' dialectical demonstration and the failures of discourse—indicated by the omnipresent suggestion of fallaciousness— together define the sense in which ontology is conceived to be possible by Plato, and in what sense it is not even attempted. For this reason, the provocative ambiguities and contradictions, especially in Parmenides' dialectical game, cannot simply be ignored: Parmenides' odd juxtapositions of various modes of intelligibility indicate finally, by means of reflection on time, that *chōris* is irreducible. And his mimicry of sophistry shows by contrast the possibilities and limitations of Plato's conception of the way of *alētheia*.

Parmenides' exploration of logos and being is thus an exploration of the being of philosophy; Plato's *Parmenides* is a dialogue about the philosopher. The aim of the present essay is to show how the discussion of the consequences of the existence of any entity, any one, points beyond itself to a disruptive moment of insight that exceeds rational discourse. The topic of the dialogue is crucial, central for philosophy itself: namely, the 'relation' of ideals of intelligibility to existence. The *Parmenides*, notoriously the most difficult of Plato's dialogues, anticipates twentieth century philosophy in focusing on the problematic relation between language and time. Given the importance of language and time for contemporary philosophy—in the Continental, Anglo-American, and Pragmatic traditions—it is time to question the tradition's reception of Plato. The adequate interpretation will acknowledge that the Platonic dialogue's indefinite plurality of deductions within deductions manifests its significance only in the unity of the dialogue as a whole—a unified wholeness in which literal and figurative elements are juxtaposed throughout. The *Parmenides* is an ironic comedy with profound philosophical import.

Chapter 1

Troubling Play

"... I have never written of these things; there is not and will not be
any written work of Plato's. What are now called his are the works of
a Socrates made fair and young."

—*The Second Letter*

Paideia in the *Parmenides*

In studying Plato's dialogues, especially later dialogues such as the
Parmenides, we learn that whatever aspect of being we focus on, we always
seem to uncover a dialectical interplay of what flows and what abides. For
example, unity in the *Parmenides* manifests as many senses as "to be" does.
Apparently, to exist at all, in whatever manner, is to stand out as a unified
individual from a multiplicity. Not only does unity always seem to be displayed alongside being in any entity, but insofar as "unity" and "being" signify distinct natures, "difference" is also implicitly manifested alongside
these two. Along the same lines, Socrates indicates in the *Philebus* (beginning at 23e) that not only does "the limited" reveal itself as an interplay
of the limited and the unlimited, of the definite and the indefinite, but
even "the unlimited" appears to be a synthesis: the unlimited is in a sense
limited, just as the limited is, in a sense, unlimited. The *Parmenides* indicates that inquiry into logos and being is a motivated path that discloses
a plurality of modes of being, and that these are not subsumable under a
single category.[1] And yet ambiguity is only part of the story: Parmenides'
humorous equivocations still always revolve around a one. In showing
Socrates how logos misses the mark, Parmenides indicates by ironic *via
negativa* the way of *alētheia*.

In order to evoke this dialectical interplay of unity and multiplicity,
the language of philosophy must be both literal and figurative. Plato's dialogues show how to learn and how to teach (*paideuein*) this discourse. The
persistence and striving of dialectic as demonstrated by the mature Socrates
in other dialogues (and by Plato's Socratic caricature of Parmenides) shows

19

that metaphor lies at the very core of the literal. The priority of being in
Platonic dialogue means that the supplementarity of the origin does not
imply an unreasonable regress because intelligibility is complemented by
a different mode of being. But although participatory being toward the
good is one with the goal-oriented strivings of dialectic, being exceeds conceptualization.

Consequently, Plato's reinscription of Eleatic negative dialectic
implies much more than the logical method of reduction to absurdity:
elenchi are supplemented by irony and other nonliteral uses of discourse,
such as Socratic analogy. In Socrates' image of the divided line in the
Republic (509c–511e), modes of disclosure are related both up and down
with contrasting modes which serve to contextualize. The icon of the line
itself complements the likeness of the good to the sun because orientation
toward the good is the occasion for *alētheia*. This convergence of axiology
and ontology holds throughout the Platonic corpus; and it becomes especially clear if we remember that the stated aim of Parmenides' game is the
philosophical training of Socrates.

But the spirit of philosophy as dialogical (or the unity of logos as a
one in many) is an analogue for being itself. For that spirit is neither in
the teacher's mind, nor in the thoughts of the learner. Socrates is engaged
in philosophical training (*gumnasia*) through dialectical provocation.
Because Socrates has arrived independently at the distinction between
intelligible meanings and the presence of an entity, Parmenides judges that
he is reflective enough to benefit from this troublesome game. Parmenides'
pivotal reduction to absurdity of efforts to represent the being of time
shows why the distinction between literal and figurative must be reconfigured, but not dispensed with: these poles prove to be inextricable in
that the ambiguity they imply is a property of even the most rigorous discourse.

Plato's use of the dialogue form is not insignificant, for philosophical *poiēsis* is explicitly justified within the dialogues by repeated emphasis
on the incompleteness and ambiguity of modes of disclosure in logos. In
the *Phaedrus* Socrates questions the supposed stability and reliability of the
gramma (written text), and leads Phaedrus toward the insight that active
involvement in living dialogue (275c–277a) engages the learner and more
adequately gives insight into the many modes of logos and being. The composition of a text is one form of the decomposition of being because written words can only remind one who has already achieved insight through
active engagement. But it is not only the mummification of truths in treatises that reduces and misrepresents the being of philosophy. The impli-

cation is that the *gramma* and the engagement in living dialogue are distinct modes of the being of philosophy. Socrates is not simply privileging speech over writing; rather, he is warning Phaedrus of the dangers inherent to any detachment from active engagement, i.e., the reliance on reminders or representation in any form. Similarly, in the *Seventh Letter*, distinct modes of disclosure concerning beings—names, descriptions, visible figures, and concepts—are said to manifest existence in various limited ways, all of which are inadequate to revealing the *alētheia* of being as such (342a–344d).[2] Plato's *Parmenides* is also an inquiry into the supposed reliability and permanence of logos.

In the dialogues, Plato says nothing, and even his Socrates rarely—if ever—says anything that is unambiguous. This means that, in order to grasp the implications of that which is said (*logoi*), we need to consider the motivations of the interlocutors in relation to the whole dramatic situation as this develops through (and beyond) the dialogue. Temporal situatedness is invoked by references to a whole cultural context familiar to Plato's contemporaries and by allusions to previous texts, including his own dialogues. The *Apology* purports to be an historical account; Socrates, in the *Phaedrus*, ostensibly recounts the speech of Stesichorus from memory; and in the *Symposium*, we have what purports to be an accurate recounting of a conversational round of discourses. The *Theaetetus* is also an account of a previous conversation, as is the *Republic* and the *Parmenides*: such temporal intercontextualizations are too numerous to be insignificant.

Plato's complex temporal framings are most significant in the *Parmenides*, because the inquiry into time itself shows why goal-oriented repetitions of sameness in logos necessarily imply difference and discontinuity. In light of Plato's intentional ambiguities, one might go so far as to say that his primary logos is that logos itself is inadequate to comprehend the truth of being, for a repeated theme of the dialogues (and of the *Parmenides* in particular) is that even philosophical discourse is necessarily incomplete: the reformative remembering (*anamnēsis*) that is truth (*alētheia*) is simultaneously a forgetting.

Disclosure in logos implies the effort to achieve commensuration between the sign world and human action in a developing (and purely individual) situation; learning involves the ongoing effort to transcend the inadequacies of signs and the habitual practices that are their contexts of significance. But because what drives this process—throughout the Platonic dialogues—is being toward the good in the nonpresence that is transcendence, there is no Platonic "doctrine." Instead, the dialogues exhibit ironic dialectics that destroy efforts to define transcendence. Like the *Parmenides*, the *Sophist* shows that although no form may be said to be identical to any other, still the *eidos* would not be what it is except for dialectical differentiation from other *eidē*. This negativity is more fundamental than any positive account of essence or 'whatness.'[3] Platonic *dialektos* exceeds conceptual dialectic because it is oriented by the goal of invoking the limitations of representation (*mimēsis*).

All of this throws into question Heidegger's declaration, in the introduction to *Being and Time*, that the ancient way of interpreting being as presence requires a thoroughgoing destruction.[4] According to Heidegger, in Greek ontology being is reduced to the potentiality for discourse. Interpreting being as presence was due to the Greek's total lack of understanding of the ontological significance of time.

But *chronos* is made thematic in the *Parmenides* precisely to underscore the Platonic insight that being has no single, foundational principle of explanation, no ground. Any representation of being is necessarily a misrepresentation.[5] The being of *chronos* may not be reduced to the now, or represented as a dimensionless time-point (or a line composed of such nothings) without leading to *aporia*. The *Parmenides* indicates that neither the visible presence of an entity nor the intelligible meaning of the *eidos* is intended by Plato as an answer to the question of being. The unity of the *eidē* is hardly seen at all; it is indefinable.

Difference and the Good as *Telos*

In the Eleatic dialogues (*Parmenides, Theaetetus, Sophist, Statesman*), the Socratic skepticism of Plato's negative dialectic is supplemented and informed by reference to the transcendence of being. Similarly, in the *Republic*, skepticism and political cynicism are overcome not only by indicating the organically interconnected nature of human existence (e.g., the social covenant), but also by remembering the transfiguring moment of insight that informs being toward the good. Is this moment of insight independent of social practice and circumstances? If knowing involves a purely individual moment that exists independently from all external relations, then insight cannot simply be told or learned by example. And yet the *Parmenides* indicates repeatedly that there is no being pure and simple; nothing exists or is intelligible in itself (141e–142a; 159d–160b; 164a–b; 165e–166c). But on the other hand, if there can be no purely private knowing, this need not imply that transformative insight into the whole can be learned by repetition, mechanically, or be memorized.

What is usually referred to as Plato's virtue ethics contrasts with the truth-as-consensus implied in conceptual dialectics. But in what sense is the health of the individual *psuchē* another modality of disclosure of the good? Does Socrates in the *Republic* ever really unify or adequately synthesize an individual perspective with the social *ethos*? If we claim that both *psuchē* and social orderings are reformed in an ongoing process of learning or transcendence, isn't it still the case that the individual dimension of being exists only in oppositional practice that contrasts with the public dimensions of shared practices, language, and conceptual thought?

But the conversion toward the light of *alētheia* depicted in the allegory of the cave (514a–521b) is a long, painful, and to some extent solitary process. The prisoner is freed by an anonymous rescuer and subsequently dragged up the slope to the light and left there blind and lost. When he achieves insight, he immediately returns to the cave to attempt to liberate the others. The prisoners in the cave cannot see each other; they cannot turn their heads and look into one another's eyes. Their fettered isolation is the antithesis of the *kallipolis* that is Socrates' just city. They have no community and no true communication: they know only their meaningless—but habitual—competition over shadows.

In contrast to this failure of community, Socrates uses analogy to indicate what he ambiguously evokes as both the idea and the *habit* (*Republic* 509a5) of the good. Although his remarks indicate that the offspring of the good are what we desire, and that desirous striving guides and sustains existence and knowing, Socrates also says that the good is not a being, it is "beyond beings," or *epekeina tēs ousias* (509b9). Socrates has already brought out the external, public aspect of justice (and of the meaning of ethical terms generally), when he sketched a social covenant hypothesis of the foundation of justice in the state (*Republic* 369a ff.). But if this agreement is constituted by shared practices, then the transcendence of the good indicates that interactions already signify preconceptually.

Significantly, Socrates' account of shared praxis is complemented by poetic images of the just life that indicate the wholeness possible when logos and proportion moderate the unlimited, monstrous passions of the *psuchē*. But this apparently straightforward distinction between two modes of being toward the good, the social covenant and the ethics of individual *aretē*, is anything but clear. Both modalities are in fact based on oppositions between the sameness of the *eidē* and the differences of the circumstance or context. The forms are that by which we measure, evaluate, and moderate whether our judgments pertain to our own individual condition or to the present state of the polis.

If it is asserted that any rational morality (e.g., the social contract) necessarily fails insofar as it cannot consistently either incorporate or ignore the purely individual dimension, this argument is neutralized if it is true—as Parmenides repeatedly indicates—that the purely individual does not exist except insofar as formal repetitions are implied in the disclosure of differing circumstances. Similarly, if it is asserted that any virtue ethics fails insofar as it cannot consistently either ignore or incorporate the public dimension, this claim may obviously be supplemented by the counterclaim that widespread consensus is no guarantor of justice. But in both cases it is the juxtaposition of differing contextualities that gives meaning to the standard; in short, these ethical perspectives differ only in privileging opposite poles of a fundamental ambiguity they both share.

Such oppositions, that reveal the limitations of conceptual dialectics, are characteristic of Plato's *erotic* dialectic. Erotic dialectic involves that which is precognitive; it is the lived interaction with what is chorismatic, or otherwise, in which both the socially mediated self and the individual aspect of *psuchē* are continually reformed. What exists implies both an immanent group logic (a public dimension) and a transcendental logic. If existence and disclosure itself is dialogical in that it involves utter singularity as well as reciprocity, nevertheless transcendence is the moment of insight when both the socially mediated self and the order that is *kosmos* are seen through; for this moment involves the apprehension of *to heteron*: the other as other.

But one consequence of Socratic critique is that even the sameness of logical identity is shown to be permeated by nonlogical otherness. Here too differentiation in action is more fundamental than conceptual dialectics insofar as the actuality of thought arises in opposition to its own potentiality. The analogical likenesses of being toward the good are *aitia*—the occasion—for intelligibility, as illustrated by the divided line: orientation toward the good is the condition of possibility for *epistēmē* and *alētheia* (*Republic* 508e). Socrates' analogies indicate that goal-oriented existence is more fundamental than the disclosures of empirical correlations and formal relations; such knowing is occasioned by the striving for the good.

This shows—as the divided line illustrates—that any representation or argument also implies its own role within the contextuality of being toward the good. This axiological vectoring is ontologically prior to the spatial, temporal, and logical arrangements it discloses. The metaphor of the vector indicates a precognitive correlation and differentiation that is neither expression of identity, nor hypothesis, term, or sign. Rather it is something utterly different, without which sign, term, hypothesis, and logic itself are all completely unintelligible. This preconceptual projecting or orientation—though informing every moment of every disclosure—can only be thought as negativity, as pure transcendence; it is the "otherwise," or beyond (*epekeina*) of existence itself. The limited intelligibility of participatory being is informed by this heterogeneity.

The unification of the *Parmenides* is informed by this governing dichotomy: the analogicity of interpretations of existence over against the negativity of intelligibility. Parmenides recasts Socrates' initial distinction between thing and form into a differentiation between modes of disclosure in logos: an orientation toward form in itself as opposed to disclosure as activity or use. This dichotomy is itself challenged insofar as Parmenides shows that intelligibility partakes of the *poiēsis* of imagination—time in itself is nothing—apart from the projections and reorientations of temporal activities, there is no *chronos*. Time "is" in the correlations and differentiations of teleological existence. Neither the separately existing *eidos* nor the materialistic reduction of form to presence allows a univocal account of time, for the instant neither is nor is not (155e–157b).

Moreover, even if conceptual unity is not, the precognitive syntheses of *eikasia*—imagination—persist (164b–165e). But that which is disclosed as correlated and differentiated for preconceptual active engagement, is for thinking merely odd juxtaposition—not intelligible synthesis—and yet persistent thought reveals its own analogicity.

Parmenides makes the incompleteness of intelligibility evident for Socrates by exploiting the indefinability of the notion of the individual as such. But if the individuality of the individual eludes definition, nevertheless the pure singularity of form—in its nonpresence—would seem to be a condition of possibility for definition itself. And yet how is singularity disclosed except by way of differentiation in varying circumstances and relations? If it seems obvious that there would be no shared practice, no consensus, no logos and no categories of explanation without individuals, nevertheless Parmenides shows Socrates repeatedly that meaning involves a play of differences between signs that are empty in themselves. There is no universal meaning apart from active embeddedness in a whole of contextuality that exceeds representation.

If it initially appears that learning is simply the ongoing effort to achieve commensuration between socially mediated categories and the individual *psuchē*—the reevaluation of meanings and critique of the shared practices from which consensus is derived—it must also be acknowledged that this activity of differentiation cannot be understood as a private mental process. Being toward the good, for Plato, gives logos its contexts of significance; logical identity is derived in opposition to existence. The *Parmenides* shows that intelligibility is not in itself foundational; but its reductions to absurdity leave standing the Platonic insight that orientation toward the good is the occasion of *epistemē* and disclosure (*Republic* 508e).

Why is there something good, rather than merely something? This may be the leading question of Plato's earlier dialogues.[6] Does Socratic dialogue indicate that individual moments of insight do not occur except in and through the erotic relation to the other that informs and constitutes *psuchē*? Or if being toward the good is always already socially mediated, does this imply that *kosmos* simply names the orderings of *ergon* (action) and logos that arise and inform human habits of prudence? After all, *erōs* (desire) is the divine artist who transforms chaos into *kosmos*, and the sphere of his art is human action. Significantly, for Plato this entire process is informed by transcendence—the apprehension of heterogeneity—and consequently the ordering is never simply a human ordering, public or private. The pursuit of self-interest—whether calculated or not—has as its condition of possibility the apprehension of *to heteron*, the otherness that informs all disclosure.

Even if it is true that desire is always my desire—it implies my existence—nevertheless Socratic *eros* involves neither hubristic self-indulgence nor slavish conformity. And Plato avoids relativism because both the particular and the universal exhibit an immanent *and* a transcendent aspect: in a different situation, different relations of ideas are disclosed. If *alētheia* involves formal repetition in reference to differing circumstances, the *Parmenides* indicates that any disclosure in logos, whether logical or empirical, can only be disambiguated insofar as it is contextualized both up and down. This is consistent with the claim that the only Platonic absolute is this *lived* differentiation: orientation toward the good as otherwise than beings. The erotic dialectic indicates this archaic unity of axiology and ontology; being and knowing are informed by the prereflective engagement with the other as potentiality for disclosure.

The *Parmenides* indicates this by showing that the distinctions between opposed modes of being may not be developed to the point of reducing one dimension to another. Form is neither entirely separate from nor reducible to the presence of entities. Because the proportionality that is rational discourse is not a synthesis but a juxtaposition that preserves difference, Parmenides' various examples of reasoning ironically highlight irreducible ambiguities as well as inevitable privileging; and Parmenides shows Socrates that the effort to definitively eliminate these simply multiplies contradictions.

Plato has Socrates allude to this paradoxical feature of ontological discourse at the beginning of the discussion.[7] Socrates remarks to Zeno (with characteristic irony) that Parmenides furnishes many proofs that the all is one, while he (Zeno) offers many proofs that it is not many; for the young Socrates this simply means that each says the same thing with only the appearance of difference. But in what follows, Parmenides vindicates Zeno and metastasizes this kind of paradox, showing Socrates that all disclosure is dialogical but chorismatic: the disjunction or separation (chōris) that Socrates affirms to exist between the ideal and the real permeates even the eidē.

Because transcendence as such is never manifest, the dimension of otherness is not reducible to presence or ousia. But habits of thinking and action blind us to to heteron, consequently philosophy involves the ongoing effort to remember the erotic dialectic that arises in and through being with the other. Socratic critique disrupts humanly constituted orderings and allows transcendence, the reforming of the whole that occurs with recognition of the other as other. Such disruption is the beginning of learning. Aporia and contradiction are the immediate goals of Socratic critique because they facilitate the fundamental reinterpretation that is learning.

Transcendence as the Overcoming of Dialectic

In the Parmenides, a very young Socrates learns that existence is not derived from the idea as from a ground or principle; entities do not resemble ideal originals that exist separately. Rather, participatory being is shown to be an activity of differentiation; Parmenides shows Socrates that the individual, as such, is as elusive as the idea itself. Socrates initially asserts that the individual is known by means of the universal; he is one even though he has different aspects (129c–d). But Parmenides' game demonstrates that nothing exists or is intelligible in itself (141e–142a; 159d–160b; 164a–b; 165e–166c).

Viewed in this light, the noēsis (thought) of the earlier dialogues becomes an odd kind of dialectic indeed, for it involves the freedom to overcome dialectic itself. At the limit of this overcoming lies a new field of disclosure: being toward the good that is beyond beings. This field of disclosure is otherwise than entities, for in this modality of existing toward the good, the object of knowledge and the mode of knowing are one. This freedom of thinking and being is the goal (telos) of philosophy; but such transcendence is neither simply above the divided line as its goal, nor beneath the line as its condition of possibility. Rather, as the occasion of knowledge and *alētheia*, it informs every moment of being and knowing, however we choose to schematize these. Any spatial, temporal, or logical schematism implies its own embeddedness in a deeper, precognitive contextualizing. In showing Socrates the limits of conceptual schemata (by way of repeated reductions to absurdity), Parmenides clears the way for a transfiguring moment of insight into the whole that cannot be adequately conceptualized, but only lived.

This does not imply that the *elenchi* of the *Parmenides* are overcome by a Platonic rational morality. It is true that for Plato the transcendence of the good is not simply the name for an indefinitely repeatable function of the sign; and both the learning of information and the overcoming of hubris involve a fundamental transformation that involves the ongoing reevaluation of the meanings of terms. But, against a simple moralistic interpretation of Plato, we need to recall that the habit of the good not only indicates the teleology and transcendence of knowing; the transcendence of the good primarily refers to the fundamental teleology of human existence. In the more complete *alētheia*, distinct modes of inquiry converge in a wholeness that eludes partition and the conceptualizations of *logismos*. The *Seventh Letter* states that inquiry into virtue must be supplemented by study of what is true and false about existence itself (344b). Plato's later dialogues invoke this dimension of existence that is otherwise than entity by showing ontology to be more fundamental than epistemology. The *Philebus* indicates this intercontextuality by showing that accounts of the ethical are simultaneously also ontological. This is so because the ground of both knowledge and morality is participatory being toward the good.[8]

But if social interactions are oriented toward the good in its transcendence, they will instantiate reflective dialogue by allowing the otherness of the other to be preserved. And in the ideal community, the truly just polis, the openness of this approach would allow a social covenant governed by philosophy. But this ideal in no way implies that dialogical morality constitutes an ethical theory that serves as the basis for distinguishing philosophy from sophistry. The *Parmenides* indicates that no conceptual discourse could be foundational, either for itself or for other modes of disclosure. The discontinuous nature of *alētheia* means that strictly speaking, there are no foundations: modes of being are bounded by otherness, and differing modes of disclosure have unique criteria of significance. The Platonic dialogues show that logos is exceeded by, bounded by, and permeated by *muthos*: for the surprising result of the *Parmenides* is that every moment of every disclosure is irreducibly ambiguous and aporetic. The nonpresence of *to heteron* informs every moment of disclosure. This result reiterates the Socratic injunction that learning is only possible on the basis of humility. Because the offspring of the good are simultaneously also non-good, wisdom involves recognition of one's own ignorance: knowing is founded in being, and existence exceeds the grasp of conceptual thought.

Only dialogue that preserves this radical differentiation allows transcendence. If Socratic *elenchos* cannot prevent the disasters that political arrogance wreaks in human life, at least it can expose the cynical hubris that underlies ideology. On the one hand, negative dialectic is employed as a logical corrective in order to unseat the sophistries that are used to justify disproportionate individualism; for singular being "is" only in opposition to the generality of universality. On the other hand, Platonic *dialektos* is apophatic insofar as it clears the way for insight into a dimension of being that withdraws from perception and thought. The mind must be humbled by *aporia* before it is elevated by philosophical *poiēsis*: neither of these moments is adequate in itself.

Because Socrates' defiant critique is oriented toward the transformation of human existence in this axio-ontological wholeness (and not merely a revision of particular beliefs), his wondering contemplation of being never degenerates into estrangement. After the effort to know the divine otherness—the unmixed good in itself—the philosopher descends again into the dialogically mixed *kosmos* of human social praxis. The *aretē* (excellence, function) of the philosopher is this movement between the good in itself (that may not be known conceptually) and the tragic twilight realm of cave society. Only those capable of this movement, of turning the eyes of the *psuchē* both upward and downward in this way, should be guardians (*Republic* 501a–c).

In the *Philebus*, both pleasure and intelligence are shown to be informed by this dialogical reciprocity. Socrates argues that the opposition of the one and the many is a necessary feature of language (15d). Every entity is both a definite one and an indefinite many (16d). The difference between a merely contentious discussion and philosophy is both moral and intellectual (17aff); because the philosopher loves the truth more than personal power, reputation, or victory in argument, he is granted recognition of the intermediate forms between the one and the many. The implication is that being itself is analogous to an opposition or mixture arising from the juxtaposition of formal unity and an irreducible plurality of possible contextualizations, for Socrates asserts this analogy holds whatever one we take as thematic for investigation (17d–e). If the opportunistic individualism of the sophist leads him to exploit one or another term in this odd proportionality, nevertheless the wholeness of the disclosure is deformed if a self-centered, disproportionate desire (e.g., *philoneikia*, contentiousness) is privileged over the desire for *alētheia*.

Therefore the question as to what constitutes a good existence is both more important and more difficult than hedonists realize. For the movement from the sick *erōs* to the divine *erōs* is not simply a conceptual movement. Not only is it the case that pleasure is in the differentiation from pain, but even intelligence itself intimately involves its opposite within itself (60d-e). This means that any possible conceptual dialectic is inherently incomplete: form, like number, is always of something. Therefore the good life is acceptance of this mixed and ruptured economy, the multiply-differentiated struggle for well-being and limited intelligibility (61b).

Although the *Parmenides* does not explicitly develop the axiological dimension of participatory being, the introductory exchanges between Socrates and Parmenides (130b-137c) accomplish at least two things that are essential. First of all, they depict Socrates as owing something to the community simply by virtue of the fact that, in the aging Parmenides, he had a teacher; he was educated in a tradition. Parmenides' game involves repetition; it is not simply free spontaneity. Socrates is initiated into the customs and uses—the discourses—of a philosophical tradition. And, as suggested in the *Republic* (520b), only the spontaneously formed philosopher would be free of an obligation to return to the cave.

But in terms of the content of the *Parmenides*, the chorismatic moment of participatory being is underscored in another way, insofar as the dialectical play will reduce to absurdity any nonteleological (or unmixed) schematism of time. Parmenides shows Socrates that no idea in itself is knowable; existence is odd mixture. The game shows that logos is differential; it involves the interplay of dialectical and transcendent dimensions. If disclosure in logos implies both irreducible individuality and transcendent universality, still singularity is only by way of universality. The precognitive orientations that contextualize linguistic disclosure are themselves informed by a restless ecstasy; Dionysian unification is pure action, and such engagement tolerates no inward-turning distraction. Erotic interplay is living in advance of oneself.

It is thus the opposition between the chaos of the *agora* and the focused quiet of philosophical conversation that informs the dialogues; there is no Platonic monologue because existence itself is differential, prior to linguistic articulation. The Eleatic dialogues throw into question the notion of simple self-identity—just as, in the earlier dialogues—Socrates' *aretē* is manifested in his preference for the confusion of the marketplace and loquacious dialogue with others over the silent solitude of hills and forest. Socrates chooses death rather than exile. The estrangement from the mixed wholeness—the unity in opposition of dialogical interplay—is the death of the philosophical spirit, even if the motivation for this exile is the desire for an individual experience of transcendence.

It is precisely because all existence is differential *metechein*, or partnership, that Plato's *Parmenides* evokes this sense in which neither individual entity nor ideal universality has being or admits of definition. Being is only in the activity of differentiation between the formal repetition of a nexus of ideas in developing circumstantial relations. Existence is in this way disclosed as a momentous opening of teleology and transcendence. But because the effort to know the wholeness of any one probes the bounds of being, the *Parmenides* indicates that this activity of differentiation may be the only necessary condition disclosed to thinking. If every mode of disclosure has its own irreducibly unique criteria of significance there can be no overarching discourse that unifies all possible modes of logos. The *Parmenides* shows this to be the case: for intelligibility participatory being is disclosed as juxtaposition, not synthesis. What is lived as precognitive analogicity is, for thinking, only negativity. The comic irony of Parmenides' troubling play is therefore isomorphic with the mature Socrates' ironic dialectic, for the goal of both is undercutting the ideology (or idolatry) of efforts to define transcendence.

Being as a Dialogical Relating To the Other

Plato's dialogues show that the individual in knowing only approaches the fullness of *alētheia* by remembering the a priori interrelations of significance and the organic connectedness of the mixed wholeness that is the disclosure of being. These relations to the other (*pros allēla*) do not inform only the ethical and communal dimension of human being. Socratic critique involves a recognition of the transcendence that is learning, the otherwise than of logos itself and of being. But transcendence is only possible in relation to immanence: there is no unmixed presence, and nonpresence in itself may not be known conceptually. Meaning itself involves this play of incommensurables: it is more than a dialectical interconnection of relations.

Because the activities of reason are situated, goal-oriented, and temporal, Parmenides demonstrates that the misguided effort to achieve a univocal reduction of dialogical being (especially in representations of *chronos*) leads to irreducible *aporia*. His troublesome game of negative dialectic exposes the impasse, and in this way remembers transcendence. The dangerous purpose of Parmenides' troubling play, then, is to carry logos beyond its limits, to evoke the nonhuman origins of human intelligibility: the whole that may not be thought. The transcendence of the good means that the conditions of possibility of intelligibility are not themselves intelligible; the darkly comical discussion of the one in the *Parmenides* evokes these limits, the beyond of logos and being. The irony of Parmenides' dialectical demonstration hinges on the sophistical omission of the teleological dimension of being toward the good. Parmenides' comedy of errors is a miming of conceptual reductions of being's transcendence to intelligible presence.

Many interpreters of Plato miss the significance of the dialogue by ignoring or downplaying the playful irony that signifies the priority of difference and absence over simple presence.[9] Thus one strategy in interpreting Plato's *Parmenides* involves the claim that contradictions are implicit to the systematic, dialectical revelation of the whole that is truth. Hegel, for example, understood contradiction to be a necessary feature of the method of ontology.[10] Similarly, Viggo Rossvër argues that contradictions are the result of the inherent limitations of dialectic.[11] Robert Brumbaugh interpreted the contradictions as indications that the scope of the method of inquiry must be extended beyond that of any merely formal system to its completion in normative evaluation.[12]

Other interpreters attempt to resolve the contradictions between hypotheses by emphasizing that claims are made about unity in many different senses. This line of interpretation, with minor variations, may be discerned in Cornford, Allen, Miller, Meinwald, and Turnbull, among others.[13] But a deficiency that both streams of interpretation share is that of suppressing or even completely ignoring the comic irony and the mimings of sophistry in Parmenides' provocations. More seriously, none of them adequately consider the ontological significance of the dialogue's third beginning on the instant (155e–157b).[14] But the dialogue is intentionally crafted in a way that is both aporetic and ambiguous, and Plato had good reasons for ensuring such interpretive controversies. The content of the *Parmenides* explains why its form eludes schematism, why neither the noncontradictory (but thoroughly ambiguous), nor the allegedly univocal (but thoroughly contradictory) interpretation stands alone. Inquiry into time, being, and logos leads to the insight that meaningful discourse is essentially chorismatic: the disclosure of being in language implies both repetitions that are equivocal as well as the discontinuity of *aporia*.

Parmenides' style of training, his provocative play, indicates that the notion of nontemporal (or nonteleological) identity in itself is deeply aporetic; if the presumption of such temporal location without dimension is a necessary condition of ratio, still in itself it is not rational. Parmenides reveals the antinomic nature of the instant in the dialogue's third beginning (155e–157b). The third beginning on the instant evokes the ontological significance of heterogeneity, and indicates the paradoxes implicit to any schematism of time. The third beginning is central in the development of the theme of the *Parmenides*. The account of the instant demonstrates the closing over that occurs alongside the disclosure of truth in logos: both ambiguity and contradiction are implied in representations of time.[15] Because Parmenides repeatedly appeals to the principle of non-contradiction and its implicit notion of simultaneity, the application of formal representations to existence (especially in the second beginning) involves the notion of pure presence in an instant. But by the law of the excluded middle, the instant should either exist or not exist; and yet it is neither being nor nonbeing (156e–157b).

The existence of the instant is logically impossible, and yet its existence is required by the intelligibility that shows it to be impossible. The third beginning shows that when a formal system is applied to beings, this resolves some ambiguities, but at the expense of producing contradictions.

Consequently, it is not only Pythagorean mathematical cosmology that Parmenides throws into question, but also the ordinary discourse of mortals. But why does Parmenides ironically juxtapose different modes of logos, not only within deductions, but even within statements? If, with the silently observant Socrates, one tries to think one's way beyond the ambiguities and paradoxes of the *Parmenides*, one discerns an awareness on Plato's part that no term in itself is a sign.[16] Expression directed toward itself signifies nothing: logos is meaningful only as dialogue, in the mode of toward-another, that is, in relation to the other. The intelligibility of experience and discourse that it is absurd to deny (*Parmenides* 135b–c) is analogous to a proportion. But this analogicity of existence itself arises in and through interrelations with entities, indicating that the *eidos* is an archaic projection of future possibilities of experience based on the materiality of past encounters. This movement of confirmation, failure, and transfiguration is permeated by negativity insofar as the very presence of the present is a project. Parmenides indicates this by showing that no term has meaning in isolation; apart from its differences in relation to a network of other terms, and apart from imagined possibilities of future experience, logos would be insignificant gesture.

The relation of ideas implicit in the network of signs, their mutual interdefinition, proves to be limited, derivative, and to some extent arbitrary. The *Parmenides* indicates the reasons for the sophistic privileging of terms that are in fact only significant in opposition: unity / plurality, form / formlessness, knowledge / ignorance, mastery / slavery, and so forth. Terms signify in their differences in relation to one another, and in the context of an organically interconnected whole metaphorically described as participation (*metechein*).[17] This implication of the dialogue's inquiry into time—that the *eidos* in itself is nothing—means that the approach to the question of being in the Platonic dialogues develops as an inquiry into the dialectical interrelation of language and human action. Consequently Parmenides' troublesome game, in exposing the inadequacy of representations of existence, is in many ways isomorphic with a phenomenological description of transcendence.

Parmenides enhances Socrates' insight by demonstrating a negative dialectic that discloses unity in opposition without succumbing to the pitfalls of any positive method. Negative dialectic reduces some hypothesis to absurdity by showing that it implies a contradiction. In such a method, positive correlations are incidental: necessary conditions are revealed by way of a double negation. This procedure reveals a necessary condition to be a hypothesis whose inadequacy is sufficient evidence that a second is inadequate. Parmenides demonstrates for Socrates the inadequacies of a variety of modes of logos, including finally dialectic itself. Parmenides' negative dialectic survives these *elenchi* only to the extent that it is the thinking that attempts to expose even its own inadequacies. Like the Platonic Parmenides, the mature Socrates of other dialogues displays a ratio that is informed by the ongoing re-cognition of its own lack of proportionality.

Parmenides' troublesome game shows, on the one hand that interrelations of ideas are never really present because they are a potentially infinite manifold defined by differences; moreover, the intelligible presence of a structural whole—an ideal matrix—is ultimately shown to be paradoxical insofar as this would imply a contradictory account of time. On the other hand, Parmenides suggests that his doubly negative mode of variation and difference is compatible with disclosure of unity in opposition, for it is absurd to employ intelligible discourse to deny the possibility of intelligibility (135b–c). But such unification implies an oddly mixed integrity, because it is a whole that exceeds the sum of its parts. This unity in opposition simply cannot be grasped by thought (*noēsis*), because the act of reducing ambiguity produces contradiction: Parmenides' account of the instant implies that thought itself essentially involves unintelligible nonpresence.

The demonstration's central reductions to absurdity of efforts to represent time (151e–157b) develop the references to *anamnēsis* in earlier dialogues.[18] The fact that terms for memory and recollection are used imprecisely in the dialogues need not prevent us from acknowledging that Plato's accounts of the process of learning are teleological. If generalizations based on experience and dialogue are themselves treated as images, this will mean that the trust (*pistis*) based on past confirmations will be supplemented by the ironic detachment that accompanies the imagination of future failures in confirmation. This theme of repetition and discontinuity is introduced in the first lines of the dialogue (see 126c–127d).[19] Because logos itself is a system of images or icons,[20] the study of meanings involves inquiry into the uses and abuses of signs (*sēmata*). Parmenides not only shows Socrates that any semantics presupposes an interpretation of existence, he also demonstrates that discourse is irreducibly plural because being is ambiguous: it is the intercontextual juxtaposition of modes of disclosure that allows significance in logos.

Recollections and projections of imagined possibilities are implicit to the disclosure of truth in logos; and *alētheia*–especially with regard to the problematic of time–is the overarching theme of the dialogue. Parmenides agrees that it is the unifying form that makes possible intelligible discourse and therefore philosophy (135b–c). The impasses relating to the metaphor of participation then, are surmountable in some way. Consequently, it is not the fact that there are forms of disclosure in language that is to be thrown into question; rather, it is how this disclosure of being is to be understood that presents difficulties. The *Parmenides* unpacks the metaphor of sharing in being (130e ff.), and reveals in a negative way–by reductions to absurdity–how participatory being may not be understood. Parmenides demonstrates repeatedly and in a variety of ways that being–the *ontos on*– is not reducible to the presence of the *eidos*: dimensions of irreducible heterogeniety are implicit to the meaning of every representation of sameness in logos. If we cannot reason without some notion of presence or actuality, nevertheless actuality itself is impossible to conceive.

Therefore the metaphor of participatory being does not simply indicate the variety of human activities in and through which entities are disclosed. Parmenides' dialectical demonstration shows Socrates that even ideal being exhibits the one-in-many, teleological structure implied in the perception of entities; consequently it is not the distinguishing of various modes of disclosure that ends in *aporia*, but the effort to make one mode foundational. The notion of being as participation is not a theory; it is a descriptive account of the disclosure of what exists. Similarly, the *chōris-*

mos is not a problem that admits of a solution; it is a feature of all disclosure in logos, including even the meta-semantic inquiry into the variety of forms of discourse. The primary Platonic insight that informs the *Parmenides* is that modes of disclosure are finite and oddly mixed. Strictly speaking, there is no disclosure (*alētheia*) in itself: truth as disclosure is transcendent, not true. No observation of phenomena could falsify such conditions of possibility of intelligible experience. The descriptive, metaphorical notion of participatory being toward the good evokes the situated, goal-oriented character of both logic and sense perception. But the transcendence that is learning is only possible alongside the *aporia* that is *chōrismos*.

Logos Toward Itself versus Toward the Other

Parmenides' demonstration will vindicate Zeno by reducing to absurdity Socrates' attempted solution of Zeno's paradoxes. Socrates distinguishes the *eidos* in itself from the entities that share in the being of the idea (128e9–129b1). Prior to demonstrating the absurdities implicit to Socrates' initial understanding of being, Parmenides sharpens the focus of the distinction between an idea in itself and the entity that instantiates it. Parmenides recasts Socrates' initial distinction between form and thing, and orients it toward two modalities of the activity of disclosure, characterized briefly at 136a–c as the analysis of a hypothesis toward-itself as distinguished from verifying its meaning toward-another, or *pros hauta kai pros allēla* (136b1).[21] Parmenides' subsequent demonstration will reveal that the hypothesis analyzed in relation to itself refers to the intelligible meaning of an event or entity: a word, for example, expresses the meaning of the entity or event with which it may be identified. But the *pros hauto* expression seems inherently to bear this sense. For unlike the sign that merely points to an entity or event, an inherently meaningful sign would bear intelligibility without presupposing the actual existence of what it signifies.

Is there any inherently meaningful sign? How could this toward-itself function of logos relate to the presence of entities? In fact, Parmenides' dialectical demonstration will show that logos directed entirely toward itself ultimately signifies nothing. We can get a sense at the outset as to why this is so by considering the following example. If I have a hundred yen in my pocket, I know many things in an a priori way about this amount of money. I know that it is twice as much as fifty yen, and half as much as two hundred. Such ideal relations may be produced indefinitely, even in relation to one moment of an entity's existence (*Parmenides* 143c–144c).

But such relations of ideas, even when they are commensurable, do not themselves inform: I do not know how much money I have unless I also know many other things in an experiential sense, for example, what the money will buy in the local economy.[22] This emptiness of the sign in itself is why the troublesome game focuses on time: Parmenides makes *chronos* central to his analysis in order to throw into question his own beginning; namely, the distinction between formal repetition and differentiation in context.

The representational unity that allows enumeration or countability, is derived by abstracting from the very contextual wholeness that gives significance to the representation. The *Parmenides* shows that the intelligibility of experience (participatory being) is analogous to a proportion that involves both the toward-itself and toward-another modes of disclosure. But Parmenides demonstrates other modes as well, for differentiations are also disclosed within these two thematic orientations. The difficulty is that this notion of proportion is merely an analogy: intelligibility has another aspect as well; it is also simultaneously a disproportion. The *telos* of thinking—the end of the effort to achieve commensuration—is recognition of thinking's own incommensurability (*to mē metechon*). Parmenides invokes this limit by testing his own beginnings (*archai*). Two apparently opposite orientations in logos are finally shown to be oddly unified in an inexpressible turning (*tropos*)

The toward-another (*pros allēla*) mode of inquiry is not the effort to isolate intelligible meaning in itself, but rather to indicate significant interrelations between natures (or characteristics) that exist. In Parmenides' demonstration, this mode of signification indicates correlations and contiguities among both entities and meanings: this usage shows that the toward-another function of logos indicates the interconnectedness of being. In this way the indicative sign points beyond itself toward a different nature, its other. The toward-another mode of logos articulates the differentiations that inform both experience and dialectic. No meaning is implicit to the term in itself; its function is to point beyond itself to something different that exists. The indicative function of toward-another discourse is to gesture toward the immanence of other characters or meanings.

One effect of Parmenides' dialectical demonstration is that this relational (toward-another) mode of disclosure seems to engulf the idea in itself. This occurs insofar as the idea in itself loses content as it is abstracted from the contextual relations that give it significance. And yet without the unique singularity of a nature or a feature (indicated by the *eidos*), there could be no dialectical differentiation of meanings. But even if it is true that there is being only where there is the logos of being, nevertheless this logos is derivative: meaning is relative to context. Relations of ideas, even if tautologous, are nevertheless relations, and it is the differences between *eidē* in a particular context that allows disclosure.

So on the one hand, apart from its contexts of significance the idea in itself is nothing, and the real interrelations that allow significance seem to overcome the empty idea in itself. The attempt to disclose all the relations implied by even one fact is an impossibly enormous task. But on the other hand, every disclosure of difference may apparently be named and described in logos. This seems to imply that an idea accompanies every feature of every entity. Indeed, Parmenides indicates precisely this at various points in the dialogue (e.g., 130b–131a, and 143c–144e). But this implies that the *eidē* are an indefinite and potentially infinite multitude. Because any entity might be enumerated and categorized in indefinitely many ways, ideal potentiality now seems to engulf real actuality; any one may be counted as a whole or indefinitely many. The metaphor of participatory being is a phenomenologically accurate basis for the articulation of this paradox. The *Parmenides* evokes a radical heterogeneity that is irreducible; for it informs both real and ideal relations, and therefore limits the philosophical effort to disclose it. Rationality is analogous to a ratio; but this ratio implies a juxtaposition of representations that masks the nonrational conditions of possibility that inform rationality itself.

What then is the precise character of this interrelation of logos functions, and in what way, exactly, does the inquiry into language involve questions about the being of time? Or, to put it differently, why should the reflection on time and being involve inquiry into modes of discourse? Parmenides' *gumnasia*, his troubling game, will show the young Socrates that his initial distinction (between idea in itself and particular instantiation) implies absurdities and must be reconfigured, but not dispensed with. In this dialogue, the figure of Parmenides critically examines his own hypothesis: he throws into question the sameness of *noien* (to think) and *einai* (to be). Plato's *Parmenides* reinscribes the words of the goddess of *alētheia*. Beyond the provocative irony of Parmenides' troubling play is Plato's transformative insight into the legacy of father Parmenides.

Given the explicitly pedagogical framing developed in the first part of the dialogue, can the mode (*tropos*) of training that constitutes the major part of the *Parmenides* (137c–166c) be construed as an example of the culmination of the familiar (but ambiguous) Socratic account of the training of the guardians? In support of this construal, it is surely no accident that the most important fact we are given about the young Aristotle, who is

Parmenides' uncomprehending respondent throughout the dialectical demonstration, is that he later became a member of the Thirty Tyrants.

Analysis of the *Parmenides* will reveal that its form and its content are unified, and that the humorous and ironic reasoning it exhibits evokes an ambiguity implicit in being. The dramatic device of conducting a discussion with a minor interlocutor (Aristotle) as an educational demonstration to engage the major interlocutor (Socrates), heralds the ironic nature of the discourse. The ambiguous character of the discourse is also suggested by the distinction that initiates the demonstration in the first place; for Socrates' distinction between intelligible meanings and the presence of an entity, which is developed in the first third of the dialogue, is not dropped once it is disqualified as a way to disarm Zeno's paradoxes. On the contrary, though it is no solution to the dialogue's *aporiai*, the distinction between eidetic and phenomenal disclosure is not eliminated but radically reconfigured in the troubling dialectical game that constitutes the remaining two-thirds of the dialogue, where the discussion focuses on the being of unity. In Parmenides' game, neither young Socrates' conception of formal unification nor Zenonian paradox is simply eliminated: both these moments are transfigured and enhanced by his troubling play. Parmenides' own hypothesis about the being of the one is chosen as the subject of the exercise because the metaliteral character of philosophical reflection becomes inescapably obvious on consideration of the nature of unification.

The responsibility that is both prerequisite and result of *dialegesthai*, as conceived by Plato, involves the recognition that the troubling play of philosophy is, in a vital sense, its own reward. A Socratic intellectual humility tempers the audacity of the most rigorous inquiry. Humility and wonder accompany the Platonic insight that the nature of philosophical discourse springs from an original ambiguity in being itself; and in this way, wonder facilitates the development of modes of *erōs*. It is this process of transcendence that is traced in this essay.

Chapter 2

Logos and Existence in the *Parmenides*

"We might put it in this way: if there would be a logic even if there were no world, how then could there be a logic given that there is a world?"

—Ludwig Wittgenstein, *Tractatus Logico-Philosophicus*

Paideia and Paradox

Aristotle's discussion of being as *energeia* is founded on the Platonic insight that being is participatory (e.g., *Physics*, 202b). But the *Parmenides* had already shown that the unity of philosophy, its being, may not be understood as a matrix of *eidē* defined in their mutual interrelation. The being of philosophy is the participatory, or dialogical activity simultaneously in teacher and taught.[1] The metaphors of *metalambanein* as substitution or interchange, and *metechein* as making commensurate, signify the Platonic insight that the intelligibility of existence is like an exchange or trafficking. For the event of manifestation that is existence is neither primarily in the mind nor grounded by its position in absolute *chora* or *chronos*. The primary unifying event of logos is intercontextual: as when *ousia* is revealed simultaneously both as phenomenon and *eidos*. Like the *Theaetetus*, which reduces to absurdity attempts to make *aisthēsis* (perception) foundational, the *Parmenides* reduces to absurdity efforts to make the intelligible the ground of being. Parmenides provokes the silently engaged Socrates by reducing to absurdity many modes of reductionism, but his *elenchi* leave standing the metaphor of being as substitution, or interchange (*metalambanein*).

In the *Republic*, a mature Socrates claims that if unity could be apprehended adequately, it would not draw the mind to a greater understanding of what-is. But because paradoxes are easily evoked in the discussion of the nature of any one, the mind is drawn into thought, inquiring what unity, as such, is. In this way, the study of unity converts the soul and guides it to the contemplation of being (524d–525a).

41

In his inquiry into the integrity of the form, Parmenides evokes many paradoxical consequences implicit in his young interlocutor's pretensions to knowledge. It cannot be maintained that only some manifestations of being are in accordance with *eidē* (130a–e). *Metalambanein* may not be construed as the resemblance of separately existing entities, *eidos* and participant (131a–c). However, the distinction between eidetic and phenomenal discourse may not simply be collapsed, for *eidos* is not divisible into parts in the same way that a thing is (131c–e). We cannot claim that the *eidos* exists apart from its sensible manifestation, for then the intelligible meaning and its perceptual manifestation could only be related by means of another *eidos*, and so on (131e–132b).

But in order to avoid this regress we may not simply reduce the *eidos* to a thought (*noēma*), for then either all beings are thoughts and thinkers are everywhere, or else these thoughts exist independently of thinkers, and so are unthought. But both alternatives are absurd (132b–c). Similarly, the *eidē* are not conceptual models (*paradeigmata*) woven into the fabric of being. In this case again participatory being would be implicitly reduced to a relation of resemblance between particular manifestation (image) and universal being (original), and this would again lead to an unreasonable reduplication of *eidē* (132d–133a). Furthermore, if the *eidos* existed apart from the particular manifestation, then *eidē* would be distinguished entirely in their mutual interrelations and would be unknown by us (133a–134e). But this would contradict the intelligibility of experience that it is absurd to deny (135b–c). Parmenides dramatically emphasizes this point in another way for Socrates: if *eidē* exist apart from participatory being, even a god could not have *epistēmē* (134d–e).

The failures that inevitably result whenever one attempts to articulate being positively indicate the need for another way of speaking: a mode of discourse in which the passionate drive toward clarity and distinctness is complemented by a sober recognition of the incompleteness of various modes of logos and being. A philosopher of such wonderful abilities will, according to Parmenides, still affirm that the *eidos* is the *genos* of each being, so that it is one with the particular being (*ousia*) considered according to itself, or *kath' hauten* (135a7–b1). But in spite of his approval of the notion of forms, Parmenides repeatedly mimes sophistry in his efforts to bring Socrates to *aporia*. Yet the young Socrates does not capitulate; when he cannot offer discursive insight, he replies with brilliant analogies, such as his comparisons of the being of the idea to a day, a thought, and to a paradigm, or model.

This last comparison is especially interesting since it implies that being itself involves an analogical dimension. The *Parmenides* indicates that figurative speech (such as the famous analogies, myths, and dreams Plato often weaves into the dialogues) proves necessary due to ambiguity inherent in the nature of being. Insofar as what exists is intelligible, it is disclosed in and through the *eidos*. Yet the very intelligibility of being shades into unintelligibility; the idea in relation to the phenomena serves as a unifying principle or measure, but the unity of the idea itself, considered in abstraction from *aisthēsis* and from other *eidē*, yields no intelligibility and has no being.[2]

Matrices of *eidē* are disclosive of being, but only insofar as to be is to be intelligible and measurable. But Proteus-like, the being of what is, the unity of unity, eludes efforts to grasp it. The inquiry into modes of logos and the limits of intelligibility involves figurative discourse and ambiguity insofar as eidetic and phenomenal discourses are only two (of indefinitely many) modes of the discoverability of what-is. Socrates initially hopes that the separation (*chōris*) of form and phenomenon would allow univocal discourse, but Parmenides shows him that the separation is not between the ideal and the real, for *chōris* is implicit to the disclosure of ideal being as well. How could logic and analogical indications of existence be irreconcilably separate if goal-oriented unification in differentiation informs them both? Parmenides shows Socrates that unification cannot be understood as composition; all unity is differential.

The analogies employed by the young Socrates in the *Parmenides* remind the reader of the high place Plato grants to nonliteral discourse in the dialogues. The priority Plato grants to philosophical *poiēsis* is evidenced not only by the presence of various forms of figurative language throughout the dialogues, but also by the content of these dreams, myths, analogies, *elenchi*, and ironical pseudo-inferences. Based on this pervasive use of nonliteral language in the dialogues, it is reasonable to infer that according to Plato the philosophical use of ironic, ambiguous discourse in some contexts facilitates *paideia*: for the unity of the individual form seems to imply a principle of unity itself that is not only too general to be defined, but is disclosed only in opposition, as a one in many.

But such philosophical *poiēsis* is performative; it is active engagement, not simply *mimēsis*. The uncompleted form of the Platonic dialogue ensures that we undergo the act of learning ourselves. Even if a discussion like the one depicted in the *Parmenides* is exactly memorized, memorization is not philosophy, as Plato indicates at the outset by the example of the horseman Antiphon (see 126c–127a). Behind the text—informing it—is a philosophical life (*psuchē*). Modes of existence inform any possible logos. The goal of the Platonic text is the transfiguration of this oddly mixed wholeness.

Modes of Logos and Being

If thinking and insight begins with what is apparently plain and obvious and present for all, such as time or unity, still it may happen that the understanding at one's disposal proves inadequate to explain some feature of what shows itself. What was first taken as self-evident then appears to be something remarkable. If the wonder this evokes is the beginning of the widening of everyday understanding into hypothesis, then philosophy involves the ongoing, revisionary effort to more fully articulate in and through logos the disclosure (*alētheia*) of what-is. But precisely because the question of the unity of any being leads to paradox, or *aporia*, discussion of the topic is good training for developing the minds of beginning philosophers. The failures that inevitably result if one discusses being in terms of images, objects, numbers, or abstractions, indicate the necessity of a more comprehensive mode of disclosure—a form of discourse in which the passionate drive toward clarity and distinctness is complemented by a sober recognition of the incompleteness of rational speech.[3]

The desire to know drives philosophical inquiry: this dialectical progression is characterized in the *Republic* (510b–511d) as a hypothetical way up and a formal way down. At 487d, Socrates figuratively describes truth as a proportion (*emmetria*). This metaphor is subsequently developed into an account of truth as disclosure through logos that facilitates a dialectical progression. This movement not only involves both the hypothetical way up and the formal way down; it is also informed throughout by transcendence, for the *telos* of the good is beyond beings (509b9).

In the *Parmenides*, the intelligibility of experience that it is absurd to deny is metaphorically described by Socrates as the participation of thing and *eidos* (129a–d). But the young Socrates conceives the *eidē* as existing separately, and in this way privileges the purely formal way down. The troubling play of Parmenides' dialectical demonstration corrects Socrates' misunderstanding of the distinction between idea and thing by showing the impossibility of the separate existence of the *eidē*. But, although the metaphor of participatory being survives Parmenides' ironic reductions to absurdity, so does the *chōrismos*. The *Parmenides* indicates the negative way that dialectic reveals the limitations of more context-bound modes of logos.[4] And yet the limitations of dialectic are revealed as well; positive dialectic is the context that reveals—by contrast—the significance of negative dialectic. Consequently, the distinction between thing and idea (and the corresponding distinction between the way up and the way down), are neither to be dispensed with nor rigorously developed.

The moment of transcendence evoked by negative dialectic is the recognition of the radical incompleteness of the positive dialectics that constitute the way up and the way down. But Parmenides' ironic equivocations and paradoxes still revolve around a one; and even the effort to deny intelligibility would implicitly appeal to that which it explicitly denies (135b-c). Nevertheless, the transcendent dimension of being and the inherent limitations of logos make any knowledge of being as such impossible. The self-critique of philosophy is fulfilled in the evocation of the limitations of positive dialectic; and reflection on time shows that any positive dialectic involves analogies of experience. Philosophy involves the ongoing effort to achieve this ironic detachment in relation to the possibility of the disclosure of truth in logos.

The ironic and occasionally comical parodies of *logismos*, or reasoning, in Parmenides' dialectical game disclose ambiguities that evoke the limitations of both formal and experiential inference. Not only does Parmenides indicate that the purely formal is empty of significance, he also shows Socrates that the representation of time by formal relations is implicitly contradictory (151e-157b).

If, as the *Parmenides* indicates, rational discourse itself is necessarily and radically incomplete, how could philosophical discourse articulate this? How does a mode of inquiry achieve a meta-status relative to all others, and to itself as well? If philosophy is a mode of language, then in disclosing the limitations of language it is revealing its own limitations. Even the most comprehensive dialogue is selective; it implies ongoing evaluations and reevaluations. *Dialegō* means "I pick out one from another," but does this imply that this selective gathering never fully recognizes its own implicit valuations?

If philosophy is not a mode of logos, it would apparently culminate in silence. In the *Parmenides*, Socrates is silent throughout the dialectical demonstration; his last lines are at 136d3-4, only slightly more than ten pages into a dialogue that is more than forty Stephanus pages in length. Such emblematic silences are a dramatic device that recurs throughout the Platonic dialogues. What insight does Socrates gain in the *Parmenides* that allows meaningful comparisons with his discourses (and silences) in other dialogues? The question as to how Plato intended this dialogue to conform with—and differ from—his earlier writing is itself another way to artic-

ulate the problematic that informs the *Parmenides*: how is the inexpressible singularity of one moment of existence unified with other moments?

In the main body of this dialogue (137c–166c), the figure of
Parmenides is ostensibly demonstrating for the silently attentive Socrates
a method of testing the consequences of his own hypothesis that a one
exists. But how do we explain Parmenides' irony and the omnipresent suggestion of sophistry in a dialogue aiming at the education of the initiate
to philosophy? Did Plato conceive philosophical *logismos* to be nothing
more than noble sophistry?[5] The *Parmenides* is a provocative challenge,
rather than an attempt to articulate a monologic doctrine or theory. Does
this indicate a more skeptical Plato than the one portrayed in traditional
reinscriptions of Platonism? But the provocation in the *Parmenides* is not
random, for it involves the difficulty of expressing in logos the insight that,
because being involves a transcendent dimension, the disclosure of being
in logos is necessarily ambiguous. Insofar as it makes these difficulties thematic, the form of the *Parmenides* itself is ambiguous; it is an ironic dialogue that demonstrates how not to do philosophy. By implication alone,
it shows us what philosophy is.[6]

The character of Parmenides represents the experienced philosopher, and Socrates the initiate. The irony of Parmenides' effort to further
Socrates' development signifies the priority of difference and absence over
simple presence. The being of philosophy is the unity of this discourse,
but this being is evoked in a negative way, by showing what it is not. The
being of philosophy is not represented adequately by Parmenides, or
Socrates, or the *logoi* that pass between them: the *Parmenides* throws into
question the notion of intelligible adequation by dramatically invoking
the transcendence—or nonpresence—of form.

The *Parmenides* is a discourse devoted to the education of Socrates
(see 135d–137c). Although the dialogue, like the paradoxical logos of Zeno
that initiates the discussion, reduces to absurdity many modes of reductionism, the metaphor of participatory being remains. And yet, though
the role of Parmenides in this dialogue is Socratic, the *Parmenides* includes
no explicit reference to the teleology of participatory being toward the
good. Instead, Parmenides indicates absurdities that result from a nonteleological, unmixed account of the being of time. The silently observant
Socrates is shown that the philosophical approach to such fundamental
questions involves the reduction to absurdity of various positive accounts
of being.

The central analogies of the *Republic* indicate that the goal-oriented
(temporal) striving of being toward the good unifies and makes possible

acts of knowing (509a5). But the use of such rhetoric (and the dialogue form itself) suggests Plato's interpretation of the limits of the analyses conducted by his characters.[7] Figurative discourse is necessary due to ambiguity inherent in the meaning of any term (such as the one), for the otherwise of the good means that the origin of intelligibility is always futural.[8]

Insofar as the disclosure of beings is intelligible, it unfolds in accord with the forms. And yet the limited intelligibility of any being points beyond itself. The idea in relation to the phenomena serves as a unifying principle, but the unity of the form in itself eludes analysis. Insofar as form differs from its every instantiation, it is like the proverbial negative that may not be proven. The idea in itself is a signpost of the bounds of being, and yet because *eidos* names the intelligibility of experience and discourse, to claim that form has no mode of being whatsoever is absurd. The negativity of form is implicit in Parmenides' challenging of Socrates' initial formulation of the separable existence of the *eidē* (130a–135d). But the insight is also explicitly developed throughout the *Parmenides*. The process of abstracting from the lived temporal context and from implicit interrelations with other intelligible meanings results finally in a sign with no significance.

Parmenides reconfigures Socrates' initial distinction between form and entity in a number of ways. Initially, Socrates not only misconceives the idea as existing separately from the real entities to which it gives being. In addition, he also allows the possibility that some entities (that are apparently unformed or worthless) might exist without there being an *eidos* for them at all (130a–e). Socrates' initial understanding of the *eidos* implies that an entity derives its being from an ideal original, and consequently there are degrees of being immanent to entities, according to their worth and presence (insofar as they are definable or fully formed). Parmenides indicates for Socrates some typical difficulties implicit to this initial formulation, but also indicates that to deny intelligibility is absurd. But the doubtful questions must be recast in relation to the ideas themselves (135e), and this will culminate in reflection on the being of *chronos*.

Parmenides' troubling play involves the further articulation of the distinction of ideality: in itself the *eidos* is nothing. And yet, transcendence—the movement of *chronos*—involves the remembering actualization of this nothing. In learning, the significance of an entire matrix of meanings is transformed when a network of interrelated ideas (that represent future projections based on past experience) are reevaluated and fundamentally revised. This is the encounter with the other (*to heteron*) that changes the soul of the learner and reconfigures the ordering that is cosmos. Socrates' initial distinction is insightful insofar as the disclosure of being in logos implies both the singularity of form and the indefinite ambiguity of that which is informed. Parmenides' demonstration shows that language involves both of these moments. This is due, in part, to the fact that any *eidos* is disclosed through differentiation from its own instantiations, other *eidē*, and *archai* oppositions. *Alētheia* involves *to heteron*, the differential, as contrast of being with being.

But moreover, because the truth of any logos is unified with its temporal context, the world as disclosed is always transcending itself. If we assert that *alētheia* does not change, then we must also acknowledge that the same words uttered at two different times do not articulate the same proposition. But how could it be that the truth does not change, if the truth cannot be separated from its context, and this (e.g., the phenomenal world) is in a constant process of change? Zeno's paradoxes evoke this problematic relation between the sameness of the representations of logos and the differentiations of *chronos* implicit to processes of motion.[9]

If hypotheses based on past experience are the materiality of future projections of experiential confirmation, still the *aporiai* disclosed by Parmenides' negative dialectic indicate intentions impossible to fulfill. These reveal the limitations of both empirical generalizations and any formal deductions based on them; for if there is no singular being, the truth of both empirical and nonempirical disclosures is threatened. The descriptive metaphor of participatory being is a response to the inadequacies of attempts to theoretically ground logos by means of either the *eidos* or *aisthēsis*. In the *Parmenides*, impasses relating to time show why this chorismatic aspect of disclosure may not be eliminated: *chōrismos* is not a problem to be solved, but a feature of all discourse. One the one hand, if we privilege identity, then the idea in itself is unknowable; but this implies a paradox of self-reference, since the *eidos* names the intelligibility of experience. On the other hand, if we privilege difference, logos is always necessarily equivocal because time constantly revises the contexts of significance that give logos meaning. The transcendence of the *eidos* in itself thus seems to imply an absolute that is nothing to us, and a presence that is everything to us but nothing in itself. The intelligibility of experience is analogous to an odd proportion between a univocity that implies contradictions and a plurality that is irreducibly equivocal.

Socrates' analogies in the *Republic* indicate in what way the dialectical opposition between the hypothetical way up from experience and the purely formal way down must be supplemented and enacted in the transcendence of being toward the good.[10] *Alētheia* involves ongoing reformation of the whole through repetition as teleological reenactment. Similarly in the *Parmenides* a young Socrates learns that this transcendence of existence exceeds the representations of logos. In short, Parmenides shows Socrates that logos implies representations of the being of time that are either simultaneously true and untrue in the same sense, or irreducibly ambiguous. Worse still, apparently neither of these unreasonable extremes may be definitively eradicated. The problem of time implies that the very effort to eliminate equivocation metastasizes contradiction, and the attempt to resolve contradiction multiplies ambiguities.

Parmenides reduces to absurdity Socrates' initial separation of meaning and entity in order to demonstrate, by means of his dialectical game, a more philosophically productive development of the questions. This framing in the initial exchange means that the demonstration will develop the problem of *chōrismos*: intelligibility is granted to us, and yet the presence of moving, changing entities is also given. To deny either of these is absurd. But reflection on the being of time will show precisely what was wrong with Socrates' initial distinction between *eidos* and entity by developing the insight that all being is differential. Problems relating to the *chōris* of intelligibility are developed in relation to the ideas themselves—by means of reflection on time—so that Socrates' initial notions of both entity and idea may be reformed (133a8-b3; 135c8-136a).

In Parmenides' demonstration, participatory being proves itself original in an entirely unforeseen way. There is no substantive being, no individual, and no self that subsists in isolation from participatory being; the many meanings of being do not disclose an intelligible ground, for transcendence as such is never present. The implication is not only that what-is cannot be conceived as a collection of atomic individuals. Moreover, the wholeness of form cannot be understood as a composition of parts. Being exceeds the dialectical interrelations and existential correlations disclosed logically and empirically. This heterogeneity is irreducible insofar as existential transcendence—the negativity of intelligibility—informs the very effort to conceptualize this radical "otherwise," or *chōris*.

The metaphor of *metalambanein* indicates the odd supplementarity that allows comprehension: it signifies the finitude of being. The *Parmenides* shows that in Plato's dialogues Eleatic negative dialectic exceeds itself; the progress of questioning the meaning of "to be one" discloses even the unifying ideas as analogous to figures on the wall of the cave. The Platonic original—the metaphor of participatory being—means that thinking overcomes itself by recognizing its own oppositional intercontextuality with poetry. This was already implied by the supplementary role the idea of the good played in Plato's thinking from early on. The significance of participatory being toward the good in Plato's dialogues means that the beginning of *alētheia* is a primordial insufficiency.[11]

Ambiguity as Unity in Opposition

According to Aristotle, the Pythagoreans identified pairs of opposing *archai* that are beginnings or origins of being (e.g., *Met.* A5.986a22–986b8). Aristotle subsequently mentions these examples of such contrarieties: unity / plurality, good / bad, limit / unlimit, odd / even, rest / motion, straight / curved, light / darkness, male / female, square / oblong, right / left. There is no reason to assume that this list was intended as complete, or that these founding contrasts were thought to be manifested according to a single mode of disclosure.

This seems to change, however, with Parmenides' poem on being, which indicates the priority of ontological discourse over other forms of cognition, including the mathematical cosmology of the Pythagoreans.[12] But because the goddess distinguishes between modes of logos and explicitly grants priority to a discourse that makes existence and oneness thematic, we may affirm without controversy that Parmenides exploited the ambiguity of the meaning of *to hen* and developed the notion in a dialectical direction. But these noncontroversial observations imply Parmenides' realization that ontological discourse involves reflection on the limitations and possibilities of various modes of logos. This ironic exposure of the inadequacy of cosmological discourse (because of its reliance on unexamined ontological presuppositions), combined with negative and indirect efforts to evoke the transcendent wholeness of *alētheia*, also characterize Platonic reflections on unity and being. And insofar as the speech of Parmenides' goddess indicates that the possibilities of distinct modes of discourse are defined by different criteria of significance, her account is dialogical, not univocal. In ironically relating the limitations of the ambiguous and ontologically naive discourse of mortals, she exceeds the limits of a literal monologue.[13]

The subordinate role of natural or cosmological discourses and the priority of ontological discourse are conveyed explicitly by the goddess as well as implicitly, in the fact that the language of the way of opinion section ironically mimes statements from the way of *alētheia* (Fr. 8). This ironic relationship of contrast between the way of *alētheia* and the way of opinion is thematic, for the cosmological, or natural claims of typical mortal discourse are offered as part of an account that is plausible (for its time).

We do not need to engage in controversial interpretations of a fragmentary text if we simply affirm that the poem of Parmenides makes thematic not only the unified manifestation of what-is, but various contrasting modes of the articulation of being in and through logos. Thus one distinction implicit to both the poetic logos of the goddess and to the analogies of Socrates in the *Republic* is the distinction between various modes of disclosure and disclosure as such.

Poiēsis and the Power of Dialectic

In the poem of Parmenides, the goddess informs the youth that the route of what-is is marked by signs, or *sēmata*, that reveal the unity of being (Fr. 8). The being of the one, however, transcends phenomenal qualification. But furthermore, discourse that indicates relations of phenomena presupposes unexamined ontological principles: only if being is will entities manifest characters. The way of opinion is subordinate to and dependent on the way of truth because nonphilosophical discourse is informed by unexamined ontological principles.

The priority of ontological discourse over ordinary and cosmological modes of logos is conveyed not only in explicit remarks made by Parmenides' goddess, but also implicitly, as for example in the fact that the language of the way of opinion ironically mimes statements from the way of *alētheia*. The most obvious example of this involves the cosmological opposites fire and night. Like being according to the way of truth, fire is described by mortals as "the same with itself in every way, and not the same with the other," in other words, night (B8. 56–58). Plato, of course, makes this ironic contrast between the way of truth and the way of opinion thematic, but even for Parmenides the cosmological, or natural claims of typical mortal discourse are not completely uninformative, as claims about nonbeing would be. Instead, they are presented as part of a plausible but inherently ambiguous account.

In the poem of Parmenides, the ambiguous discourse of the goddess indicates why no mortal can speak the wholeness of *alētheia*, for this would involve a complete grasp of everything relevant, a god's-eye view of a total context. Because the ability to say how *to eon* (what-is) is would require an awareness of what-is in its wholeness—and this is impossible for mortals—the goddess communicates insight negatively: using irony, negations, and likenesses, to contrast incomplete mortal intelligibility with the fullness of *to eon* and *alētheia*.

The structuring of the Parmenides poem, in its articulation of modes of discourse that correspond to ontological distinctions, is developed in the organization of Socrates' image of the divided line in the *Republic*. The prologue of Parmenides' poem, which describes a chariot ride to the boundary of the phenomenal realm and beyond, is an analogical presentation of the discourse of the goddess, just as Socrates' parable of the cave and of the ascent toward the lighting of being are figurative developments of a literal account.

The central analogies of the sun, the line, and the cave (*Republic* 506d–521b) may be viewed as figures which reveal why the language of philosophy must be figurative: they are images that illustrate the philosophical re-cognition of imagery. These passages in the *Republic* describe the highest stage in the education of the guardian class. The analogy of the divided line illustrates the Eleatic contrast between philosophical *alētheia* and more context-bound, conditional modes of disclosure. The cave analogy is a development, in a social and political direction, of implications of the line; but it also serves to elicit, in a vivid and dramatic way, the ontological distinctions of the line. If political motivations—for example, overcoming the relativism of the sophists and curbing what was perceived to be the decline of the polis—prohibit taking Socrates' rhetoric in the *Republic* as Plato's last word on the nature of philosophy, there is also no reason to presuppose without question that Socrates is simply Plato's mouthpiece. On the contrary, given the irony of his performances, there is good reason not to presuppose even that the character of Socrates is unambiguously uttering his own views. And in the *Parmenides*, Socrates' notion of forms is reduced to absurdity.

Socrates' comically impractical proposals in the *Republic* can only be understood as ironical. Often the explicit argumentation is aporetic, and must be read in light of what is not being said; and dramatic action supplements verbal arguments. Other examples, already mentioned, of Platonic negative and indirect meaning are reductions to absurdity and the mimicry of sophistry in order to produce puzzlement. Throughout the dialogues, Plato approaches the topic for discussion in this manifold, rhetorically subtle way. His characters break open revelatory accounts repeatedly (and in a variety of ways) precisely to acknowledge the limits of manifestation and the irreducible differences of various modes of disclosure. Discourses oriented toward-itself and toward-another are not peculiar to the *Parmenides*; these are developments of a reflexive differentiation of contextuality that is discernible throughout the Platonic corpus.[14] Such distinctions show Plato to be concerned with many forms of logos and being; no single category grounds the various modes of disclosure.

The *Republic* indicates, and the *Parmenides* makes clear, that the most fundamental conditions of the possibility of intelligibility are not themselves intelligible. "In the realm of the knowable, the good is the last thing to be seen, and yet it is hardly seen at all" (*Rep.* 517b8-c1). Socrates has already claimed that the good is not *ousia* (509b8), and that we have no adequate knowledge of it (505a7-8). But the unifying principle of the good gives meaning to all manifestation, without being present as an entity (508b-509c). The implicit teleology of Socrates' account means that the disclosure of truth is simultaneously a closing over; we do not know *alētheia* itself. The comparison of the sun with the origin of disclosure is presupposed and developed in the icon of the divided line. Modes of disclosure are variable; the divided line shows that there are stages of possibility (layers of interpretation) by which things are discoverable in their being.[15]

But making thematic many senses of being is not equivalent to reducing these senses to one primary sense. Insight arises in the movement between—the differentiation—of modes of disclosure. The imaginative associations of *eikasia* are not the trusted correlations of *pistis*. Nor are the conceptual representations of *dianoia* simply to be identified with—or reduced to—the insights allowed by *noēsis*. Similarly, in itself the good is said to be unknowable; it is beyond beings. But as lived it is ambiguously disclosed as immanent teleology. The line itself—as an image—implies that neither conceptual representation nor discursive reasoning subsumes or definitively overcomes *eikasia*. None of these modes of disclosure are invalidated by their occasion: being toward the good in its transcendence. In its repeated reductions to absurdity of various positive accounts, the Platonic dialogue indicates that even *archai* oppositions themselves are signifying relations, not epistemological foundations. But the crucial aspect of these relations is negativity—opposition itself—dialectic as differentiation, not synthesis. This implies that interpretation is prior to presence. Obviously, if this is so, the use of irony and other nonliteral discourses might have philosophical significance that exceeds the limitations of literal discourse. We need to remember that father Parmenides was not only a logician and a lawgiver, but also a poet.

The shadow of Parmenides looms over the pivotal analogies of the sun, the line, and the cave in the *Republic*, where a mature Socrates asserts that knowledge is of what is; opinion is of what is and is not; and ignorance is of what is not (477a-b). The first way is analogous to Parmenides' path of it is, and it is not possible for it not to be. The second way is the mixed route of mortals, which lies between and mixes being and not-being. But the path of it is not and it is right that it should not be, is the way of complete ignorance and therefore not really a way; it is nonway.[16] It is perhaps these Eleatic distinctions between modes of disclosure that most influences Plato. Mortal discourse never achieves the wholeness of divine *alētheia*, nor does logos ever entirely transcend *aporia*. The *Parmenides* develops ontological insight by showing that both discourse and the disclosure of what-is in experience involve signs defined in relation to each other in a negative way.

The Platonic figure of Parmenides will show Socrates that the ideal in relation to itself yields no intelligibility. It is therefore not the case that *eidē* are intelligible solely with respect to their mutual relations. In light of all these implications of the *Parmenides*, the Aristotelian paradox of the third man—if it is intended as a critique of Plato's thinking—is simply irrelevant. Parmenides' inquiry into time raises more serious difficulties than the regresses with which he initially humbles Socrates. His game shows Socrates that regresses arise from an inadequate way of conceiving both intelligible meaning and entity. The demonstration is intended to show Socrates why the significant development of the problem of *chōrismos* arises in relation to forms themselves. The interesting separation is not between ideal and real being, but between the presence and nonpresence of form itself. This is why the doubtful question must be developed in relation to the *eidē* themselves (135d9-e5). Parmenides does precisely this in his dialectical demonstration for Socrates, and the problem of time reveals a radical incommensurability implicit to all intelligibility.

Parmenides shows that any possible disclosure exhibits a double aspect: to be is to be both signifier and signified. *Pros hauto* and *pros allo* are finally sign functions, not terms. Although Parmenides employs a family of such names from the outset, and highlights ambiguities and *aporiai* throughout his troubling play, nonetheless these provocations orient the potential philosopher toward analysis of sense and reference, and inquiry into meaning and intentionality. Because the game shows that any being exhibits a one in many (teleological) opposition, the efforts of Vlastos and others to ignore intentional analysis and the goal-oriented nature of cognition by focusing on formal structures of inference are repetitions of Socrates' naive effort to separate two necessarily parallel aspects of signification; disclosure in logos is this unification in differentiation. Such efforts thus repeat the very mistake that Parmenides' demonstration is intended to correct. Parmenides' inquiry into time implies that self-referential paradoxes are symptomatic of the reduction of teleology to representations of presence. All unification is differential.

The pivotal ambiguity of the *Parmenides* is already discernible in the *Republic*. Practitioners of mathematics postulate certain theses which they then regard as assumptions for the sake of discourse, although they do not give any further account or justification for these assumptions (510c). But the power of dialectic (511b4) is capable of revealing the merely conditional or hypothetical moment of discourse. But if *philosophia* involves the intercontextual differentiation of various forms of being and logos, then philosophical insight is not simply another mode of discourse. If discourse necessarily involves such notions as same / different, and unity/plurality, then dialectic itself implicitly involves *archai* of identity, difference, and presence, and an explication of such general notions is obviously impossible within a discourse that employs or presupposes them.

The freedom of philosophy to transcend itself, already indicated in the *Republic*, is developed in the *Parmenides*. Parmenides' *gumnasia* develops, not as positive explication but as negative ontology: the one—or any beginning—is not seen through without an inquiry into the consequences of its nonbeing in addition to an examination of the consequences of its being. Clearly a certain character might be displayed alongside another character, without an essential relation between them. The game demonstrates that if one abstracts the character in question (unity, plurality, etc,), and shows thereby that the other character would not occur, this indicates that the character in question is a condition of the possibility of the other.

How is the possibility of phenomenal apprehension correlated with the identity necessary for predication? Are *eidos* and particular manifestation ontologically unified in that the ground of the possibility of both is identical? Parmenides' game indicates that neither the transcendental subject nor the transcendental object serve as such a grounding principle. The condition of the possibility of intelligibility and presence is disclosure itself; but participatory being toward the good defies conceptualization. Is it then the case that, for Plato, being and beings are differently located? If it is the articulated and informed realm of what-is that is accessible to philosophical inquiry—if only being exists for thought—nevertheless *archai* such as unity are too general to be defined; therefore it is *poēisis* to call the hardly seen source of unity an idea, or an intelligible principle. Is it pedagogical or political rhetoric to identify this nonentity with what is good? Or is it an indication that the *eidē* let the world reveal itself through our goals and projects, as Heidegger claimed? Is the good simply the idea of ideas that makes something useful?[17] In the *Parmenides*, Socrates' initial understanding of the *eidē* involves an illegitimate privileging of forms for things that are agreeable and dignified. Parmenides admonishes him for this (130c–e).

Meaning, Entity, and the Ungrammatical *Chōris*

In asserting his initial conception of the forms, the young Socrates affirms confidently that *eidē* exist for "likeness" in itself (*homoiotēs*), "one" (*hen*), "plurality" (*polla*), and the other (unspecified) abstractions of which Zeno spoke. In addition to these intelligible meanings, Socrates is also willing to claim the existence of ethical-aesthetic forms such as rightness and beauty and goodness. Yet about the existence of forms for other things Socrates expresses doubt. He is not sure whether to assert the existence of *eidē* for entities, not even the most valuable of these, things such as man, fire, and water. Further, Socrates expresses certainty that *eidē* do not exist for ugly or worthless things such as hairs, soil, and filth (130c–d).

But Parmenides informs Socrates that the range of the *eidē* comprehends even such apparently unformed and worthless entities (130e). Socrates has unthinkingly granted to these entities an existence independent from the formative, unifying influence of the idea. Parmenides' demonstration will expose the consequences of this assumption of the nonexistence of formal unification.

Parmenides' game shows Socrates that the range of unity (and therefore of the forms, as unifying principles) is coextensive with the range of presence, or *ousia*; no unformed material in itself can exist in this sense. But if presence implies unification by form, his demonstration also shows that form exceeds presence. Notions such as unity / plurality, being / nonbeing, sameness / difference, and form/instantiation are only disclosed alongside one another, in their opposition. Moreover, apart from the manifold differentiations of existence, there is no intelligibility or form. And apart from unity, the many in themselves cannot be conceived in any way; they cannot even be said to be many.

If the one has no being in any sense, then there could be no appearance, opinion, conceptualization, or existence of the many as such (165e–166c). The *chōrismos* of meaning and entity infuses ideal relations because these are representations of being, and existence may not be represented without misrepresentation. If the articulations of participatory being are ontologically prior to ideal relations, this would cast in a different light the fact that the learning that is the disclosure of *alētheia* is described metaphorically in the dialogues as remembering. Such poetic descriptions are phenomenologically justified, for even before we learn to interpret distinctions that are articulated linguistically, we seem to have always already lived them.[18] This would be the case if matrices of ideal interconnections are implicit in any present instantiation. The paradoxical movement of disclosure—its indefinite finitude—is indicated poetically in the Parmenides poem (Fr. 5), when the goddess asserts that it doesn't matter where she begins, because she will get back there again. Another way to figuratively indicate this coherence in correspondence would be to claim that being is a whole, like a sphere.

The *aporiai* evoked by Parmenides in the introductory exchanges with Socrates (130b–135c) result from either attempting to reduce the *chōrismos* between form and thing or to widen it so far that the limited intelligibility of existence would be impossible. Parmenides' subsequent exploration of the distinction between ideal expression oriented toward-itself and indication of relations toward-another reveals the sense in which transcendence is conceived by Plato. On the one hand, the ungrammatical *chōris* does not imply that intelligibility is impossible, for that is not something we could think or communicate (135b–c). On the other hand, Parmenides' provocative mimings of sophistry (especially relating to the notions of whole / part and temporal / atemporal) show Socrates the consequences of attempting to ignore the *chōrismos* between intelligible meaning and the presence of an entity.

But sensual presence and intelligibility are distinct modes of disclosure insofar as the notions of whole and part apply in one way to things, and in another to the form. Socrates senses this, and responds with his analogy of the form to a day (131b). This use of analogy is the first indication that Socrates is moving toward the employment of a language appropriate to the way of being: form is analogous to the way the day is present as a whole in many places at once.

The young Socrates' analogy comparing the form to the day recalls not only the mature Socrates' image of the sun (*Republic* 508 ff.) but also the imagery of light and darkness in Parmenides' poem. In Socrates' analogy the form, like the day, is equally present everywhere that it is not absent: as day is to night, so the form or, more generally, the unity of being, is to nonbeing. This recalls the goddess's assertion about *to eon* in Parmenides' poem—that where being is, not-being is not. Being is this presencing out of what is not.

In that being is universal, it is analogous to a sphere equal on all sides from its center; it is not more or less anywhere, since nonbeing cannot prevent it from reaching uniformity. The Platonic Parmenides throws into question the notion of degrees of being that is implied by Socrates' initial conception of the forms. If the wholeness of being—in the fullness of *alētheia*—implies that nothing would prevent it from symmetrically resting evenly in its bounds (like a sphere), still the Parmenidean one is manifested in the Platonic dialogue as the one in many of various modes of logos and being. Thus there is a touch of irony when Plato's Parmenides casually suggests his own hypothesis on the unity of being as a means of illustrating dialectic and thereby developing the young Socrates' initial conception of the form.

The lesson of the regress arguments is that attempts to reduce eidetic to phenomenal discourse or vice versa leads to absurdity. The relationship described figuratively as the participation of physical things in the idea does not entail, and cannot accommodate, a relation of resemblance between form and thing. Material things may be said to resemble one other, if they have a share in the same *eidos*, but the idea resembles nothing. The paradox of the third man results from a misguided attempt to reduce to univocity distinct modes of discourse. The *eidos* is no thing. Paradox leads the potential philosopher toward the insight that all disclosure involves an odd supplementarity of various significations of unity and difference.

But analogy alone is not the way to the disclosure we are seeking. Parmenides makes this clear in his rejection of Socrates' untrained likenesses of the form first to a day and then to a thought. Socrates says that if we understand the *eidos* as a thought, this allows us to assert that the idea is unique and whole (132b). Furthermore, the unreasonable consequences that result when we speak of the form as though it were a thing are now irrelevant. A thought possesses a unity that, like the unity of being, does not lend itself to division; for a thought cannot be cut in half as a thing can. Socrates already recognizes that the wholeness and unity of intelligible meaning extends completely through its range, like the wholeness and unity of the day. But one problem with his untrained analogy is that the intelligible form always implies more than just the particular thought of a particular mind at one instant in time.

The *chōrismos* is not simply a gap between ideal and real entities; rather, anything that is disclosed in any sense—including an ideal of intelligibility—is revealed according to differing criteria. If we develop our questioning toward-itself (*Parmenides* 136a–c) then opposed *archai* pairs will be disclosed. But, although these *archai* oppositions inform the being of every *eidos*, in themselves the *archai* are not ideas. Instead they are indicative of the bounds of both existence and logic: they signify what we are, not only how we think. Since discursive reasoning is only possible by way of archaic differentiation, no *archē* in itself may be thought, but only disclosed in a negative way. Inquiry directed toward-itself then, involves a negative dialectic that leads to signposts of the bounds of being: any singularity is distinguished only in opposition to that which it is not. But if the negativity of archaic opposition also informs any *eidos*, how could any singular idea be thought in itself?

If our discourse is toward-another, does it simply indicate the existence of entities and their various features? But since paradoxes of perception are not resolved except by thought, phenomenal disclosure is informed by dialectical eidetic interrelations. Because phenomenal disclosure "is" in relation to the dialectically interrelated *eidē*, it is informed by difference and absence. This means that the persistent effort to resolve *aporiai* of perception inevitably unfolds as negative dialectic. Consequently, these interwoven modes of disclosure are not separate worlds that lie on either side of an unbridgeable gap; they are two inflections of the verb "to be," two ways in which being manifests. The many tenses and moods in the discussion of unity in the *Parmenides* indicate in what way and to what extent the discourse of philosophy may meaningfully articulate ontological ambiguities.

Although present entities may be seen to resemble one other, and this indicates that they share in the same intelligible meaning, the *eidos* looks like nothing. The meaning of a particular entity does not resemble the thing. Meaning cannot be cut into pieces as a sail can (131b ff.). Largeness is not large because meaning has no size. The more adequate modes of discourse Parmenides is attempting to indicate must not contradict what is given: a philosophical disclosure of being and unity must constantly refer to the meaningful experience of entities. To deny this given is absurd (135b–c). Such inquiry will not limit itself to metaphor because it is the erotic striving after knowledge, and likeness alone cannot account for intelligibility. For if a relation of likeness is asserted to obtain between *eidos* and entity, paradox is inevitable. On the other hand, we must acknowledge the implicit ambiguity in terms such as unity and being, and therefore we cannot pretend to more precision than the subject matter admits. Parmenides' game finally indicates that the systematic effort to eliminate ambiguity simply multiplies contradiction.

Explicitly, on the surface of the *Parmenides*, we are shown only what philosophy is not.[19] If one were to accept as literal Parmenides' ironical summations at 160b and 166c, the dialectical demonstration as a whole would amount to nothing more than an instance of the forbidden non-way of nonbeing in the Parmenides poem. For the way of it is not, is not a way at all, but an impasse. But is philosophy itself radically limited like other modes of logos?

There is an apparently reasonable stance toward time indicated by this dialogue that upon reflection leads to *aporia*. This reduction is a representation, or hypostasis of time. Parmenides intentionally and repeatedly lapses into thing-language in his accounts of unity, being, the *eidos*, and *chronos*. If we reduce *chronos* to a now, we reduce a manifold to a representation in which only what is present, thinglike, and imaginable has significance. But apart from beings that change, *chronos* is nothing; and Parmenides' account of the instant implies that time cannot be understood as a linear succession, for there could be no contact between atomic instants. He shows Socrates that time considered as a thing in itself is unintelligible. And any attempt to represent *chronos* leads to paradoxes that are irresolvable as long as the representation is taken in a literal way, for the reduction of temporal modes of repetition and discontinuity to a pure singularity undercuts the intelligibility it purports to allow. Therefore the only way beyond *aporia* is by way of nonrepresentational, nonmimetic insight. The ubiquitous negativity of being simply cannot be represented.

Is it the case that, after the provocative preparatory work of ironic dialectic, the only mode of logos that proves adequate to the disclosure of being is mystical silence? Or does silence speak also, in the context of a discourse to which it is opposed?

Chronos and *Chōrismos*

If every mode of disclosure in logos is bounded by *archai* oppositions that stand as signposts, then even the effort to cross the boundary and see through these differential beginnings would itself be informed by signifying oppositions. Plato's dialogues indicate that the reforming of the whole *psuchē* in a moment of insight is facilitated by the progress of ironic dialectic. If the divided line is said to depict stages of transcendence—for example, from disclosure that involves unfounded conjecture, through the trust that reliable generalizations allow, to knowledge of dialectical interrelations of *eidē* and toward the philosophical revelation of being—nevertheless manifestation as such is never manifested. Ironic dialectic is itself a rung or stepping-stone toward an act of differentiation that exceeds conceptualization.

Even in the *Republic*, the origin that Socrates names *to agathon* eludes disclosure, for the good is only indicated negatively and analogically. The *Parmenides* shows that because each of the indefinitely many possible modes of disclosure has its own criteria of significance, philosophical insight does not imply a moment of univocity. But the recognition that disclosure is differential in no way implies an overcoming of the negativity of being itself. On the contrary, no matter where we begin, we are always brought back again to this *chōrismos*: for even if it were the case that the real is the rational, then the disclosure of the incompleteness of rationality exceeds rationality. If Socrates' rhetoric in the central analogies of the *Republic* occasionally tends to obscure the finitude of the power of dialectic to disclose *alētheia*, Parmenides' troubling play highlights its own intercontextualization without univocity.

At the culmination of the initial discourse between Parmenides and Socrates, Parmenides states that Socrates does not yet comprehend the difficulties that ensue if the *eidos* is said to exist as a separate independent entity. The greatest difficulty is that if ideas are distinguished as existing separately from entities, they are unknowable (133b–134c). Thus the intelligibility of experience that it is absurd to deny (135b6–c4) is not accounted for by relations of *eidē* if they exist separately (*chōris*) apart from entities. The idea in itself is unknown to us (134b15–c2). If the relations of ideas themselves (such as mastery/slavery) could obtain apart from the presence of entities, not only would the intelligibility of our experience be impossible, but even a god could not have knowledge (*epistēmē*). Even if knowledge of the ideal in itself were possible, and a god possessed it, this would allow no divine understanding of real relations in human affairs (134c–e).

The implication is that being is a coherent unity-in-opposition informed negatively by differences. What-is manifests itself in many ways, and these must be considered according to different criteria: when we articulate being toward-itself (136a–c) interrelations of intelligible meanings are expressed, such as mastery/slavery. But if a term or relation is abstracted from the whole context of participatory being, it signifies nothing. If it is abstracted from this wholeness of context, any one has no being and no intelligibility: one is not even one (141d–e). Socrates' distinction, therefore, between intelligibility and presence may not be collapsed or dispensed with; but neither may it be rigorously developed: *chōrismos* necessarily accompanies correctness in the disclosure through logos.

Parmenides indicates to Socrates in their initial exchanges that the philosophically significant development of these difficulties will not be by means of a rigorous distinction between the ideal and the real. Rather, the questioning must be focused on the being of the ideas themselves (135e). This problematic is articulated in the subsequent demonstration by means of a reduction to absurdity of efforts to represent time.[20] The import of

Parmenides' demonstration will be to show Socrates precisely why, even if a god could possess all possible ideal relations in an instant, this would still not be knowledge.

The theme of temporal discontinuity within repetitions of sameness in logos is indicated dramatically in the dialogue's introductory passages (126a–127d). Cephalus narrates the dialogue; it was recounted to him previously by the horseman Antiphon, who heard it years earlier from Pythodorus, who came in when Zeno's reductions to absurdity were nearly finished. Thus the initial lines of the *Parmenides* evoke the problem of origins, or beginnings (*archai*). Zeno's paradoxes initiate the philosophical discussion because they imply that the being of a motion or change, which it is absurd to deny, cannot be unambiguously explained by the mathematical representations of the Pythagoreans.[21] It is not simply the unification of the disclosure of being, but rather the hypothesis that being is a plurality of singular, atomic units that leads to the absurd conclusion that motion is impossible. Parmenides' dialectical game reintroduces Zenonian paradox by reducing to absurdity efforts to represent time and being. Parmenides shows Socrates that if one conceives being as presence—ideal or real—not only is the intelligibility of experience not accounted for, but paradoxes and unintelligibility result. Socrates' conception of separately existing ideas—the originals of which phenomena are the images—implies contradiction.

If the theme of original and image (that structures the figure of the divided line in the sixth book of the *Republic*) remains important in later dialogues such as the *Sophist*, this does not imply a doctrine of degrees of being. *Eikasia* involves the ability to recognize an image as an image, and this applies to the image of the divided line as well. The line closes around onto itself insofar as the ways up and down the line are interrelated: they are different ways of contextualizing the intelligibility of disclosure that it is absurd to deny.

Similarly, Parmenides' troubling play indicates that even the *eidē* may be viewed as images, but if they are interpreted this way, then they are images of an original that is not an idea. Any logos depends on *archai* oppositions that are definitive of not just what we think, but also what we are. If the nonhypothetical opposition between good and nongood articulates prelinguistic experience, then the fact that the newborn does not yet understand what is good for it illustrates the Platonic theme of transcendence, and of knowledge as remembering.[22]

Intelligibility—moments of which are named by the *eidē*—intimately involves conditions of possibility, such as archaic opposition, that are not in themselves intelligible. But no overarching univocity, no unambiguous and noncontradictory mode of discourse subsumes all possible modes of *alētheia*. This makes every claim to truth an *eikōn*. But the image is that which *is not what it is*. *Alētheia* in and through logos is irreducibly chorismatic; it is permeated by difference as well as sameness. The good—in its opposition to the nongood—indicates the prelinguistic differentiation of existence: the futural origin of knowledge is being toward the good.

The reduction of this teleology implies absurdities. If we conceive time as the presence of a line of successive nows, we reduce being to a picture in which only what is present, thing-like, and imaginable has significance. Similarly, if we claim that the past has a share of being in the same way that what is present does, we involve ourselves in obscurities. The goals that unify and give experience its intelligibility are projections of futural possibility; in an important sense, they are not. Therefore, if the presence of an entity is the standard for a logos of *epistēmē*, the account undermines itself by resulting in entities characterized by an absence of intelligibility.

Socrates' initial formulation of two separate modes of disclosure (the presence of an object to sensation and the presence of an objective intelligibility to thought), cannot survive reflection on the being of time. Only if these two modes of signification could be unified in a dimensionless and atomic instant would such an account seem to be possible; and yet if this were the case, the account would be undermined. Socrates' initial conception of the ideas refutes itself; it implies an impossible and contradictory metaphysics of presence.

Reflection on the being of time indicates that oversimplification and pseudo-precision leads to paradoxes that are irresolvable as long as the image or likeness is taken in a literal way. If figurative discourse proves indispensable, it nevertheless may be recognized to be figurative. The dialogue's evocation of the being of time shows the extent to which even apparently literal discourse is figurative. In bringing into relief absurdities inherent to attempts to represent being, the *Parmenides* also discloses the way of *alētheia*: in showing how not to do philosophy, Parmenides is revealing what philosophy is. It is no coincidence that being is invoked in the dialogues by ironic reflection on various modes of human existence: actor, rhetorician, friend, angler, statesman, lover, man of courage, philosopher. Moments of *alētheia* are occasioned by goal-oriented strivings with and against others. Parmenides engages Socrates and evokes the being of philosophy negatively, by ironically reducing to absurdity discourses that do not recognize the ontological significance of *to heteron*.

The dialogue indicates why the being of anything is only disclosed in a negative or indirect way.

Though goal-oriented action (*ergon*) and logos may be distinguished in thought, still existence cannot be conceived apart from the intelligible meaning named by *eidos*. Socrates initially believes that one can conceive intelligible meaning in abstraction, apart from any particular bearer of this sense, and apart from other ideal significations. But Parmenides' game indicates that even if the intelligible form could be conceived singularly in abstraction, nevertheless in both the unspoken confirmation of meaning and in any communication, the expressive "toward-itself" and the indicative "toward-another" functions are strangely unified in differentiation. If prelinguistic disclosure were utterly undifferentiated, still *alētheia* in logos implies the ongoing effort to achieve commensuration between some unifying form and the bearers of its sense. And if all discourse is differential, there can be no pure soliloquy and no pure silence; being is singularly contextualized from within by the negativity and silence of its other. An absolutely unique signification would signify nothing; meaning involves repetition in differing contexts.

Parmenides' game shows that only insofar as phenomena are unifiable instances of a toward-itself (*pros hauto*) sense does the being that is disclosed bear intelligible meaning; we cannot think the singular percept apart from universal signification. But in intelligible experience, many unique expressive possibilities are opened for realization in confirmation or falsification. Similarly, in discourse a toward-another (*pros allo*) sign function like a gesture or a sound bears an intelligible meaning and also serves to indicate existence. Parmenides' troubling play will show Socrates that without this potential for unification of expressive and indicative functions, there would be no communication of intelligible sense.

Nonetheless these two aspects of signification are distinct (as Socrates initially senses), even though in both intelligible experience and in discourse their functioning is juxtaposed. An analogy may serve to indicate this teleological unity in opposition. In the multiplicity of real entities there is no number; being may be enumerated indefinitely many ways (143a–145a). Nevertheless it is that which exists, in its multiplicity that permits unification as enumeration. Participatory being is the intelligibility that arises in orientation toward (*pros*)—and differentiation from—unintelligibles, such as pure unity and pure multiplicity. Unification in relation to existences involves indefinite possibility of naming, enumeration, and measure: Simmias is tall in relation to (*pros*) Socrates, so it is not insofar as he is Simmias that he is short, but only because he is short in differentiation from Phaedo. The potential for differentiation indicated by such precognitive *tropoi* or orientations allow us to truly utter the claim that "Simmias is short."[23]

This freedom to name and enumerate in indefinitely many ways does not imply that humans as a group or individually control the ordering or logic of disclosure in logos; *pros hauto* signification is never simply a result of a decision or consensus. Nevertheless, any mode of signification is supplemented by other differing modes, and this substitution (*metalambanein*) involves evaluation. But if the *archai* oppositions that inform the dialectical differentiations of *eidē* are privileged because of their generality—their indefinite repeatability—nonetheless their power to disclose intelligible presence does not extend to themselves. And however we choose to name archaic oppositionality, we cannot think it.

But if we take seriously Parmenides' exhortation to Socrates at 135e–136c about the manner of dialectical inquiry into opposed ideas, would an inquiry into likeness reveal that the orientation toward likeness in itself leads to unintelligibility? Each *archē* taken by itself can only be named, not defined. But there is no basis in the *Parmenides* for assimilating all these heterogeneous names for archaic opposition. On the contrary, one effect of Parmenides' game is to show Socrates the irreducible ambiguity of intelligible experience. If inquiry oriented toward-itself into any form (or, alternatively, into any *archē*) would reveal paradoxes analogous to those Zeno evoked in relation to objects and their characteristics, this does not imply that *to heteron*—the differential moment of disclosure—may be overcome in an assimilative account of fundamentally indefinable names.

The effort to think the intelligibility of experience culminates inevitably in *diairesis*, or differentiation. If an *archē* is a simple indefinable name that does not get its meaning from constituent expressions, still there is no fundamental *archē* because any selection of a name (e.g., "one") is disclosed only in differentiation from its other (e.g., "many"); in itself the name has no being or intelligibility. The heterogeneity of any moment of disclosure implies that the dialectical differentiation between one *archai* opposition in itself (e.g., one / many) be not be completed: "one / many" has no intelligibility in itself, apart from the differential disclosure of being. How can the difference between one *archai* opposition and other *archai* oppositions (e.g., between one / many and same / different) be comprehensively thought, if the contextuality that gives significance to this opposition is existence? Parmenides' game implies that there can be no complete list of *archai* or Platonic indefinable names (*megista genē*) because fundamental oppositionality is what we are, not just how we think.

Parmenides demonstrates this primarily by showing that even the opposition between existing / not-existing cannot be comprehended, because the instant neither is nor is not. Similarly, the differentiation of an *archai* opposition and a form cannot be completed, (e.g., one / many versus beauty). The good and the beautiful are lived differentials, not conceptual foundations.

There is no purely formal expression of identity because disclosure oriented toward-itself and away from existence yields no significance whatsoever.[24] Moreover, the irreducible ambiguity of toward-another interrelations permeates toward-itself identity in disclosure of existences (142b–155e). If the negativity of intelligibility in itself is disclosed only over against the unintelligibly ambiguous positive of analogical indications of likeness / unlikeness in being, the question that remains is whether Parmenides also undermines this dichotomy—between the negativity of thought and the analogicity of existence. Parmenides shows that the consequences of the assumed existence and *nonexistence* of the one imply that there are finally no Platonic beginnings (*archai*) of thought. The intelligibility of experience itself implies the unintelligibility of experience: contextualization cannot be completed. The substitution involved in signification—as *metalambanein*—implies not only that the good itself is *epekeina tēs ousias*; the otherwise of the origin also means that negative dialectic culminates in a supplementary moment of *poiēsis*.

Chapter 3

𝕃𝕃𝕃𝕃

The Game Begins

"By a strange paradox, meaning would isolate the concentrated purity of its *ex-pressiveness* just at that moment when the relation to a certain *outside* is suspended."

—Jacques Derrida, *La Voix et le Phénomène*

Modes of Logos, Modes of *Chronos*

Parmenides' troublesome game ostensibly unfolds according to the schema he outlines briefly at 136a–c. In response to Socrates' question as to the proper mode (*tropos*) of philosophical training, Parmenides indicates that the development of his dialectical demonstration will be determined by the following three pairs of oppositions: (1) what follows if the one exists, and what follows if the one does not exist. (2) Under each of these opposed conditions, what follows for the one and what follows for the others. (3) Under these opposed orientations, what follows toward-itself (*pros hauto*), and what follows toward-another (*pros allo*). But this eightfold oppositionality will itself be challenged by the odd nonpresence of the instant (155e–157b).

The division of the exercise by the first of these opposed orientations indicates the significance of Parmenides' exhortation to Socrates at 135e–136a that the consequences of the nonexistence of unity must be examined as well of its existence. If both the existence and the nonexistence of the one imply the same consequence, that consequence may be assumed to obtain. However, on the most literal reading of the explicit results as summarized by Parmenides, this dialogue achieves nothing but contradiction. A further complication arises from the fact that many of the arguments in the discourse on unity may be interpreted in both a fallacious and a nonfallacious way: Parmenides suggestively mimes sophistry throughout.

This clue into the philosophical significance of the dialectical game may be developed in the following way. The ostensible results of the examination of the hypothesis of the existence of the one (137c–160b) must be compared to the ostensible results of the examination of the hypothesis of the one's nonexistence (160b–166c). Whatever results follow from both the assumption of the one's existence and from the assumption of its nonexistence may be regarded as at least ostensibly true. For if both p implies q and not-p implies q, then q is apparently true.

The qualification arises from the fact that the inferences used to support these results are ambiguous. For this reason, we must regard the explicitly stated results which Parmenides summarizes at various junctures as ironic. Though Parmenides' exercise differs in significant ways from his projected schema, it also remains true to the projection insofar as the game is structured throughout by oppositional orientations. By means of this differential or *diairetical* alternation of orientations—that informs both the projection of the exercise and the carrying out of it— Parmenides indicates the unusual persistence of archaic opposition even when the one is assumed to not exist. In this crucial respect, Parmenides' provocative and indirect way of *alētheia* is unified with that which is disclosed by means of it.

The reasoning in the sections (allegedly) exhibiting only disclosure oriented toward-itself (137c–142a; 159b–160b; 163b–164b; 165e–166c) is informed by the intention to isolate the singular meaning of a term. These sections ostensibly proceed by considering only what belongs to an intelligible meaning in itself, by eliminating other fundamental characters that are distinct from the nature in question. These passages are isomorphic insofar as isolating a singular meaning is shown to be impossible. However, the orientation toward singular meaning in itself—in every one of these allegedly *pros hauto* passages—only proceeds by way of its other: the orientation toward-another (*pros allo*). Moreover, the conclusion of these passages that follows from this (essential) mutual interpenetration of opposed orientations is the same in every case: for thinking, nothing exists in itself.

These passages allude ironically to Socrates' initial conception of separately existing *eidē* insofar as they get underway by attempting to consider only what is expressed in statements of identity depending on the subject's own nature, as opposed to how this nature is related to others. Thus the first beginning (137c–142a) purports to show that the meaning of unity considered in itself does not imply and cannot without contradiction admit of plurality, being a whole of parts, being in time, etc.

Parmenides shows that various characters do not belong to the meaning of unity (or plurality) considered in itself. The subject considered in itself, apart from time and existence, is shown to yield no knowledge, intelligibility, opinion, perception, or even meaningful speech. The implication is that, although a single idea may apparently be distinguished in thought, it is only defined within some nexus of ideas. But the inquiry into *chronos* indicates that this ideal matrix itself is disclosive only in and through participatory temporal existence. If a whole network of interrelated ideas is implicit to the temporal and goal-oriented striving that is human existence, nevertheless this whole can never be made explicit, for the matrix partakes of the impossibility of the antinomic instant.

In this way the game shows that the metaphorical notion of participatory being is not intelligibly reduced either to *eidos* or to phenomenon: disclosure implies both presence and the possibility of unification of future presences. But the very effort to make presence intelligible culminates in the recognition of heterogeneity, for the meaning of to be (*einai*) involves both to not be (*mē einai*) and an odd, unintelligible *nonpresence* that Parmenides names *to exaiphnēs*, "the instant." Being then is ambiguous in that its disclosure (*alētheia*) has many modes; being is transcendent in that its disclosure involves negativity. Thus the unity of the dialogue—the being of philosophy—is not Parmenides, or Socrates, or the totality of *logoi* that passes between them. This and the emphasis on many modes of logos and being argues against the thesis that Plato reduces *alētheia* to the presence of the ideas.[1] The *eidos* or *archē* considered toward-itself is unknowable because it is not.

The other type of assertion distinguished by Parmenides, namely, toward-another, ostensibly corresponds to the perception of various properties of an entity as it relates to others, as for example in the claim that Socrates is short. This mode of logos suggests the discourse of typical mortals satirized by the goddess of Parmenides' poem as the 'two-headed' way of is and is not. Such disambiguated, naively uncontextualized disclosure is also indicated by the visible (*horaton*) section of the divided line, where prereflective trust (*pistis*) coupled with active—but nonphilosophical—engagement, masks the indefiniteness of correlated phenomena. Parmenides' game begins on the assumption that discourse in the toward-another sense does not involve relations of identity that depend on a nature considered in itself. Rather, this discourse (allegedly) simply indicates manifestation of various characters as they are related to each other.

Near the beginning of the dialogue Socrates audaciously informs Zeno that there is no difficulty in showing paradoxes and ambiguities implicit to phenomenal disclosure. Socrates challenges Zeno four times to develop such difficulties in relation to the ideas themselves (129b–130a).

Zeno defers, but Parmenides accepts Socrates' challenge, and invokes Socrates' initial distinction in order to subsequently reduce it to absurdity. Parmenides' dialectical game shows why the attempt to separately conceive intelligible meaning (apart from entity) implicitly depends on an incoherent conception of *chronos*.

The crux of the overall *elenchos* involves the insight that Socrates' initial conception of intelligibility depends on a moment of pure presence in an instant. But Parmenides shows that the problematic interrelation of time and logos implies that even if such a punctual instant of pure signification were possible, it would make itself impossible. This is because the collapsing of expression in itself and indication of relations toward others in the dimensionless instant (that Socrates' initial account of intelligibility requires) would allow no signification at all, of either type.[2] Parmenides' account of the instant vindicates Zeno by showing that if what-is were a collection of atomic individuals, change would be impossible. Because unification requires heterogeneity, each of the two thematic aspects of intentionality (*pros hauto* and *pros allo*) requires the other, but there is no simple unity or synthesis of the two. Disclosure in logos is inherently ambiguous and aporetic insofar as to be implies to not be as well as that which neither is nor is not.

As metaphor, participatory being preserves the insight that all discourse is simultaneously both toward-itself and toward-another. But these intercontextualized modes of discourse must be rethought in light of time; and Parmenides' subsequent investigation into *chronos* discloses the operant ontological distinctions of this dialogue to be developments of the analogical accounts of the good beyond being in the *Republic*.

In his descriptions of the remedial dialectical training (136a–c) Parmenides refers to these two modes of disclosure in a variety of ways. First, beginning at 136a5, he illustrates the oppositionality of the mode of dialectical training by referring to the treatise which Zeno has just presented: "Take, for instance," he replied, "that hypothesis of Zeno's." The consequences of the assumed existence of a many must be examined in a twofold way: first, *pros hauta*, or toward themselves (136a7); and secondly, *pros to hen*, or toward the one. Furthermore, the consequences must also be developed on the assumption that such a many does not exist, and these consequences must be examined both for the one and for the many. These consequences must also be articulated in the same twofold way: toward themselves (*pros hauta*), and toward one another (*pros allēla*).

After offering this illustration of the dialectical development of Zeno's hypothesis, Parmenides applies the same type of proposal to the concept of *homoiotēs*, likeness (136b). Informative results may be disclosed only oppositionally, for example, by considering both the existence and the nonexistence of likeness. Such coimplications (*sumbainonta*) must be examined for whatever "one" is chosen and for its others; moreover, the subjects chosen and their others must be approached both toward themselves (*pros hauta*) and toward the others (*pros allēla*). At 136b–c, Parmenides generalizes, claiming that such dialectically opposed orientations will also disclose the truth about unlikeness (*anomoiou*), motion and rest, becoming and perishing, and to be itself (*einai*) as well as to not be (*mē einai*). Socrates should posit both the existence and nonexistence of these, and then consider what follows for the subject itself and for that which is other than the subject. Implications must be dialectically differentiated—both for the subject toward itself and for the subject toward the others—and developed for these others both toward themselves and toward the subject.

Parmenides says to Socrates at 135b that if anyone were, because of difficulties like the ones he himself has just raised, to deny that there are *eidē*, then that person destroys the possibility of discourse itself. But this would be absurd; it would be to use discourse to deny the possibility of discourse. Parmenides says (at 135a–b) that only an individual of very great natural gifts is able to overcome the kinds of difficulties he has raised and recognize that everything has both a *genos* (type) and existence in itself (*kath' hauto*).

The main body of the dialogue (135d–166c) purports to be a demonstration of the style of training prescribed by Parmenides as requisite for the beginning philosopher. The hypothesis chosen as the subject of the troubling game is Parmenides' own thesis that the one exists (137b3–6). Although the game ostensibly corresponds to the scheme projected by Parmenides, this correspondence is undermined throughout. For example, the sections do not later occur in the order in which Parmenides initially mentions them: on the assumption that the one does not exist, the consequences are examined first for the one toward the many (160b–163b) and only then for the one toward itself (163b–164b). In addition, Parmenides generates apparent paradoxes by including discourse toward itself in sections purportedly devoted to inquiry toward another and vice versa. And the actual development of the game suggests (at least) nine beginnings, not eight. But according to the oppositions Parmenides generates in his projection of the exercise (at 136a–c), there should be only eight reorientations.

The section of the dialogue dealing with *to exaiphnēs*, "the instant" (155e–157b) does not simply fall out from the threefold division that yields eight reorientations. Like many of Parmenides' arguments, the third beginning is an *elenchos*. The failure of any attempt to represent *chronos* without *aporia* indicates that the being of time may not be reduced to a representation without misrepresentation. The reductions to absurdity in the dialogue clear the way for the development of this insight and a questioning that views *chronos* as manifested through participatory being, rather than as existing in itself. Being determines the now through a teleological unforgetting.

What, one might ask, is the purpose of such elenctic cleansing? We should call to mind that Socrates is not Parmenides' only interlocutor in the dialogue. The other, the young Aristotle, later became a tyrant (he was a future member of the Thirty Tyrants). We are perhaps meant to recall Parmenides' reputation as a lawgiver. The demonstration that constitutes the second and longer section of the dialogue can thus be read as a test—one that Socrates passes but Aristotle fails. The intent of this test is clearly not simply logical; it is also *psuchē*-logical. The aim of every step in this gymnastic might be condensed and expressed in one question: "Which do you love more, *alētheia* or authority?" On the one hand, Parmenides and Zeno both admire the spirit of the young Socrates and his impulse to argument (see 130a and 135d). On the other hand, Aristotle's dutiful acceptance of Parmenides' provocations and reductions is hardly philosophical. Does this imply that tyranny is analogous to the sophistic attempt to reduce many modes of being and logos to univocity?

Parmenides' indirect and negative method is a way beyond the limitations of more context-bound forms of disclosure; it is orientation toward the fullness of *alētheia*. Its goal is not a univocal theory of being, or any other form of sophistry, despite appearances to the contrary. The irony of Parmenides' provocations and the failures of discourse—the suggestion of sophistry and the *aporiai*—define the sense in which ontology is conceived to be possible by Plato, and in what sense it is not even attempted.

The discussions of *chronos*, in particular, prohibit taking what is present as the standard for the meaning of being. The presence of the now (*nun*) does not determine being; on the contrary, the moment of presence is informed teleologically, by repetition and discontinuity. Because being as participatory allows the disclosure of *chronos*, the insight that disclosure in logos involves an odd interchanging (*metalambanein*), remains standing throughout the *elenchi* of the *Parmenides*. The possibility this discloses, for development of the being question, is the justification for Plato's style of philosophical *poiēsis*: the erotic dialogue. The unity it discloses cannot be thought; it is an irreducible plurality of forms of logos and being, each defined by difference.

Ungenerable, Unperishing, Indivisible, Unmoving

Philosophical discussion in the *Parmenides* is initiated by way of Zeno's paradoxical treatises. The conversation begins after the reading, when a very young Socrates asks for a repetition of the beginning. Zeno rereads the first hypothesis of the first logos, and Socrates shortly thereafter challenges Zeno four times. There is nothing marvelous, he says, in showing that things that share in (*metechein*) ideas are characterized by opposition. But if it could be shown that likeness itself involves interchange (*metalambanein*) with the unlike, or unlikeness itself with the like, that would be a portentous sign (129b1–4). If someone could show that both kinds and ideas in themselves (*en autois*) are affected in this way, then that would be a marvel (129c2–4). If someone could first distinguish separately (*chōris*) the ideas of likeness and unlikeness, multitude and unity, rest and motion, and all other such, and show that these ideas themselves are capable of both mingling and division, that would be marvelous (129d8–e5). It would be truly amazing, Socrates says, if ideas, in themselves, could be shown to be an intertwined manifold as are the things distinguished by sight (129e6–130a3).

Parmenides, after a show of reluctance, takes up the challenge for his friend Zeno, and first humbles the *philoneikia* of the young and enthusiastic Socrates by reducing him to confusion (130a–136c). When the initiate to philosophy has been made ready for insight in this way, Parmenides demonstrates for him precisely those marvelous consequences Socrates had challenged Zeno to demonstrate. Parmenides accomplishes this by means of the troubling play that is the mode (*tropos*) of training he recommends to Socrates (135d–136c). The dialectical game (137c–166c) demonstrates that all discourse involves both identity and heterogeneity: there is ultimately no rigorous distinction possible between expressions of identity based on a subject's own nature, and indications of relations between the subject and other natures.

Parmenides demonstrates this in a number of ways. For example, these two ostensibly distinct modes of discourse interpenetrate every section of the dialogue. Furthermore, the method based on the distinction between meaning and entity undermines itself in another way. Which hypothetical orientation—toward-itself or toward-another—is the third beginning (on the instant) ostensibly intended to exemplify? The nonhypothesis on the instant (155e–157b) reconfigures the eightfold hypothetical method, as well as the apparently straightforward distinction from which the method is developed. It is the lack of content in the ideal representation of a now that allows its infinite repetition, or applicability to any possible moment.[3] But this absence of content undercuts the notion of the punctual instant, and shows exactly what the metaphor of participation implies. Parmenides' reductions to absurdity preserve the Platonic insight that the moment exists only insofar as humans engage in goal-oriented activities in the totality of supplementarities that is participatory being toward the good. If time is one way entities are interrelated, still, time in itself is completely unintelligible.

Pedagogically useful puzzlement or the provocation of Socrates are not adequate explanations for the fact that discourse toward-itself and toward-another are juxtaposed throughout the dialectical game, for Parmenides' inquiry into time shows this intercontextuality to be inevitable. Socrates' initial distinction presupposes the identity of what-is to be foundational. Parmenides' troublesome game undermines the foundational role of identity by showing that disclosure which indicates one's interrelation to other natures is more fundamental. Even if a completed expression of identity could be intelligibly present in an instant (in the mind of a god), this instant would make signification of any kind impossible. Parmenides demonstrates that Socrates' initial distinction must be radically reconfigured because both identity and otherness structure all manifestation, whether the entities disclosed are ideal or real.

The One Toward-Itself

Parmenides begins by making a show of adhering to Socrates' distinction between the disclosure of essential features on the one hand, and on the other hand, the disclosure of whatever different characters an entity might exhibit. Parmenides gets underway by noting that if one is[4] then it will not, according to its own nature, be many. This is ostensibly what will occur in this section; the meaning of the one will be distinguished in itself simply by eliminating all other characters.

Parmenides next explains that the one cannot be said to be either a part or a whole, for a part is one of several parts of a whole, and a whole is composed of more than one part (137c). Therefore, to be either part or whole means to have a share of multitude. But if the one as such is precisely that which by nature admits no plurality, then the account of the meaning of unity does not require, and could not admit, the notions of whole or part. Therefore, unity is neither a part nor a whole composed of parts.

After first purporting to disclose only the one in itself (*pros hauto*), Parmenides immediately argues that part and whole are interrelational notions, and may only be understood in relation to the other (*pros allo*). The first example of reasoning in the game introduces a precedent that fundamental characters are meaningfully disclosed only in differentiation from other such characters: this means that the *archai* are founding contrasts and not unambiguous principles defined entirely in themselves. The argument at the outset of the demonstration (137c4–d5) depends on this: the interrelational status of whole / part is used to support the claim that the one according to its own nature cannot be many. One is defined only in opposition to many other characters. This initial reasoning in the game already implies that Socrates' distinction cannot be rigorously maintained; discourse toward-itself and discourse toward-another are indicated by the first inference of the demonstration to be unified in their opposition, and not completely separate (*chōris*).

The one has no beginning (*archē*), middle (*mesos*), or end (*teleutē*), Parmenides now argues, since these would be parts of it (137d6–7). But beginning, middle, and end are significant only in relation to one another, and this unification in oppositionality itself only signifies in relation to some one that displays them. And is part (*meros*) to be understood here in a spatial or a temporal sense, or both? How can the term *archē* (beginning) be conceived as a 'part' without reference to space or to time? Again Parmenides' actual procedure renders dubious his allegedly straightforward method. Parmenides' style of training depends on the ability to distinguish a nature separately—in itself—apart (*chōris*) from other natures or characteristics. But Parmenides first showed that whole and part are defined only in opposition to one another, and now he has claimed that beginning, middle, and end are parts. The problem is that these may not be conceived except as unified in their opposition to one another; moreover, they cannot be called parts without reference to something else other than unity: namely, space or time. Already it is clear that the orientation of logos toward-itself cannot be simply the isolation of a singular intelligibility.

Or perhaps the claim here that *archē* (to take one example), is a kind of 'part' might be derived from considering the natures, in themselves, of beginning and part? In that case again, discourse toward-itself discloses the interrelations of natures, for example genus / species relationships. But these relations are also differentiations; they obtain between natures that are not identical. And if disclosing genus / species relationships is what discourse toward-itself is, then the negative procedure of differentiating other natures from the nature of the one is not an example of discourse toward-itself. What Parmenides is ostensibly doing in this first beginning is simply considering what belongs to the meaning of unity. If it is argued that the first beginning really is an example of discourse toward-itself, then it must also be the case that something about the nature of *to hen* makes it a fundamentally different kind of *pros hauto* inquiry than is the reflection on the natures of beginning and part, for these natures are defined only in relation to other natures: beginning implies a spatial or temporal reference, and part is defined only in relation to whole. The ostensibly straightforward method appears to require further refinement; but this refinement will be by way of disclosing further differentiation of sign function within the *pros hauto* orientation.

But, Parmenides claims, beginning and end are the limits of each one (137d8–9). Does this mean that the ideas of beginning and end are each the limit of the other, when these natures are considered in themselves? Or does it mean that any one that exists may be observed to have a beginning and an end, or both? In either case, or both, the allegedly unproblematic method is again exceeded.

Since the nature of the one, in itself, implies neither beginning nor end, Parmenides now asserts it to be *apeiron* (137d10). Just seventeen lines into the demonstration of the method required for proper training as a philosopher, the subject of the discourse is said to be without definable limit! We are making progress. Or perhaps the intelligible meaning of unity is indivisible and omnipresent like the day, which is in many different places at once as the same being? If so, why did Parmenides replace Socrates' illustrative analogy with the misleading one of the tangible and divisible sail (131b8–c1)? No doubt we can trust him now not to mislead us, in this demonstration of proper philosophical method.

Then why does he next describe various shapes displayed by objects at 137e2–6? Parmenides claims that the one is without shape (*schēmatos*), because possessing a shape means having definite boundaries and limiting parts. The one has no shape, since it has no parts and therefore no limiting parts. The inference here (at 137e) implies that shape may only be understood in relation to other natures. The meaning of *schēmatos* is itself shaped insofar as it may not be conceived or defined apart from other terms such as "part" and "limit." Therefore it is not only the nature of the one that may not be defined positively—in itself—for it is only in relations of contrast with other natures that shape is defined. But this is also another example of inquiry directed toward-another, used in an ostensibly toward-itself orientation.

And again the meaning of unity is indicated only negatively. Does this imply that the nature of any one in itself is determined only by contrast with characters that are displayed by other natures? Is this what inquiry directed toward-itself is? Or is it the case that, in itself, a mode of discourse is nothing, and that it exists only in differentiation from a whole of discourse? If so, how might this whole of logos be known? Obviously it could not be heard or spoken or actually present all at once; is it the case that any one is like this? The unity of logos in this dialogue is an analogue for the unity of any being. After all, if *kosmos* is truly one, it is so in spite of the fact that we never see it or know it in its totality. The dialogue indicates that *kosmos* is one only insofar as *chaos* is ordered: *kosmos* is oppositional unification of the indefinite.

What is this unification in itself, apart from how we experience and think it? Parmenides answers this question repeatedly in this dialogue. His answer is that whatever any being in itself might be, we can have no knowledge of this. Parmenides shows Socrates that his initial conception of the *eidos* implies this paradoxical contortion of language: "In itself, any being is nothing to us." How does one avoid this grafting of meanings? Parmenides' game nowhere does.

The *Chōra* of Singular Intelligibility

Parmenides argues that the nature of the one cannot be in any locus; for it cannot be either in itself or in another (138a–b). Parmenides here ironically alludes to the discussion with Socrates that preceded this demonstration: for "in another" (*en allō*) and "in itself" (*en heautō*) suggest the variety of characterizations of the two contrasting ways of considering an *eidos* in itself or in relation to another nature (see 129a–136c). The game is Parmenides' counterchallenge to Socrates; and the young philosopher's task is to keep these two modes of intentionality separate, if he can.

Parmenides asserts that if the one were contained in another, it would be observed to contact points of its container with points of itself; but if the singular meaning of unity does not involve the notions of part or shape, unity could not be contained within another in this way. Here again we have reasoning that juxtaposes an orientation toward meaning in itself against indications of existential relations toward others: if the meaning of unity does not have limiting parts, the one could never be observed to be encircled within another and spatially contained.

Neither does the one contain itself, Parmenides continues, for to contain is one thing and to be contained is another, and in order to do both, the one would need to be two. The same entity cannot be both the container of itself and contained by itself. Is the principle introduced here (138b4–5)—that a whole cannot be both active and passive (*peisetai kai poiē-sei*) in the same action—intended as a metaphysical or a logical principle, or both? If both, the thematic opposition of the method is again thrown into question. If a principle of existence is also simultaneously a principle of logic, then obviously a rigorous separation between meaning and entity is impossible. This impossibility is even clearer if the distinction between active/passive is simply a metaphysical principle being employed in an ostensibly logical discourse toward-itself.

But even if the distinction between active / passive indicates a characteristic of logos, how is this related to the isolation of the meaning of unity in itself? This would imply that the process of eliminating other characters from the one is governed by rules or principles that are themselves never eliminated. But if every moment of the game is governed by such beginnings (*archai*), then they are implicated in the disclosure of whatever one we consider. If even the meaning of unity in itself implies relations with another beginning or principle, then there can be no singular meaning or disclosure. Just as we cannot think either one or many in itself, so we cannot think any archaic opposition; though we cannot think without this. What would pure activity or passivity signify? Parmenides claims that even a god could have no knowledge of such separate intelligibilities (133a–134e). Alternatively, what is the being that is both compelled (*peise-tai*) and creative (*poiēsei*) simultaneously, in the same act?

Parmenides shows Socrates that principles such as noncontradiction, identity, and simultaneity are necessarily implicit even to a discourse that purports simply to eliminate all other characters from the meaning of unity. The very process of eliminating other characters from the meaning of a term in itself necessarily involves others: these beginnings are not eliminated because they are principles of the process of elimination. The apparently simple expression of an identity in itself (e.g., "the one is the one") implicitly involves other conditions of possibility, such as the being of time.

Can the one be said to be at rest or moved? At 138b10–c2, Parmenides asserts that alteration and change of place are the only motions (*kinēseis*). But the one could not alter its character and still be one, since oneness is its character. Therefore, motion in the sense of alteration is ruled out. But how do we know that these are the only two kinds of motion? Is this an empirical generalization, or is this principle derived from *a priori* reflection on the nature of motion in itself? When did this reflection occur? We are supposedly considering only what is implicit to the meaning of unity in itself, and eliminating all other characters. Is the principle introduced here that "motion means either alteration or change of place" unrelated to the nature of oneness, or implicit to the meaning of unity in itself? If it is completely unrelated, why is it employed here? What is the justification for introducing it at all? And if it is related in some essential way to the nature of unity in itself, then once again, the very process of eliminating character A from the nature of the one implicitly involves characters X, and Y, and so on. Toward-itself discourse then, involves dialectical differentiation, rather than expression of singular meaning.

Does the logical method of eliminating other characters from the meaning of the one implicitly involve reference to terms based on empirical generalization? If the *pros* distinction that structures the eightfold hypothetical method were adequate in itself, the claim that alteration and change of place are the only two forms of motion could be justified either by reflection on oneness in itself, or else by considering a one as it is related to others. In either case, the apparently straightforward method, based on Socrates' distinction between an idea in itself and an idea in relation to others, has been exceeded from the outset of the dialectical demonstration. Why should the isolation of the nature of unity in itself involve indications of how a one that exists is observed to move? The first beginning is inconsistent with the method it purports to demonstrate: not only is it the case that logical principles are necessarily implied in the effort to isolate a single meaning; in addition, the effort to isolate an *eidos* in itself involves reference to terms that have their meaning only in relation to lived experience and the differences between temporal phenomena such as movements and changes.

Parmenides asserts that if it were to move by changing place, the one would have to either revolve in a circle or go from one place (*chōra*) to another (138c6–8). But again, how do we know these are the only two kinds of change in location? Is this principle analytically true or empirically verifiable? In either case its employment here reconfigures the method. Since this first beginning purports to be simply a consideration of the meaning of unity in itself, why are other principles and characters being introduced at all? Apparently the nature of the one in itself necessarily involves differentiations within a whole: of principles, forms, and phenomena. This implies that what anything is implicitly involves what it is not. The *eidē*, then, are not a collection of atomically independent entities. Even the (apparently) univocal disclosure of a system of ideal relations presupposes logical principles—and the implicit notion of simultaneity—and the ideal whole gets its meaning in relation to possibilities

of lived experience and observations of phenomena. No ostensibly positive account can avoid such differentials.

Parmenides states that to revolve means to rest on a center and to
have parts which go around that center (138c8–d1). The idea of revolu-
tion then is defined in relation to motion, parts, and center, (in addition
to principles such as identity, noncontradiction, simultaneity, the law of
the excluded middle, etc,). Since neither middle nor parts belong to the
one as such, unity cannot be said to revolve.

Becoming and Singular intelligibility

But neither can it move by passing from place to place; for inasmuch as it
was seen to be impossible for the one to be located in anything, it is all the
more inconceivable that it should come to be (*gignesthai*) located in something (138d6–7). Still another claim is introduced and employed here, in
an account that purports to merely eliminate extraneous characters from
the meaning of the one: namely the assertion that becoming is more difficult to conceive than being. The point is not to consider whether this
assertion is supported adequately or not. Parmenides has already inferred
that a one cannot be contained in any location. And he now argues that
a one could not come to be in a location except as a whole or part by part;
but since neither part nor whole belongs to the nature of the one, it could
not come to be in a different location.

Since the conclusion here about being in a different location was
already implied, the interesting question is why Parmenides refers to the
greater impossibility of coming to be in a different location. The implication is that something about becoming makes it more difficult to understand than being. But again, what is it about the effort to isolate the nature
of the one in itself that necessitates the introduction of such apparently
unrelated claims? It is not immediately obvious why motion might not be
eliminated from the meaning of unity in itself without introducing apparently extraneous principles. Again the expression of identity and the indication of relations to others seem to be inextricably entangled.

If a thing is passing into a location, parts of the thing are observed
to come to be in the place while other parts are seen to be not yet there.
Therefore, only wholes composed of parts move (138d8–e5). Again, this
reasoning mixes discourse toward-itself and discourse toward-another. Is
the process of changing place that is indicated here disclosed by a priori
reasoning on the nature of unity in itself?

It would be not only irrelevant but futile to defend Parmenides' procedure by claiming that he might have limited his discourse to the meaning of unity in itself, except for some ulterior motive such as simply producing puzzlement. The question as to why the character of Parmenides exceeds the apparently straightforward method is crucial because this *why?* leads to the transfiguration of Socrates' distinction between idea and entity. Is all disclosure informed by the odd interchange or substitution of *metalambanein?* If, as the game indicates, such supplementarity is inevitable, then participation is no ordinary metaphor. If there can be no singular signification, and logos involves both repetition and discontinuity, this development puts us in a position to see the significance of the game's central reductio of the effort to represent time as a punctual instant.

The one then, Parmenides now claims, cannot move by changing place, or by revolving, or by changing character; in short, neither motion nor change can be said to pertain to the one. Furthermore, since we cannot say that unity is ever in anything, it follows that it is never in the same (139a7–10). Again, Parmenides seems to be provoking someone to object: never being in the same (*en tō autō*) makes plain the ironic juxtaposition of toward-itself and toward-another criteria of significance in these inferences. The first beginning shows Socrates that this proximity cannot be overcome by a definitive separation without complete loss of significance.

A similar effect—on a rudimentary level—was achieved in the introductory discussion with Socrates, when Parmenides provocatively employed phenomenal criteria to refer to the disclosure of the *eidos* (e.g., the sail analogy). Now Parmenides suggestively infers that because the one is never in the same, it can never be at rest, therefore the one is neither moving nor at rest (139b3–4). The irony is that because it is never in the same the one could be said to be in constant motion. Parmenides again plays on the distinction between thing and idea. This ongoing juxtaposition of two apparently distinct modes of disclosure suggests that the distinction between them may not be rigorously developed, and prepares the way for the demonstration why: the instant of univocity implies neither intelligible presence nor the absence of nonconsciousness.

But this neither / nor of singular signification has already shown itself. Neither sameness nor difference belongs to the nature of unity (139b–c). Unity is not the same as itself (*heautō*), the same as anything else, different from itself (*heterō*), or different from anything else. If it were different from itself, Parmenides says, it would be other than one, but this is impossible. The one cannot be the same as anything else, Parmenides infers, because if the one were the same as anything else, it would be other than itself and so not one. If oneness were identical to some nature that is other than unity (i.e., sameness), unity would be identical to not-unity; but this is impossible. But furthermore, unity is not different from anything other than unity. Difference—*to heteron*—is not part of the meaning of unity. But only by otherness, Parmenides asserts, is anything different from another: *alla monō heterō heterou, allō de oudeni* (139c6).

The sheer emptiness of the notion of singular intelligibility becomes more and more apparent. This movement will culminate in the disclosure of the nonconsistency of this intention: singular signification could not signify.

Parmenides infers that it is not by being one that a thing is different, *alla monō heterō heterou*, "but only in virtue of difference that it is different." If it is not by virtue of itself that a one differs, it is not as itself that it differs, and if the notion of unity in itself does not imply difference, there is a sense in which unity is not different from anything else. In itself, unity is neither same nor different (139c-d). Because these inferences demonstrate a mode of disclosure in logos that eludes genus / species relationships, it is now clear that *pros hauto* signifies a range of orientations, rather than a singular linguistic modality. As Parmenides abstracts the meaning of *to hen* away from all relations of ideas (e.g., genetic / specific differentiations), and away from time and being, the movement culminates in a name empty of significance.

But he is only able to accomplish this *via negativa* by means of constant differentiation of the one from other natures, by employing logical principles and empirical generalizations that he nowhere attempts to justify. Parmenides suggested near the culmination of his initial exchanges with Socrates (at 135c) that denying the intelligibility of discourse presupposes such intelligibility. It is now apparent that if such self-referential inconsistency is an argument against anyone who denies the intelligibility of experience and discourse, then it is also an argument against the separate existence of the ideas. But Parmenides' reasoning throughout the first beginning distinguishes the significance of unity in itself only by constant reference to other natures, that is, by means of significance toward-another. Parmenides nowhere demonstrates any logos that avoids such discontinuity.

If noncontradiction implies simultaneity, nonetheless the critical participant will ask why reasoning based on observations of becoming and change are implicit to the distinguishing of the meaning of unity in itself.

Parmenides argues that if the natures of unity and sameness were identical, then whenever something came to be (*gignesthai*) one, it would become the same, and whenever something came to be the same, it would become one. But if something came to be the same as the many, then it would become many and not one: therefore unity and sameness are not identical (139d4-10). When something comes to be the same, it does not thereby become one; for if something comes to be the same as the many, it comes to be many, not one.

Because something can come to be the same without thereby coming to be one, we not only know that unity and sameness are not identical, but we also know that sameness is not a species of unity. Similarly, if unity were a type of sameness, then when something came to be one, it would thereby come to be the same. But Parmenides claims that if the one itself were the same, it would not be in itself oneness (139d10-e1).

The toward-itself orientation demonstrated by Parmenides does not expose the intelligibility of the singular idea, but evokes the limits of disclosure oriented toward-itself. What these arguments show Socrates is that the meaning of *to hen* is lost entirely when it is considered in itself, and distinguished from other fundamental characters. To be is to be unified as an idea unifies a many: to stand forth as a unity out of a multiplicity. Apart from this ontological differentiation, there is no being and no intelligibility.

Moreover, unity is not a species of difference, for it does not follow from the unity of a thing that it is different: it is not as one that anything differs, but only insofar as it is different (139c). In itself, unity cannot be said to be like or unlike either itself or another (139e-140b). To be like, Parmenides argues, means to be affected (*paschō*) in the same way, but the one has no share of sameness and so is in no sense affected in the same way as anything else.[5]

If unity had any affection distinct from its oneness, it would not be what it is, namely, unity as such. And since to be unlike means to be affected in a different way, the one cannot be unlike, for it is not affected at all. Again the meaning of the one in itself is distinguished only in differentiation from empirical correlations. Parmenides indicates in these inferences not only that ideas are defined in relation to one another, but also that the nonempirical singularity of form only signifies in juxtaposition with empirical contextuality. But Parmenides' claim that the meaning of likeness / unlikeness implicitly involves reference to observed affections (*ta peponthata*) of an entity might be extended to the one as well. Does unity/plurality also only have meaning in the context of participatory being?

Nor will the one by nature be equal or unequal either to itself or to another (140b–d), for to be equal means to have the same measure. Since unity does not partake in sameness, it cannot be said to have the same measure as anything. Furthermore, if to be unequal means to have more or less measures, then, since a thing has as many parts as measures, only divisible, spatial things should be said to admit of a measure, and therefore unity itself is not unequal, not even to things with which it is not commensurate (*mē summetron*). Nor can it be said to have one measure, for it would be equal to this measure, and unity has been shown to have no share of equality.

The theme of time was introduced in the first lines of the *Parmenides* by reference to the history of the repetition of this discourse, transmitted by persons who were not present at its occasion. The motif of temporality as repetition and discontinuity suggests the problem of beginnings, of non-presence at the origin. Difficulties relating to representation of the being of time also inform Zenonian paradox: that moment that precedes but begins the discussion. The thematic moment of beginning as presence / nonpresence is constantly reintroduced throughout the first beginning by reference to becoming, as well as by the frequent appeal to the notion of simultaneity that is implicit to the principle of noncontradiction.

Time and Singular Intelligibility

But if the one has no equality or inequality, Parmenides continues, and no likeness or unlikeness, it cannot be the same age as itself or another, nor either older or younger than anything. In short, the nature of unity possesses no temporal qualifications, since these all admit of measure, but unity itself does not. But any one that is, any one that has a share of being, possesses temporal characteristics, and comes to be older than the entity it once was (141b). If to have a share in being means to become, that is, to be generated, to endure for a time, and to perish, then the being of any entity is inextricably bound up with time in this way, so that *metechein* in being also means to have a share of temporality, and vice versa (141e). But the one as such—since it has no equality / inequality—is never younger than, or the same age as, or older than. If *to hen* as such is entirely separated from time and being, its singularity does not even allow the tautologous claim that one is one (141e13–14). No logos, no perception, and no opinion of it would be possible. If the one in no way *is*, it may not even be named (142a). Parmenides has effectively barred the initiate to philosophy from proceeding further in this direction: considering a nature solely according to itself is a way of complete ignorance, and therefore not a way at all.

Parmenides' Synopsis at 142a

The passage, which is both the conclusion of the first beginning and the transition to the second (141d–142a), does not simply indicate that a merely tautologous identity is void of informative content and, in this sense, may be said to yield neither perception, nor opinion, nor *epistēmē*. If *to hen* in itself does not imply being a whole of parts, being limited or unlimited, being shaped, being in itself or in another, or being in time in any way, then the one is nothing. Unity in itself is not disclosed in any way; and no truth in logos is possible about it, not even the uninformative claim that one is one. If oneness is abstracted from *chronos* and *ousia*—apart from the many and apart from all the other oppositional natures invoked throughout the dialogue—the one allows no logos, is not one, and cannot even be named (141d–142a).

Inquiry into the one toward-itself implicitly involves differentiation from others. Not only is the process of eliminating other characters from the nature of the one impossible without discussion of these other characters, but moreover, the eliminating itself is only carried out by employing the principle of noncontradiction and presupposing its implicit notion of simultaneity. This means that the actual practice of disclosure in logos oriented toward-itself is thoroughly informed by that which it is not; namely the orientation toward-another.

But the synoptic summary of the results of the first beginning is simply negative in character. The synoptic overview of the first beginning as a whole is formulated negatively, even though the praxis of toward-itself disclosure in logos involves apparently positive correlations insofar as Parmenides' practice employed principles and generalizations that are not shown to be implicit to the meaning of unity. If it is by way of noncontradiction that Parmenides isolates the singular meaning of *to hen*, paradoxically—at the moment of isolation—even this relation is suspended. The one in itself is not one (141e). Parmenides climbs up a ladder and kicks it away. If logos involves singular intelligibilities, such singularity is nonetheless unintelligible.

Because Parmenides will disclose these antinomic beginnings (*archai*) repeatedly and in different ways, it will be useful to compare and contrast

Parmenides' summary synopses, which occur at the end of every beginning. But at this point, in order to reorient ourselves within the whole dialogue, it is important to note that the synopsis itself constitutes a different
mode of disclosure from that of which it speaks.

Reorientation within the Whole

The one abstracted from being may not even be said to be one. This otherwise is being's withdrawal; such closing over necessarily occurs alongside the disclosure that is truth.[6] If disclosure of being in logos is not
possible apart from logical identity, still this identity itself is not intelligible. Expression of identity, pursued beyond the odd juxtaposition that is
participatory being, is a nonway. This movement in the *Parmenides* is analogous to the ascent indicated by the central analogies of the *Republic*, the
transition from discursive reasoning to the figurative discourse that seeks
to illuminate the conditions of the possibility of dialectic itself. What the
power of dialectic can disclose only negatively, philosophical *poiēsis* evokes
indirectly.

Socrates in the *Republic* evokes these bounds of being for his young
interlocutors by means of the analogies of the sun, the line, and the cave.
In what is presented dramatically here as perhaps the most significant
encounter of Socrates' youth, Parmenides delineates the possibilities and
the limitations of literal discourse. Parmenides made it clear at the outset in his remarks to Socrates that the range of the ideas extends throughout being (130e–131d). But Parmenides shows that signification implies
an oppositional whole that exceeds intelligibility: disclosure of this
exceeding involves differentiation of principles from each other and from
forms, *eidē* differentiated from each other and from phenomena, intentional orientations (*tropoi*) juxtaposed in linguistic disclosure, etc. In itself
none of these moments has being or intelligibility; but nevertheless the
sameness of repetition in logos is disclosive of that which is always becoming different.

The structure of both meaning and entity is identical in this essential respect. It is not only that experience involves the dialogical interpenetration of ideal possibilities of disclosure with the presence of entities,
and that neither pole of this separation is reducible to the other. In addition, the presence of the unified manifold is informed by nonpresence
because what anything is necessarily involves what it is not. Parmenides
translates the question of *chōrismos* beyond the separate existence of the
ideal and the real to the intercontextuality in every mode of logos—empir-

ical or nonempirical—of presence and the nonpresence that sustains and informs it.

The subject considered in itself is not even an object of significant speech (142a3–5). This apparently un-Platonic conclusion compels the critical participant in the dialogue to consider the possibility that there are various senses of being that are juxtaposed in every discourse. The first beginning's culmination—in problems relating to time and repetitions of sameness in logos—alerts Socrates to the deeper significance of Parmenides' development of the doubtful questions.

In the *Republic*, the notion of the good, as the last thing obscurely glimpsed at the limit of the knowable (517b8 ff.), indicates the precognitive teleology that differentiates and thereby unifies participatory being. Because *alētheia* is in and through this differentiation, Platonic knowing is from early on the articulation of a profound negativity. This omnipresent nonpresence, the otherwise of *chōris*, means that *to agathon*—in Socrates' familiar but ambiguous accounts—signifies neither simply an entity nor an unground.[7] Socrates uses caveat, analogy, intentional ambiguity, and deferrals of direct discourse to indicate that these accounts of the good signify more than either the goal-oriented habits of intelligent existence, or the abyss that freedom presents to intelligibility. As occasion of *alētheia*, the good transcends present disclosure; and, because disclosure as such is never disclosed, these discourses gesture toward a wholeness in which truth, existence, and axiology converge. But the incomplete form of the Platonic dialogue acknowledges that *alētheia* itself is never completed; what-is is neither simple presence nor absence.

In the *Parmenides*, neither the presence of things that are nor the intelligibility of the form is presented as the locus of being. On the contrary, Parmenides' efforts to express ideal relations on the one hand, and to indicate real relations on the other, repeatedly interpenetrate throughout the dialogue. Existence is dialogical; it is the participatory being—in accordance with *chronos*—of the nonpresence of form over against presence, over against the active engagement in a current situation that the form defines by contrast.

Against Platonism

Because the ideal is defined negatively, the predicament of the *chōrismos* occurs alongside the effort to know not only phenomena, but also the form itself. Insofar as *eidos* gestures toward the fullness of being, the notion of form exceeds its own intelligibility. And if meaningful experience is the active disclosure of meaning, still the tautology implicit here is itself a derivative mode of *alētheia*. Plato's apophatic dialectic reveals this by showing the priority of being over knowing, and of nonpresence over presence. Participatory being toward the good is ontologically prior to modes of *chronos*.[8] One manifestation of this Platonic insight in the *Parmenides* is that phenomenal differentiations such as before / after, in contact / not in contact, and so forth, are disambiguated only insofar as they are seen to be embedded contextualizations of a deeper preconceptual vectoring. In the game such moments prefigure their own undoing.

It may be that there is being only where the logos of being is, but Platonic dialogue shows the logos of being to be more than a cognitive grasp or representation of being. Being defies *mimēsis*.[9] If the Platonic dialogue indicates that modes of being are more adequately disclosed by philosophical *poiēsis* than by other, more context-bound forms of logos, the openness of this approach is brought home in the *Parmenides* by the emphasis on the questioning after being, rather than its final comprehension.

The *Parmenides* enacts its meaning by articulating layers and strata within discourse; it is a performance of dialogue that evokes the finitude of a plurality of modes of disclosure. The dialogue is a provocation. It progresses by way of questioning and *elenchos*; and on the most explicit, literal level no progress is made at all. Even so, many hypotheses are eliminated by reduction to absurdity. The notion that there is a relation of resemblance between thing and *eidos* is fully eliminated—as is the suggestion that an *eidos* is a thought.

A rhetorical style, or *tropos*, is philosophical insofar as it reveals modes of logos to be derivative: different modes of logos imply different modes of being. When Socrates asks for clarification about the manner (*tropos*) of training for a philosopher, Parmenides briefly outlines an eightfold hypothetical method (136a–c). But it is the contrast between Parmenides' apparently straightforward method and what actually occurs in his demonstration of it that constitutes the ironical framing of the dialogue's central *reductio*: the reduction to absurdity of efforts to represent time.

This ironical framing is already initiated in the introductory exchange between Parmenides and Socrates. Parmenides suggests that ideal signification may not be eliminated without destroying the power of the very discourse used to deny the possibility of ideal signification (135b–c). And yet, if ideas exist separately, even a god could not have *epistēmē* (133c–134e). Somewhere in between these poles of self-referential paradox and the givenness of the intelligibility of experience is the alternative third way of *alētheia*. Parmenides' first beginning demonstrates that the required training involves the activity of testing and exceeding the limits of logos. Socrates must practice this active play of systematically returning to, testing, and finally seeing through the *archai* (beginnings) of thought. This play with the limits of logos does not abolish the power of dialectic, but reveals its true nature. Nor does it imply the denial of the individual dimension of personal connotations and idiosyncratic associations.

In Parmenides' demonstration, the crucial role of that which is purely individual and indefinable, raises questions that will resurface in the later investigations of Aristotle (the philosopher). But, insofar as Parmenides' method exceeds itself, the *Parmenides* is evidence, not only of Aristotle's debt to Plato, but also of the superiority of Plato's dialogical approach to the question of being over Aristotelian and Scholastic categorial analysis. The Platonic Parmenides, like the mature Socrates in other dialogues, mimes sophistry in order to show the reductions implicit to *logismos* (calculative thinking). Whereas sophistry forgets the situated, goal-oriented nature of meaning, the ambiguity of being, and the negative dimension of disclosure, Parmenides' praxis highlights these very features.

The fact that being in time is repeatedly used by Parmenides to indicate the shift from toward-itself to toward-another discourse (and vice versa) shows that these two modes of intentionality involve two opposed but mutually supplementary modes of temporality. In this way Parmenides' performance indicates—even before time is explicitly thrown into question—that *chronos* is not given, but is disclosed in and through dialectical differentiation. This oppositional unfolding is the negativity of existence for intelligibility. The chorismatic instability, implied by Parmenides' repeated failures to keep his two thematic modes of intentionality entirely separate, indicates why dialectic must be negative.

In the second and third beginnings, Parmenides will mime sophistical reductionisms (e.g., Pythagorean mathematical cosmology) in order to lead Socrates to the insight that being may not be represented without misrepresentation. The predominant tendency in interpretations of the *Parmenides* is to ignore or try to explain away its irony and pedagogical mimicry of sophistry.[10] If such interpretation goes on to find fault with Plato's alleged metaphysics of presence, then it is guilty of the very type of error it presumes to detect, namely, attempting to reduce the ambiguous and tension-laden opening of the dialogue to a univocal theory or doctrine.

Chapter 4

🔲🔲🔲

From Irony to Comedy

"I would rather be wrong with Plato than right with such men as these
[Pythagoreans]."
—Cicero, *Tusculanae Disputationes* I, 17

Logos as Structure and Process

Like the *Parmenides*, the *Cratylus* raises questions about language and the
manner of learning about being. And like Parmenides, a mature Socrates
in the *Cratylus* challenges his young interlocutors with ironic and humorous reductions to absurdity. Socrates throws into question the notion that
names (*onomata*) resemble beings. Cratylus claims there must be some basis
for language in nature (*phusis*), while Hermogenes believes that linguistic
usage and naming is a matter of convention (*sunthēkē*) and agreement
(*homologia*). Socrates challenges both these interpretations of the beginnings of logos, and indicates a third alternative. But though it is clear that
Socrates' third way is intended to avoid Protagorean relativism, it is also
evident that the role of custom and social practice in the assigning of terms
is not entirely ruled out: in fact Socrates claims that discourse (*legein*) is a
kind of praxis (387b8–9).

But near the end of the *Cratylus*, Socrates discloses the reason for his
skepticism regarding hypotheses on the origins of logos. We cannot answer
such questions because we do not know the manner (*tropos*) for learning
about and discovering *ta onta*, or what exists (439b). And yet Socrates is
surprisingly earnest in urging that there must be *ideai* named in language.
The beautiful and the good are terms that indicate *eidē*; these allow intelligibility by holding their form, for the flux of *chronos* in itself is unintelligible (*Crat.* 439c–440d). In light of all this, how are we to understand this
Socratic alternative, that existence has a dimension of stable form? For the
Parmenides also involves the effort to understand *ousia* in light of time.

If the structure of the *Parmenides* is taken as being unambiguous, then
the dialogue is utterly contradictory, but if it is said to be noncontradic-

91

tory then it is thoroughly ambiguous. Plato ensured such questioning by indicating schematization and yet undermining it. For whichever interpretation one prefers, contradictory or ambiguous, the dialogue eludes the very form that it suggests. If the effort to maintain an interpretation that discounts ambiguity is carried so far as to allow actual contradiction, this would not eliminate syntactic amphiboly.[1] Furthermore, at 135e–136c, Parmenides mentions eight beginnings within one integrated inquiry, but in fact there are nine explicit and many more implicit returns to the beginnings (*archai*). *Pros hauto* and *pros allo* orientations are interchanged and juxtaposed throughout the dialogue. These considerations imply that an interpretation that purports to overcome both contradiction and ambiguity in fact takes one ever further from the actual text.

The problem is compounded by the history of the manuscripts. As is well known, research has indicated errors in copying and other changes.[2] Obviously, if a text is ironic, such issues become more difficult to determine with precision. The *Parmenides* is ironic, and there are deductions within deductions, implicitly as well as explicitly. Moreover, time and translation efface the plays on words, allusions, and distinctions that were significant for Plato's contemporaries. But, even if we divide the dialogue indefinitely by focusing on ambiguities and difficulties of interpretation, nevertheless it is informed by the wholeness of a unified theme. The only alternative is to think philosophically, along with the silent Socrates, about this unifying theme, and see which specific questions about the structure of the text are resolved. Plato, in fact, makes imperative this philosophical engagement with his texts by the use of irony and other means. What then is the philosophically significant, unifying theme of Plato's *Parmenides*?

Chronos is made thematic in the *Parmenides* beginning in the initial passages; for the account of the dialogue is related long after the deaths of its participants. The narrator Cephalus originally heard it from Antiphon who heard it from Pythodorus (126a–127a). Because Pythodorus came in when Zeno's arguments were nearly finished, the ostensible source of the repetition was present for only part of the original discussion (127d). Plato situates the *Parmenides* by means of these dramatic chronological removes because, as the *Phaedrus* and *Seventh Letter* make clear, Plato held that there can be no adequate disclosure of what exists in logos.

These texts suggest not only an awareness on Plato's part of difficulties relating to the history of the interpretation of manuscripts, but also, and more importantly, fundamental and immediate problems involving the disclosure of truth in languages. This is one of the primary reasons for the variations in mode of presentation and form throughout the Platonic corpus. Socratic irony and the dialogue form indicate Plato's concern that we follow him in questioning the subject matter ourselves, rather than attempting to reconstruct some lost univocal Platonic doctrine.

Variation in tense and mood and other ambiguities in the text of the dialogue are not insignificant because differentiation in both logos and being is, from early on, a primary theme of Plato's philosophical *paideia*. The *Parmenides* is a rhetorical performance of its own meaning: it indicates ambiguities in language use that arise from articulations in the prelinguistic contexts of discourse. But the very structure of the *Parmenides* (and especially its undermining of its own form) implies that the effort to eliminate ambiguity multiplies contradiction. The dialogue involves an effort to think being in light of time; this very effort discloses the proportion / disproportion that is rationality. But in his elimination of other types of account, Parmenides leaves standing the insight that being is participatory. If knowing is goal-oriented, situated in a context, and radically incomplete, then inquiry is the purposive effort to gain information in response to an absence of which we need not be conscious. Parmenides' game shows that such limited disclosure reveals the interconnections of beings, rather than their atomic independence or fully intelligible presence.

In the *Parmenides*, the treatment of time reduces to absurdity nonteleological, sophistic reductions of being to either real or intelligible presence. The dialogue indicates in this way that Platonism—properly understood—represents a direct challenge not only to Democritean atomism, but also to Pythagorean mathematical cosmology. But how can the rather skeptical implications of the *Parmenides* be reconciled with the rhetoric in the *Republic*, or for that matter, in *The Laws*? Does Eleatic negative dialectic provide the philosophical context for the noble sophistry of analogy, myth, dream, indirect discourse, and rhetoric?[3] Nonconsistencies, ambiguities, and irony provoke the thinking that does not depend on useful assumptions, but rather strives to go back to the beginnings (*Republic*, 511d). If negative dialectic reveals the absurdities implicit to positive accounts of the *archai* of intelligibility, philosophical *poiēsis* supplements this negativity with indirect evocations of beginnings.

Parmenides shows Socrates the impossibility of the separate existence of the forms; in this way the dialogue reduces to absurdity any substantial understanding of the ideal. If the *Parmenides* dates from about the time when the *Theaetetus* was written,[4] and the latter indicates difficulties in viewing sense perception as foundational in knowing, these considerations suggest a rather skeptical later Plato. The account or logos that supplements true belief and completes knowing involves the difference that makes any being distinguishable from other beings; this heterogeneity informs all disclosure. Because the *Parmenides* shows that nothing exists or is intelligible in itself, the forms cannot be understood as timelessly true propositions that allow *alētheia* in logos. The instant of logical identity cannot exist.

Thus the transcendence in the moment of insight is not accounted for by any possible analysis of categories. Given the suggestive name of the dialogue's minor interlocutor, some scholars have considered the possibility that the *Parmenides* was written after Aristotle had established himself in Plato's Academy, since the dialogue reduces to absurdity a theory of ideas similar to the doctrine later criticized by Aristotle.[5]

The Second Beginning 142b-155e: One toward Others

The next section of argument purports to examine the consequences of the existence of the one in relation to other natures. Instead of asking what qualifications, if any, belong to the meaning of unity in itself, the second beginning purports to examine how the one must be differentiated in opposition to other natures. Examples of such oppositions include unity / plurality, part / whole, limit / unlimit, motion / rest, same / different, likeness / unlikeness, temporal / atemporal, being / nonbeing, intelligible / unintelligible, etc.

A difficulty for interpretation is that Parmenides in the second beginning mimes sophistry by juxtaposing different linguistic intentions in a provocative and suggestive way. But especially because of the way this inquiry into the uses and abuses of discourse leads into Parmenides' central reductio of representations of time, it is important realize that there are also nonfallacious interpretations of this reasoning. As the second beginning proceeds, Parmenides' provocations become blatantly ironic. But when viewed in light of his overall intention, even these challenges show the extent to which truth is contextual. When the meaning of a joke depends on an inconsistency, this means that a unified sense—the intention of the joke—is conveyed through the disunification of another, more familiar sense.

Parmenides' game is a counterchallenge in response to Socrates' challenging of Zeno (129a-130a). This training leads the potential philosopher not out of, but deeper into the *aporiai* implied by Socrates' initial naive conception of form. But in the process, Parmenides demonstrates that *alētheia* involves much more than noncontradiction.[6] His game makes it obvious for Socrates that truth in logos is not simply a matter of one (allegedly) univocal, timeless standard of disclosure. Because the meaning of an expression or term involves both customary and new usage—social praxis as well as what an individual intends by using the term in a unique and developing situation—Parmenides highlights ambiguities as his exercise approaches the problematic of time. The second beginning develops the ironical framing of the account of the instant.

The following overview of the second beginning gives an indication of the prevailing mood of comic irony and the intentional scrambling of language games that occurs throughout this nuclear segment of the dialogue.

Looked at again from the beginning (*ex archēs*), if a one exists, then it must participate (*metechein*) in being (142b). But the meaning of being is not identical with the meaning of unity: "is" means one thing and "one" another. The question now to be examined, Parmenides says, is not whether a one is one, but what follows if a one exists. But if "to be" is said of a one because it exists, and if unity is said of any entity since it is one—and if being and unity are different—then any one that exists must be a whole composed of being and unity. Any existent one, then, will be a whole of parts. Because Parmenides names being and unity parts it follows by definition that any one that exists is a whole that has parts (142d). This shows that as he did in the first beginning, now also in the second beginning Parmenides juxtaposes toward-itself (*pros hauto*) and toward-another (*pros allo*) discourses; this interpenetration continues throughout his game.

Nevertheless Parmenides' orientation here runs counter to his previous intention at the outset of the exercise, where it was shown that the meaning—in itself—of *to hen* cannot imply having parts or being a whole composed of parts, since to be a part involves having a share of plurality (137c). Can meaning be cut into pieces like a sail, or does its wholeness extend completely through its range, like the unity of the day?[7] Parmenides has shown that ideas participate in one another insofar as—if they are disclosive at all—they must be qualified by what they are not; but how can meaning have parts unless we imagine it to be analogous to some object in *aisthēsis*? Parmenides' inquiry into time will imply that even apparently literal uses of terms, such as part (*meros*), imply a figurative moment.

If the claim that unity is divided into parts means that there are indefinitely many ways in which oneness may be predicated, then since no presently existing entity exhausts the meaning of the term one, the transcendent dimension of signification reasserts itself. Parmenides' playful interweaving and juxtaposition of logos-functions—which become more obvious as this second beginning approaches the topic of time—frame his reduction to absurdity of conceptual representations of time. In the second beginning Parmenides evokes innumerable ambiguities in order to indicate just how difficult it is for reasoning to eliminate all equivocation.

Parmenides ironically reduces the transcendence of form first to a property of an entity (e.g., its oneness, or its being), and subsequently to a synthetic *instantiation* of both unity and being in real and ideal entities. The goal of this differential strategy is reduction to absurdity: Parmenides first shows that if *ideai* are conceived as the parts or the properties of a being, these are an indefinite and potentially infinite manifold. Then Parmenides demonstrates for Socrates that if the *eidos* is reduced to either ideal or real presence (e.g., numbers or the beings that are enumerated), then the ideas will also be an indefinite, potentially infinite, and incommensurable multiplicity.

Reducing the transcendence of the idea—by conceiving the *eidos* as real or ideal presence—is shown in this second beginning to lead to an unreasonable pluralism. In the third beginning (155e-157b), Parmenides will show that the reduction of teleology to presence is not only irreducibly ambiguous, but also deeply contradictory. By these interrelated reductions to absurdity, Parmenides shows Socrates that his initial conception of the *eidos* must be reconfigured by the acknowledgement that a chorismatic moment governs the disclosure—not only of phenomena—but also of the form. The oneness of the one is not accounted for by either phenomenal or intelligible presence.

The first beginning showed that *eidos* in itself discloses nothing: this nothing signifies the transcendence of being. Ambiguities and *aporiai* are implicit, not only to accounts of phenomenal entities—as Socrates had already recognized—but also to the *pros hauto* effort to disclose form itself. Even ideal being "is" only by differentiation; all disclosure in logos of what-is implies *chōris*. This otherwise than implies that even the form of objects in experience—though it is apparently simply seen or intuited—is actually little more than a signpost for the bounds of being. Consequently, in this second beginning, Parmenides will show that though we may generate conceptual unities indefinitely (cf. 143a-145a), this does not imply Protagorean relativism, for we do not control the ordering of conceptual representations in relation to phenomena.

If *pros allo* indications of existence are to be articulated in logos, they must be informed by, or juxtaposed against, *pros hauto* singularities. If the unifications—the correlations and differentiations—in logos are to be true, then they disclose beings as they are. The first beginning showed that logical identity in itself is impossible; even if one is, the *pros hauto* orientation in logos leads to insignificance, nonconsistency, and unintelligibility when "unity" is abstracted from the differential contextualities of time and being. No term in itself signifies anything.

The second beginning will indicate that if one is, signifying differentiations are possible in logos when logical identity is related to (or juxtaposed against) phenomenal associations and contiguities. In this way the first two beginnings together will show that the two thematic orientations in logos, *pros hauto* and *pros allo* would disclose nothing whatsoever if they could be instantiated purely; only the differential juxtaposition of logos-functions is disclosive. *Pros hauto* expressions of identity—in relation to phenomenal disclosures—allows truth in logos.

But a problem arises insofar as different toward-another relations (or unifications) might be disclosed indefinitely, and in ways that produce inconsistencies. This implication of the second beginning means that even if one is, conceptual unifications of phenomenal correlations are irreducibly ambiguous. For example, the same thing might be truly said to be both moving and at rest, and the results of the first beginning (141e–142a) imply that both terms, "motion" and "rest," are in themselves completely unintelligible. The third beginning (on the instant) involves an effort to locate the source of the nonconsistencies of the first and second beginnings.

Parmenides now claims that unity and being are displayed alongside one another in all of the parts of any entity: unity is not lacking to any part which is, nor is being lacking to any part which is one. Each one of these, then, unity and being, is forever becoming two and will not stay absolutely unique, as long as we view them as exhibited in a one which is. The unity of an entity occurs alongside its being, and its being is manifested alongside its unity. But since any part of an existent one is forever becoming two, then in this sense any existent one is *apeiron plēthos*: an indefinite multitude (143a). Whereas disclosure oriented toward unity in itself allowed no intelligibility whatsoever (141e–142a), the disclosure allowed by dialectical differentiation (of the one toward the many) is now shown to be limited by irreducible ambiguity.

Although the differentiation of significations in the second beginning involves *pros allo* indications of many opposing features manifested by any existent one, still this very process also implies the *pros hauto* mode of discourse. But if an entity displays opposing characters in different senses, does this mean that the characters themselves collapse into one another? Though Socrates' initial conception of the forms acknowledged the distinction between ideal and real, Parmenides has already demonstrated that Socrates did not realize the difficulties implied by the separate exis-tence of forms.[8]

Nevertheless the second beginning will show that Socrates was partly correct when he claimed at the outset that paradoxes may be sorted out when forms are related to phenomena (128e–129d). In this second begin-ning, there are no differentiations of a multiplicity without unity; even Parmenides' most humorous equivocations still revolve around a one. But Parmenides will show, in the second beginning as in the first, that Socrates overreached himself with his challenges to Zeno (at 129d–130a). The effort to think *ousia* in light of *chronos* shows why paradoxes recur even on the level of the ideas themselves.

At 143a Parmenides gives Aristotle an imperative: Come, let us (pro-ceed) further yet (*Ithi dē kai tēde eti*). The wording suggests still another return to the beginnings, and it is a reorientation of a sort. For Parmenides now asks Aristotle to consider the one alone, according to itself (*monon kath' hauto*). Parmenides argues that a one that exists partakes of being, but considered in itself, apart from that *ousia* of which it partakes (*metechein*) this one is also a many. In any one that exists, its being is one thing and its oneness another; therefore, Parmenides reasons, one is not other than being because it is one, and being is not other than oneness because it is being. On the contrary, both are other by virtue of the dif-ferent (*to heteron*). But this otherness is not reducible to either oneness or being. On this level of conceptualization, unity is distinguished from being, but not entirely abstracted from it. Any terms that are abstracted beyond this disclosive juxtaposition—beyond dialectical differentiation—are all equally uninformative; in themselves they are indistinguishable one from the other, and are not even one with themselves. The orientation of the second beginning indicates one form of the differentiation that allows disclosure.

Because Parmenides asks Aristotle to conceive in thought (*tē dianoia*) the oneness of the existent one, this inference indicates that the two the-matic modes of discourse interpenetrate this section of the game. But moreover, the wording suggests that on the level of the understanding (*dianoia*), there is a conceptual unification that preserves the oneness of disclosure, unlike the unity of the first beginning that is abstracted from ontological differentiation and so cannot even be one (141e). This means that it is not simply the distinction between *pros hauto* and *pros allo* that differentiates the exercise, for the differences between one toward many (the second beginning), and many toward one (the fourth beginning) will also prove significant. But both of these orientations are *pros allo* in that they are differential; they both consider the way a nature is disclosed in opposition to its other (*to heteron*). In addition, there will be further important differences that are disclosed when these latter orientations are articulated alongside the assumption of the one's nonexistence (160b–166c).

Because disclosure only occurs by way of juxtaposition, the differential orientation one toward many allows oneness to be oneness, unlike the pure unity of the first beginning that is no longer even one (141e). It is this level of conceptualization that will allow Parmenides to make the transition to the subsequent generation of number (143a–145a). But the development of the second beginning makes plain that Parmenides' game has a dangerous purpose; it will test its own projected schema by finding juxtapositions within apparent syntheses. This will culminate (in the third beginning) in an inquiry into time that evokes paradoxes that show the utter incommensurability implied in any *alētheia*. Any representation of disclosure and any positive claim to truth is misleading insofar as it masks its own limitation; it masks the fact that it is only by way of the other—*to heteron*—that what exists may be disclosed.

Consequently, rather than simply implying a systematic analysis of natures and categories, the *Parmenides* ironically juxtaposes various modes of discourse with amusing and intentionally bewildering results. The purpose of this troubling game is to evoke the bounds of being and logos. But this ironic juxtaposition of discourses proves to be more profound than any systematic treatise. The form of the dialogue itself is suggested[9] and then intentionally exceeded in order to graphically illustrate that form is never simply present: because *ousia* is informed by *to heteron*, existence may only be evoked in a negative and indirect way. The *Parmenides*—like any one that exists—is a whole that exceeds the conceptual unification of its parts.

The Antinomies of Presence

Of a one which exists, its unity is one aspect and its being another. But its unity does not differ from its being by virtue of oneness, for unity as such has no share of difference. But neither does its being differ from its unity by virtue of being, for the meaning of being as such implies no difference: being is neither a species of difference, nor identical in meaning to difference. Rather, the oneness and the being of any one that exists differ by virtue of the fact that this one also has an interchange with *to heteron*, or difference (143b).

Any existent one, Parmenides claims, is a partnership (*metechein*) of unity, being, and difference. But these natures are nowhere displayed absolutely and uniquely, for the in-itself is neither expressed nor indicated as such: the one in itself is not even one (141e). By contrast, the consideration of unity in opposition to other natures discloses ambiguous plurality; any one we choose to consider will have a share of being, unity, and difference. But if being, unity, and difference are named parts of any disclosure, then a problem arises in that each of these divisions must also display being, unity, and difference. Thus the second beginning—by way of disclosure of ambiguities—mirrors the *aporiai* (such as the regresses) that Parmenides evokes in the initial exchanges with Socrates.

At 144c, Parmenides claims that anything that is, is some one being, otherwise it would be nothing; this means that being, unity, and difference are everywhere coimplicatory. But this cannot be interpreted to mean that any being is either only some one thing or nothing, for Parmenides' demonstration repeatedly shows (in a variety of ways) that what anything is intimately involves what it is not—beings are only disclosed by differentiation—the pure singularity of any individual nature in itself is nothing, it is not even itself.

But since any one we select manifests these two, being and unity, and since these always implicitly involve a third—difference—and since any one of these selections or divisions itself implies each of these, any number whatsoever must be generable (143d–144a). Any one that we select implies both an enumerable many and an indefinite, potentially infinite multitude. Unity is manifested, alongside existence and difference, in any conceivable division or selection oriented toward this indefinite potentiality (144e).[10]

The sameness of logos—unification *tē dianoia*—in relation to existence yields the possibility of ideal repetition. The form of conceptual presence, indefinitely repeatable, gives meaning to enumerations of existence, such as mathematical representations. Parmenides' dialectical game will show Socrates that representation and presence are necessarily associated and that it is impossible to distinguish them rigorously. The orientation one toward the many has now revealed that conceptual unification—or enumerability—in relation to existence (*to hen hupo tou ontos*) is itself divisible and indefinite (143a–144e).

But since any selection or division of parts is oriented toward a definite whole, a one that exists is also limited in respect to its wholeness. Any one is both definite and indefinite, limited wholeness and unlimited potential for division (144e–145a). Wholeness implies indefinitely many possibilities of divisibility; parts might be enumerated in any number of ways. Therefore wholeness is not reducible to any particular enumeration of parts. This means that any existent unity displays unlimitedness in that it is a wholeness that implies indefinitely many possible divisions into enumerated parts. But this same one has a share of limitedness in that it is a distinct and definite whole—it may be named a one. But insofar as possible ways of enumerating *ousia* and dividing being into parts (*merē*) might be generated indefinitely, such differentiations are boundless (*aperanta*).[11]

Parmenides now asks Aristotle a question that clearly ties this present exercise to his dialogue with Socrates that preceded the game: "Can the one be in many places at the same time and be one?" (144d1-2). Whereas young Socrates had argued that form is in many places at once and yet is a whole like the day (131b), the even younger Aristotle asserts confidently that this is impossible (144c2-3). The antinomic character of Parmenides' subsequent argumentation is a response to this naive reduction.

Parmenides will disclose possibility where Aristotle saw none: a sense in which the whole is neither identical to the sum of its spatially-differentiated divisions nor entirely separate from them. This inconceivable unity in opposition was what Socrates struggled to comprehend with his untrained analogy of form to daylight. But Parmenides evokes this sameness in differentiation by a negative logic: he shows the antinomies implied by attempts to reduce it. The only alternative left open then is this odd nonidentity: the whole cannot be either identical to or entirely separate from its parts. The overall effect of this reasoning by antinomies is to reinforce the brilliant insight that informed Socrates' analogy of the day: the form is like a whole that exceeds the sum of its parts. Parmenides discloses the inconceivable by way of revealing the antinomies of presence. Conceptual representations of being are implicitly nonconsistent. The puzzle of whole and part shows that the whole cannot be separate from its parts; nor can the whole be identical to its parts. Whole must be unified in the differentiation from parts.[12]

This existent one which is a limited whole will have beginning, middle, and end and therefore some shape or another (145a-b). Such a one may also be said to be both in itself and in another, for there are senses in which this one is both a unified whole and also one with all possible divisions of itself (145c). But Parmenides next discloses a sense in which the one as the whole being is not in the parts, neither in all nor any. At 145d, he points out that the whole cannot be in all unless it is in each of them: if it were not in every one, it could not be in all. But it is impossible that a part contain the greater whole of which it is a part. The whole could not be spatially contained in some one of its parts. And since that one is one among all, and the whole is not in that one, then there is a sense in which the whole is not in all.

At 145c, the whole was said to be "in" all the parts in the sense that the whole encompasses (*periechō*) the parts; it is the being they are divisions of. At 145d, however, the whole is said not to be "in" all the parts in that it cannot be spatially contained—as a whole—by one or some or all of its own parts. The meaning of wholeness cannot be exhausted by the presence of the parts. At this point Parmenides gives Aristotle a chance to try to say the unsayable, as Socrates attempted with his untrained analogy of the day. He asserts provocatively that if the whole is not in one of the parts, or some of the parts, or all of the parts, it must be in another (*en heterō*) or nowhere at all (145d8–145e1). The irony of this assertion is not only in the ambiguous juxtaposition of two senses of in, but also in the suggestive invoking of otherness.

The puzzle of whole and parts, and the antinomic conclusions Parmenides draws, are intended to provoke insight into the odd non-presence of form: if it is nowhere, Parmenides claims, the whole is nothing (145e1–2). But a one that exists is not nothing; therefore, insofar as it is the whole and not nothing, it may be said to be in another. A whole cannot be contained in itself in the same way that parts are in the whole. If the one is said to be in itself insofar as it is the parts, then it must be in another insofar as it is the whole (145b–e). One implication of these passages is that the apparently tautologous relation of the ideas of whole / part cannot be expressed univocally: the whole "is" in a different way than the composition of its parts "is." The wholeness of the whole—its self-identity—is not accounted for by the presence of all the parts. The identity of any one exceeds the presence of its parts.

Parmenides does not have to show that there is no other sense in which a one may be said to be in itself; indeed, he has already evoked another sense himself at 145d. He is not indicating conclusions here which would lose their force because of ambiguity in relation to one another: on the contrary, it is just such ambiguity which, in this section, he is trying to evoke.[13] But Parmenides has by now also illustrated how contradictions are easily evoked when a logos of unity is attempted: for if the individual entity is that which is truly said to be, then unity as such does not exist and is not one. But if only the one itself truly is, then the many motions and changes we everywhere observe (and engage in) would be impossible.

Socrates claimed, in response to Zeno's *logoi*, that paradoxes are easily evoked in relation to any existent one (128e7-130a3). Parmenides will
not destroy Socrates' insight that ideal being allows distinctions for sorting out apparent *aporiai*. But he reconfigures Socrates' initial formulation
by indicating in this second beginning (142b-155e) that eidetic and phenomenal discourses always interpenetrate one another. The puzzle of
whole and parts shows that the transcendence of the form in itself permeates even the disclosure of phenomena.

Chōris as Nonidentity

Parmenides next claims, at 145e-146a, that the one is both in motion and
at rest. A one is at rest if it is in itself, for then it is in one thing and does
not move relatively to its container, which is itself. But it has just been
claimed in the previous section of argument that, insofar as it is the whole,
a one must be said to be contained in another. Based on this, it is now
asserted that the one moves, since what is always in another (146a4) is
never in the same and what never rests in the same may be said to be in
motion. This conclusion is based on another ambiguity, to which Aristotle
fails to object. In the claim at 145e that the one insofar as it is a whole,
must be in something other (*en allō*) other means other than the existent
one. But at 146a, it is asserted that what is always in something different
is never in the same thing. Here being in something different means being
in a containment relation that is constantly changing or being replaced—
in other words, in an ongoing succession of containments. The sense shifts
from in something other than the existent one to always in something different and never resting.

Whatever is in one thing and does not pass from it may be said to
be in itself. Thus, a one in the sense of all the parts may be said to be at
rest insofar as it remains contained within the whole of itself. Since a one
understood as the whole cannot be within itself in the way that parts are
in a whole, it must be in something other. A whole cannot contain itself
in the same sense in which it contains its parts. But something that is
always in something other and never resting in the same must be moving,
therefore the one moves. This passage does not prove that a one which is
must necessarily move, or that it does move. The argument does not even
establish that a one which is might move—the argument demonstrates
nothing except ambiguity, and the need for stable forms of logos in order
to prevent miscommunication.

The next section of the discussion illustrates how the one which exists may be said to be both the same as and different from itself, and the same as and different from the others. This section begins with the claim that everything may be classified as being relative to everything else in the following way: either it is the same or different, or, if neither the same nor different, then it is part relative to whole, or whole relative to part (146b). But to which sense of being is this classification intended to apply? The third beginning will show that the instant can neither exist nor not exist; and the puzzle of whole / parts foreshadows this in its evocation of the odd nonpresence of wholeness.

But once this classification is presupposed, paradoxes are easily generated. Parmenides' initial strategy is to eliminate the alternatives one by one: in the first place, a one is not part of itself. But unless it were part of itself, it could not be said to be a whole in relation to itself. Therefore, a one is not a whole in relation to itself. Nor is a one different from itself, and so it must be the same as itself. The arguments which follow reveal another sense in which the one is different from itself, as well as a sense in which it is the same as the others, and another sense in which it is different from the others. But there is another point to be made regarding the classification that allows the antinomic conclusions; for the antinomies result from denying the inconceivable wholeness of the form. Aristotle's naive tendency to reductionism allows Parmenides to generate contradiction.

At 146b, this disjunction purports to be exclusive: something is either the same as another, or different, or is either whole relative to part or part relative to whole. However, it has already been shown that a one may be said to be both the whole which contains as well as the parts which are contained (see, for example, 145a and 145c). Although there is a sense in which the whole and the parts are nonidentical, still there is another sense in which whole and part are unified: a one which is may be said to be the whole as well as the parts.

This means that just before this ostensibly exclusive disjunction is asserted, an example is given that illustrates how any existent one may be said to be both same and different, whole and part. Parmenides first produced the counterexample, and then the sophistic bifurcation that it undermines. At a juncture such as this, when the irony of the game is so obtrusive, one cannot help but wonder what the course of this demonstration would have been like if Socrates were the respondent instead of the young Aristotle.[14]

After the explanation of the sense in which the one may be said to be the same as itself (146a–c) comes an example of how it may be viewed as being different from itself. A one which is, insofar as it is a whole, was said to be in a containment relation with another. However, there was also found to be a sense in which the one is said to be in itself (145c). This means that a one is different from itself insofar as it is both in itself and in another (146c). Yet it remains true that whatever is not one is different from what is one, and a one is likewise different from these not-ones. Therefore, in this sense, a one is different from the others.

Finally, Parmenides tries to evoke a sense in which a one exhibits sameness with the others. Since difference and sameness are opposites, there is a sense in which difference is never in what is the same, for difference is never in sameness as such. But if it is never in the same, then there is a sense in which difference is never in anything which is (146e). This means that a one that is cannot be different from the others; therefore it must be the same as the others. This inference is odd to say the least; for one thing, the notion of being was already shown to imply difference in the sense that in any one that is, its being is distinct from its unity by virtue of the implicit difference between being and unity. Therefore, although Parmenides has claimed that difference is not in sameness toward itself (because this does not have any share of being), difference has been shown to be implicit to the existence of any nature that has a share of being, since anything that is exhibits both unity and being, and these natures are not identical (143b).

If sameness, as such, implies no interchange with difference or being, then it also cannot be the same; but any entity participates in both sameness and difference. By juxtaposing the meaning of sameness itself against difference versus sameness as displayed, Parmenides effaces the distinction between the eidetic and the phenomenal that initiated this demonstration in the first place.

At 147a–b, Parmenides gives another argument to the effect that the one and the others are the same. It may be said that things not one do not have a share of unity, for then they would be one. But insofar as they do not have a share of the one, they are not parts of the one; and if unity is one and they are not one, then unity is neither a part of them nor a whole which contains them. Nor are they wholes of which a one is part. But it has already been agreed that if things are neither parts nor wholes in relation to each other, nor different from each other, they may be said to be the same as each other. Therefore, a one is the same as the things not one.

So Parmenides has evoked a sense in which a one is different from the others and itself, as well as a sense in which the one is the same as the others and itself (147b).

Parmenides next offers an amusing argument at 147c–148d to evoke a sense in which a one that exists is both like and unlike itself and the others. A one was said to be different from the others (146d). But if this is the case, a one is different from the others exactly insofar as they are different from it. Parmenides claims that this means that insofar as a one is different from the others and the others different from it, a one and the others are similar. Both alike have a share of difference, and in this at least, they are like (148a).

Furthermore, likeness is the opposite of unlikeness, and difference is the opposite of sameness. It has been shown already how unity may be said to be the same as the others (146d–147b). Being the same, though, is the opposite affection from being different. Further, it was just said that insofar as a one and the others both partake of difference, in this respect at least they are alike. But it is by the opposite of what makes it like that the one is unlike. Difference made it like; therefore, it must be by sameness that it is unlike. This would mean that not only is a one like the others in being different, but it is also unlike the others insofar as it is the same.

Beneath the ironic surface of the dialectical game, Parmenides is developing the insight that an *eidos* has meaning only in relation to another: not only to a network of *eidē*, but in relation to the context of lived experience, the concrete situation in relation to which they are disclosed. But neither a complete system of *eidē* nor the wholeness of any contextuality is ever present. Consequently, not only conceptual unification, but even the effort in imagination to reproduce an *eikōn* of being as a singular presence implies a reduction of the juxtapositional whole of contextualization that gives experience its intelligibility. Any possible representation is infused with the temporality of imagined confirmations or failures. This teleology implies transcendence; meaning is never *really* present.

Because all presence is necessarily informed by nonpresence in such ways, toward-itself signification essentially involves relations toward-another. This is precisely why Parmenides argues that, apart from all the interrelations that give it significance (apart from time and existence) the one itself is not even one (141e–142a). Parmenides is leading Socrates to the inescapable conclusion that the *eidos* is qualified by what it is not: persistent reflection on time will vindicate Zeno and show why the otherwise than of *chōris* necessarily accompanies all disclosure in logos.

But, Parmenides continues, when a thing is affected in the same way as another, it is said to be like that other (148c). And if a thing is affected in a different way, it is unlike. So Parmenides now claims that whether a one is the same as or different from the others, it has been shown to be both like and unlike the others—and similarly, whether a one is said to be the same as or different from itself, it may be said to be both like and unlike itself (148d).

The argument is not explicitly stated, but merely indicated, to the effect that whether the one is said to be different from itself or the same as itself, in either case it will appear like and unlike itself. These paradoxical results, like the other apparent contradictions in this dialogue, are intended, not to constitute a univocal and comprehensive schema of types of fallacies, but rather to provoke philosophical insight into the transcendent wholeness of form. The ideas in relation to entities are the potential for the intelligibility that is disclosed alongside multiple modes of being. Such juxtaposition is participatory being: the idea in relation to itself denotes the singularity of being. This transcendence may only be approached in a negative way. But, on the other hand, ideas generated indefinitely (without ongoing relation to the way an entity is disclosed in experience), also allow inadequate intelligibility because they are a potentially infinite and incommensurate multitude.

But there is no univocal doctrine behind this dialogue that is capable of resolving all the difficulties, and this is precisely the point of Parmenides' dialectical game. He shows Socrates that to attempt to formulate one univocal discourse that encompasses the whole is misguided; Parmenides is exposing the gaps between juxtaposed discourses in order to teach Socrates that every instantiation of logos is uniquely individual because its meaning is its context, and this is different always and everywhere. Therefore the sameness of ideal possibilities of repetition in language makes disclosure in logos also a covering over. The whole of contextual relations that informs our utterances is never present, and yet—paradoxically—it is this omnipresent nonpresence that gives meaning to all disclosures of truth in logos.

Failures of Logos

Parmenides argues at 148d–e that insofar as a one is in the others, it would touch the others, but insofar as it is in itself, it touches itself. Therefore, a one touches both itself and the others. And yet, he continues, a contact exists only when two entities occupy spaces that are directly contiguous.

Yet in order for a one to do this, it would need to be two; therefore, a one does not touch itself in this way. Since the one is one and not two, it will not be in contact with any others; for it is said that what touches is separate from and yet in succession with what it touches, and further, that there is no third thing intervening. There must, then, be two things for a contact to exist, and if a third object is added to the sequence, the contacts will then be two, and so on. The contacts will always be fewer by one than the number of objects in succession. Consequently, if the one alone exists and two is not, then contact is impossible. And yet that which is other than the one, and has no share of unity, cannot be one, nor two, nor have a share in any number whatsoever (149c–d). So unity alone is, and since there is no two, there can be no contact. Therefore, Parmenides concludes, a one touches and does not touch both itself and the others.

With his linear depiction of contacts, Parmenides' initiates the reduction to absurdity of schematic depictions of being that will culminate in his ironic account of the paradoxical instant. If the relation is more real than the things related, still no relation in itself can be thought. If causal relations over time are imagined to be linear, the intelligibility allowed by such an account also implies its own unintelligibility. For this depiction can never be completed, because the entities or events related will always exceed the relation by one. For the sake of consistency, this one would have to be entirely uncaused. The unification of entities or events by the idea of causality cannot be completed; for cause implies that which is uncaused. In the third beginning, Parmenides will develop this aporetic moment by showing that if time is imagined to be a line, its points (instants) cannot be in contact with one another. Parmenides is demonstrating the inherent limitations of any attempt to synthesize eidetic and phenomenal disclosures, and thereby indicating that the way of truth can only be negative: for positive correlations do not prove a hypothesis to be true, although one contradictory fact disproves the hypothesis.

Parmenides uses the notions of largeness and smallness ironically in order to demonstrate the paradoxical conclusion that a one is both equal and unequal to itself and the others (149e–151e). These arguments show Socrates that the meaning of an *eidos* simply may not be adequately represented in thought, not even if the idea is the meaning of something visual or tactile. For if smallness is depicted as present within a one, it is present in either a part of this one or the whole of it. But if smallness is present in the whole of a one, it must be spread out evenly through this one, or else smallness exceeds and contains it. But if it were stretched out evenly through a one, then smallness would be equal to the one. And if smallness contained the one, then it would be larger than the one. But small-ness cannot thus do the work of equality and of largeness. Therefore, Parmenides claims, smallness must not be present in the whole of a one; if it is present in a one, it must then be in only a part of this one.

And similarly, if smallness is imagined to be contained in even a part of a one, the same results follow: if it is present evenly throughout the whole of the part, then it will be equal to the part. And if it exceeds the part and contains it, it will be larger than the part. Therefore, smallness cannot be said to be present in either a part of, or the whole of a one. Parmenides ironically concludes that since smallness is never in anything that is, nothing may be said to be small except for the idea of smallness itself! But obviously this conclusion implies all the difficulties (such as the regresses) exposed by Parmenides in relation to Socrates' initial under-standing of the *eidos*. No doubt the silent Socrates realizes by now that meaning has no size and cannot be cut into pieces; Parmenides will shortly show why time may not be cut into pieces.

But, Parmenides continues, if smallness were in nothing whatsoever, largeness would have nothing to be larger than. And even if largeness were in something, then that thing added to largeness itself would make the largeness in the thing larger than largeness itself. Parmenides ironically pretends that the meaning of largeness is itself large, and Aristotle does not object, so Parmenides concludes that largeness cannot be in anything either. Parmenides exploits a materialistic conception of form in order to undermine a materialistic conception. Therefore largeness itself will not be larger than anything except smallness itself, and smallness itself will not be smaller than anything except largeness itself (150c). Parmenides begins with a materialistic depiction of the *eidos* in order to reduce to absurdity such depictions; he reduces in order to eliminate reductionism.

But his conclusion here implies that largeness and smallness are defined solely in differentiation from one another. This recalls the ques-tion regarding separation and unknowability that arose in the exchange with Socrates prior to this dialectical exercise. It was shown there that if ideas are defined solely in relation to one another, they would allow no intelligibility whatsoever of real beings. Parmenides shocked Socrates at the outset (133a–134e) by claiming that if this were so, then not even a god could have knowledge. Consequently, at 134e8–9, Socrates agreed with Parmenides (though for the wrong reason), that ideas could not be entirely separate. Parmenides is now emphasizing that forms cannot sim-ply be identified with entities either. These perplexities relating to the meanings of spatial terms are leading up to the even greater difficulties relating to time. In the third beginning, Parmenides will develop more pointedly the reasons why meanings may not be adequately represented by images in imagination.

However, according to Parmenides' present line of reasoning, the others are neither larger nor smaller than the one, since the others have no largeness or smallness in them. But if the others are neither larger nor smaller, Parmenides asserts, they may be said to be equal. It does not follow from the claim that the others do not partake of largeness or smallness that they must therefore partake of equality, but Aristotle fails to object—even when Parmenides uses the same reasoning a second time to claim that since a one has no largeness or smallness, it must be equal to itself and to the others (150e).

Since his young interlocutor obediently allows him to proceed unchecked, Parmenides claims that a one understood as the whole must be larger than itself, since it contains all the parts of itself, and that a one understood as the parts must be smaller than itself, since it is contained by itself (151a). At 145c, it was asserted that the one may be said to be both the whole which contains and the parts which are contained, but this identification of the parts and the whole clearly does not support the claim that when the one is interpreted as the parts it is smaller, but then when it is taken as being the whole it suddenly instantaneously becomes larger. If we assert that a one understood as the whole contains all the parts of itself, this apparently innocuous claim implies the absurd consequence that the one is both larger and smaller than itself.

Parmenides intentionally evokes ambiguities because the whole of what a thing is may not be made present to either thought, or to *aisthēsis*, or to a harmonious blending of these: all unification involves differentiation. The possibility of further interpretation is the possibility of transcendence. But ideas in relation to phenomena may be generated indefinitely, and all of the possible interpretations are not commensurable, not reducible to one fundamental unifying interpretation. In Parmenides' game, sometimes *to hen* means unity as displayed, by part or by characteristic, and sometimes it means one particular entity among others. And at 153b, *to hen* is used to mean the first unit of arithmetic. Sometimes it means unity as defined; and, as already indicated, unity/plurality also signifies a condition of the possibility of definition itself. It is no accident that the mere listing of these various employments suggests the schema of the divided line. But if a systematic interpretation purports to resolve these ambiguities in the *Parmenides*, it ignores one of the primary aims of the dialogue; namely, disclosing precisely this irreducible plurality of juxta-posed modalities of disclosure.

If it is true that to be is to be somewhere, and that there is nothing else besides a one and all the others, the one and the others must be contained in each other, because there is nothing else besides them in which they might be contained. But if a one were in the others, the others would be larger than the one. And if the others were in the one, the others would be smaller than the one. Therefore, Parmenides concludes that a one is larger, smaller, and equal in measure both to itself and to the others (151e).

Parmenides claims that if the one were in the others, the others would be larger than the one. If the one is taken here to mean the *eidos* of unity, then this claim is nonsense; for a thing is not larger than an idea. If we take *to hen* here to mean one entity, then it makes some sense to assume that whatever is contained must be smaller than its container, and if the others were contained spatially within the one, they would be smaller than *to hen*. However, in his conclusion Parmenides assumes that both these situations obtain simultaneously—the one is contained in the others and is therefore smaller than they are, and the others are contained in the one and are therefore smaller than it is (151b).

Ambiguities Relating to *Chronos*

The second beginning culminates in a series of ironical *aporiai* related to the conceptualization of time. These obscurities relating to *chronos* occupy a central location in the game. They are crucial to the development of the theme of the dialogue because they make unavoidable the merely hypothetical nature of all discourse that does not constantly reflect on its own contextualization. The difficulties involved in any chronology serve to make visible the kinds of reductions and oversimplifications that are always implicit to positive dialectic. Parmenides is evoking, by means of these ironical provocations, the arbitrariness of representations of time. It is in the ironical exposure of the absurdities inherent in such reasoning that the dialogue achieves its ontological dimension.

At 152a Parmenides asks whether to be (*einai*) means to have a share of being in present time, just as "was" and "will be" signify the sharing with *ousia* of the past and future, respectively. After Aristotle agrees, Parmenides asserts that a one has a share of *chronos* if it has a share of being. Parmenides then claims that anything that partakes of time as it passes is always becoming older than it was: indeed, having an interchange with *chronos* was earlier described as 'becoming at once older and younger than itself' (141b) But in becoming older, Parmenides asserts, a one never over-steps the now (nun). Yet in becoming older, and in never overstepping the now, it might be said to actually be older whenever it is in the now. In this case, it would appear that in this thing we call now, a one leaves off becoming, and simply is (152d).

But what is becoming older than must be moving away from that which is younger because older is older only in relation to a younger. Therefore, when in becoming older it reaches the now, a one may be said to have become older than itself. But whenever a thing is, it is always in the now; therefore, Parmenides asserts, a one that exists is always becoming, simultaneously, both older and younger than itself. The assumption that allows the paradox at this point in the dialogue is the presupposition that the past has a share of being in a way that is comparable to the way the present has a share of being. But if a thing were identical with—rather than merely analogous to—what it once was, would it be true to say it becomes older than itself? Even if we imagine that the being of the past could be logically identical with the being of the present, it would still be meaningless to claim that what a thing once was still exists, and that this thing that was becomes younger, as time passes, than its present identity, which is in turn becoming older. Whereas the first beginning showed that in itself a one is not even one, the second beginning shows that the ambiguity of being implies that every claim to truth involves analogicity. By exploiting the chōris between allegedly timeless propositions and the temporality of experience, Parmenides discloses the figurative dimension of every claim to truth.

He now asserts at 152e that a one exists and becomes for an equal time as itself: neither more nor less. This means that a one cannot, after all, be said to become at once older and younger than itself. Presumably Socrates, for whose benefit this dialectical game was initiated, is meant to reflect at this point on the nature of chronos: a one may be older than it was, but what it was does not exist anymore. But if what was is said not to exist in any way whatsoever, then what is there for that which presently exists to be older than—and what is the basis for the assumption (implicit to our very grammar), that an entity remains identical to itself throughout predicament? We assert an entity to be older than it once was, but if what it was is nothing now, how can it be "older than"?

In regard to this point, the de-reification of substantives is no resolution: if we are correct in claiming it to be older, how do we know this? If it is true that a one exists only in the present, it cannot truly be said to be older than it was. If a one does not exist only in the present, how can it be one? If the past continues to exist in some way, a one must be affirmed to be at once growing older and younger than itself. Parmenides exploits these vagaries of grammar in order to bring into relief the indicative function of all discourse, even that logos which purports simply to express the simultaneity of logical identity.

At 153a, Parmenides induces Aristotle to agree that the multitude of things other than the one has a share of a number that is greater than one, since they are many. This contradicts Parmenides' claim at 149c that the others are neither one nor two nor have the name of any other number. At 149c Parmenides employed the notion of being 'other than the one' as a premise to support the conclusion that the others have no number whatsoever. But now, at 153a, being 'other than the one' is used as a premise to support the conclusion that the others do have a number.

But even more ironically, Parmenides claims that because the smallest number must originate first, a one is generated prior to the multitude, and is therefore older. Parmenides shifts the sense of *to hen* from an individual entity to the number one, and then claims that since one comes before the other numbers, the one must be older than the others.

A one was said already to have beginning, middle, and end. At 145b, where this was asserted, beginning, middle, and end were taken in a spatial way: the middle holds off equally from the extremes and this is assumed to indicate that any existent one will have some shape or other. At 153c, however, this spatial reference of beginning, middle, and end is shifted to *chronos*. Parmenides asserts that in all generation, whether of the one or of the many others, the beginning comes to be first, and then the others, up to the end. The others, however, have been said to be parts of the one, which is the whole. And the one comes to be one and whole only at the end of its generation. A one therefore comes into being last, along with the end (153d). But this would mean that the one is younger than the others.

Yet a beginning, or any other distinguishable event or entity, insofar as it is, is one. Therefore, unity would have to come into being in the beginning and be present *throughout* the generation of everything, including itself. Parmenides here shifts the sense of the one from a one which exists to the idea of unity by which an entity is disclosed as one thing. In this case, the one would be the same age as everything else, for the being of anything that is always implies unity. So, by this account, unity is neither older nor younger than the others, nor the others than it, whereas by the former account, the one was said to be both older and younger than the others, and the others than it. This, Parmenides claims, is the way it is now and has already become. But what about the future; does a one continue to become older and younger than the others and they than it?

If a thing is older than another, as time passes the difference in age remains the same: the older does not become still older than the original difference. And likewise, the younger does not become still younger; for adding equals to unequals does not affect the original difference which made them unequal. But, in this case, a one is not becoming either older or younger than another.

But a one was said to be older than the others. This means, Parmenides asserts, that a one has come to be for a greater time than the others, and they have come to be for a lesser time. But if an equal quantity is added both to a greater quantity and to a lesser quantity, the equal measure which is added increases the greater quantity proportionally less than it increases the lesser quantity. In this sense, as a one and the others each grow older, the relative difference in their ages decreases proportionally when it is compared to their actual ages. But even if this proportional difference in age continued to decrease indefinitely, the difference would never become nothing.

Parmenides derives a sense in which a proportional decrease in the relative difference in ages allows the claim that the one is younger than it was, compared to those things than which it before was older (154e). There is another sense in which the others may be said to be becoming older, because, as the difference in their ages decreases in a proportional way, so, in a proportional way does the age of the others approach the age of the one, which was said to be older.

What these arguments evoke is an account in which a one becomes neither older nor younger than the others, nor they than it; insofar as they always differ from each other by the same measure of time, this is true. But the difference in their ages decreases proportionally as more and more time is added. In this sense, as the difference in their ages decreases proportionally, the older one and the younger others might be said to be growing younger and older relatively to each other. This means that a one may be said, to be and become, both older and younger than itself and the others and neither to be, nor become, older nor younger than itself or the others (155c).

Parmenides' Second Synopsis and Reorientation within the Whole

That Parmenides' game—his praxis through logos—is informed by *projected schema*, the *activity* of dialectical differentiation, and synoptic *reorientation* is evident if the summaries at the end of every beginning are compared and contrasted with each other and with his outline of the manner of training given at the outset (135e–136c). Because Parmenides' game shows Socrates that every moment of disclosure in logos involves projection, differential activity, and reorientation, the passage which is both the conclusion to the second beginning and the transition to the third involves a remembering of the results of the first beginning. In summing up the equivocal results of the second beginning, Parmenides contrasts these results with the results of the first, and it is obvious that the first two beginnings, insofar as they make thematic opposing senses of *to hen*, arrive at different conclusions.

Unlike unity in relation to itself, a one which is—that is, a one relative to the many—may be said to exhibit numerous characteristics in various senses. For example, the one in relation to other natures has a share of *chronos*: it has a before and an after and a now, since a one that has a share of being exists in time and becomes.

But at the end of the first beginning, Parmenides claimed unless something has a share of time and being, no knowledge is possible of it (142a). Like the first, the second beginning also indicates that no mode of disclosure reveals simple presence. Just as there is no pure presence in *aisthēsis* apart from the logos of being, so also there are no intelligible foundations of intelligibility, apart from participatory being.

It is precisely because the intelligibility of experience is a chorismatic ratio that persistent inquiry reveals all disclosure in logos to imply both identity and difference. It is only in relation to the uniqueness of discrete intentions that an indefinite multiplicity of conflicting interpretations is disclosed; but the relation that discloses is negative, not positive. Any disclosure of a one or a being is by way of *to heteron*, the different. Parmenides' ironic dialectic is in this critical sense a kind of *archē*-ology. The attempt to think an *archē* like unity shows that taken individually, it cannot even meaningfully be named. One is only in opposition to a many. Oppositions like unity/plurality are in no way reducible to our conceptions, because archaic opposition is what we are, not only how we think. Because being is only in and through differentiation, dialectic culminates in a negative moment: there is no otherworldly existent totality of interconnections to be made present. Such a metaphysics of presence would prevent even a god from having knowledge.

The second beginning, like the dialogue as a whole, calls forth difficulties implicit to the representation of temporal beings by means of the sameness of logos. It is no more a systematic ontology than it is an ironic

comedy of errors intended to provoke the critical participant in the dialogue. Parmenides' intentional sophistry (e.g., his mimicry of materialism)
indicates the wrong way to read the Platonic dialogue: we cannot piece
together a univocal Platonic doctrine or system of categories based on the
selection of this and that claim uttered by one or more of the dialogue's
participants. Plato breaks open various revelatory accounts in a number
of ways, and it is only by way of this disruptive moment that the philosophically significant development of the questions occurs.

For example, the insight that the *eidos*–as well as the phenomenal
thing or feature–is defined by what it is not is the way beyond the unreasonable regresses implicit to Socrates' initial understanding of the *eidē*.
The regresses evoked in the introductory exchange with Socrates (e.g., 132b
and 133a), result from the insistence that an idea cannot be subject to what
it is not. Parmenides' game shows Socrates that the notion of participation between form and thing implies an odd substitution or exchange
(*metalambanō*). But this doubling, analogous to a mixing of incombinables,
both allows intelligibility and produces difficulties, because significance
in logos involves a juxtaposition of senses that does not correspond to a
reduplication in being. There is no third form, somewhere beyond, that
allows the participation of form and thing because this sharing is an odd
interchanging that preserves radical difference. But this differential can
only be thought as negativity: form and thing may not be distinguished by
anything positive. We may try to argue, like young Socrates, that the wholeness of form is not material, it is not divisible into parts, and so forth. But
do such efforts necessarily end in figurative discourse, like Socrates' analogy of the day? If this proves inevitable, nevertheless any intelligible
account of the being of a thing is by way of the *eidos*: for the idea names
the intelligibility allowed in logos.

Nevertheless the first beginning shows that formality in itself is nothing; therefore the phenomenon cannot be a sign indicating an intelligible
presence that is signified. This implies that the odd interchange of participation involves an addition of sign functions, not a reduction of one
to the other. The first and second beginnings together show that it is the
movement of toward-itself disclosure—in addition to the movement of
toward-another—that allows disclosure of many senses of being.

The first synopsis at 142a is negative; the one cannot be named or
known. The second synopsis at 155d–e is positive but ambiguous. But the
actual practice of dialectical differentiation—that informs both beginnings—contrasts not only with these synoptic moments, but also with the
projected schema of the game at the outset. Because the praxis that is dis-

closure through logos involves both the inconceivable negativity of singular form and the unintelligibly ambiguous flux of temporal existence, every moment of Parmenides' actual performance arises out of this differentiation. There can be no moment of disclosure in itself: there is nothing pure and simple in logos or in being. Strictly speaking, there is no toward-itself disclosure and no toward-another disclosure. At the boundary of being and logic is differentiation of the inconceivable, an archaic oppositionality that cannot be named or defined. Presence is bounded and informed by nonpresence. Parmenides' schematic projection of the game's development is exceeded at each moment insofar as any synoptic overview differs from that which it is an overview of.

Socrates is silent throughout Parmenides' demonstration.[15] In the *Parmenides*, this silence does not only indicate Plato's intent that we think our way beyond contradiction and ambiguity, insofar as this is possible. The silence of Socrates dramatically invokes the moment of insight into the inconceivable oneness of form; the silencing of conceptual thought is the moment of transcendence. The dialogue is not only a universe of discourse; for its wholeness includes its silences. In the instant of insight (*to exaiphnēs*), the critical participant is led beyond the limitations of the dialectical games of discursive reasoning. The irony of Parmenides' troubling play is unified with revelation of the being of time because irony compels the critical participant to active engagement in questioning the meaning of existence—the oneness that exceeds real and ideal presence—and the limitations of logos that confine such disclosure.

Chapter 5

卐卐卐

If the All Is a Many,
Change Is Impossible

"Nonetheless, be well aware that you cannot yet say or grasp the *aporia* there is, if you are going to always set out one *eidos* for every distinction among things that exist."

—*Parmenides* (133a13–b3)

The Greatest Perplexity

In his initial exchanges with Socrates, before beginning his dialectical
game, Parmenides warned that Socrates did not yet realize the *aporia*
implied in distinguishing a singular form in itself, apart from beings
(133a–b). Suppose someone asserts that, if the forms are as we say they
ought to be, they cannot be known? At this point in their introductory
exchange, Parmenides had already raised difficulties about the extent of
ideas (130a–e); he has already invoked the dilemma of participation
(131a–c), the paradox of divisibility (131c–e), the largeness regress
(131e–132b), and reduced to absurdity Socrates' efforts to conceive the
forms as thoughts or paradigms (132b–133a). Shortly after this,
Parmenides informs Socrates that he must reorient his questioning toward
the *eidē* themselves (135e).

What precisely, is this greatest *aporia* that Socrates does not yet appre-
hend, but that he can only discover if he focuses on the forms grasped in
logos, the *eidē*? And how could this eidetic paradox be more difficult than
the regresses and other difficulties relating to how sensible particulars are
unified by the form?

The form of this greater *aporia* that Parmenides' game discloses for
Socrates invokes the paradoxical wholeness of *to eon* in the fullness of
alētheia. Parmenides is showing Socrates that if being is one in itself, then
this oneness cannot be truly spoken in mortal logos; for insofar as the disclosure of being is unified, then it is also irreducibly ambiguous / non-

119

consistent. If the formality of logos involves singularity and universality—as we philosophers say it does—then how is intelligibility possible?

Parmenides' game has decisively undercut the notion of ideal presence by showing that even if the *eidē* could allow assimilation of particulars in a perfectly consistent synthesis—as Socrates initially believed—this conception of formal universality would strip the *eidos* of its singularity. This paradox of unmixed *alētheia* implies that being itself is a sign function, not a term.

The third beginning will show that, without the contrast allowed by the anticipation of "will be" based on the retention of "was," "is" would be entirely empty of significance. The significance of any "is" depends on this juxtaposition. The existence of the one is disclosed only alongside this nonpresence at the heart of presence.

The Central Problematic: Repetition or Discontinuity?

The motif of logos as repetition and discontinuity is made thematic from the beginning of the *Parmenides*. Cephalus, the narrator, learned the discourse from Antiphon, who learned it from Pythodorus (126a–127a), who came in when the presentation of Zeno's reductions to absurdity was nearly finished. Both the first and the second beginnings culminate in exposure of the same problem: how can language disclose the nature of beings that are constantly changing? The Socratic enigma of the limitations of logos and absence at the origin—already discernible in the *Republic*—informs Parmenides' troublesome game.

The first beginning shows unification without reference to that which is unified to be utterly empty and meaningless (141d–e). And the second beginning indicates ways that logos can succeed and fail to disclose the nature of beings: unification in logos must involve acceptable phrasings, modified grammatically according to rules and with reference to the particular circumstances of their use in varying contexts. Both beginnings make clear that *alētheia* in logos depends not only on grammar, but also on logic: if a discourse is to be disclosive of the nature of beings, it must avoid absurdities and contradictions. The second beginning illustrates how these absurdities can arise or be avoided: unintelligibility about entities arises in the improper combination of terms, phrases, propositions, arguments, or more general linguistic *tropoi* such as empirical and nonempirical orientations. The first and second beginnings together indicate the need for timeless logical rules that govern the unification of expressions by is, was, and will be. These formal rules would be atemporal insofar as they would be repeatable in all circumstances, all places and times. Only such rules could allow differentiation of the many senses of being disclosed in the second beginning.

The problem is that even such ruled-governed disclosure of being implies a radical incommensurability. If one is one (137c), then in itself—apart from time and being—it is not one (141d-e). And if one exists (142b), then it is both a definite one and an indefinite many (142e-143a, 144e, etc.,). In such ways, Parmenides throws into doubt the naive reduction of being to either ideal or real presence; *alētheia* in logos about being involves a mixture of unmixables. His dialectical game demonstrates that fundamental oppositions such as unity/plurality are implicit to reasoning; consequently they stand prior to any attempt to clarify them.

Because such *archai* oppositions are basic to the process of discursive clarification itself, no *archē* admits of definition by genus and species. This indefinable archaic opposition seems to inform the disclosure of every relation, ideal or real; for Parmenides is unable to keep the two thematic orientations toward-itself and toward-another separate: apart from being, one is not one; and if one exists, it is also an indefinite many. Disclosure of oneness toward-itself is by way of differentiation; it involves relations of difference toward the many other natures, just as unity itself is implicated in disclosure of the many others.

But this means that the problem of the *chōrismos* is metastasized, rather than resolved by the first two beginnings. In the first, even eidetic discourses are shown to be articulated by way of the unity-in-opposition dialectic that is implied in the disclosure of phenomena. And in itself one is not one. But similarly, the discourse of the second beginning depends on unity: meaningful accounts of beings that change are impossible without unification according to identity and noncontradiction. The discourses in both beginnings involve this odd interpenetration or juxtaposition: being is participatory in that it involves both repetition of sameness in logos and ongoing differentiation of context. But the omnipresent differential of logos-functions in the first two beginnings raises the possibility that discourse always involves the combination of incombinables. The third beginning will indicate why all disclosure in logos is juxtaposition, not blending.

This intercontextuality also implies that presence is always informed by nonpresence; both beginnings show that reflection on time makes this conclusion inescapable. Because even the silent dialogue of the soul with itself would involve representations of identity defined by way of differentiation, a god could have no *epistēmē* if the forms existed separately

(134c8–135a3). The notion of separately existing *eidē* implies a reduction of teleology that undercuts the intelligibility it purports to explain; but, similarly, the collapsing of the distinction of form would lead to utterly unintelligible ambiguity. But if disclosure in logos is rule-governed praxis, like a game, what is the status of this governing? If formal rules for unification by way of is, was, and will be are said to be utterly nontemporal, this implies the unintelligibility of inconsistency (141d–e), but if they are thoroughly temporal, this would imply the unintelligibility of sheer ambiguity.

The dual theme of conceptual representation and time is developed in this way in order to underscore the Platonic insight that being has no simple and undifferentiated principle of explanation. Repetition implies discontinuity, and yet logos and experience are unified somehow; to deny this is absurd. Both the first and second beginnings culminate in difficulties relating to *chronos* because Plato's reinscription of Parmenides' way of *alētheia* is by way of an investigation of the unification—in logos—of disclosures of temporal beings.

The Ironical Framing

At 155e, Parmenides suggests they take up the discussion of the one a third time. But is this discussion of the instant (155e–157b) an addendum to the second beginning or a separate beginning in its own right? Scholarly efforts to resolve this issue are longstanding and ongoing, and this is in part due to the fact that Plato draws attention to this passage in a number of ways. The very existence of this third beginning as a unified section is made problematic by the difficulty of resolving the question of the dialogue's structure. Parmenides projected eight divisions in the hypothetical manner of training (136a–c). Consequently, if we insist on the coherence of the projected form of the method, then the account of the instant cannot exist as a separate and unified third attempt in its own right. But one difficulty for this interpretation is that Parmenides refers to it as the third attempt (*to triton*) at the outset (155e4). In fact, it is the only beginning in the dialogue that is explicitly enumerated this way in the text. This is not insignificant, for Parmenides shows in this beginning that time may not be represented mathematically without misrepresentation; if the instant is enumerated, the discourse this allows implies its own unintelligibility.

But if it is not a third attempt in its own right, this seems to imply that it is either simply a continuation of the second beginning, or else an entirely noncontinuous interjection. The first alternative initially might appear to allow the coherence of the projected schema of the game, except that this project was undermined and exceeded from the outset, in that *pros hauto* and *pros allo* orientations in logos interpenetrate throughout. But the second alternative means utter discontinuity; for the presence of a discontinuous moment would thoroughly undermine the projected schema: how could a disjointed moment be unified into the eightfold outline of the project? This beginning is the only one explicitly enumerated by Parmenides in the text; but if it is counted, there are at least nine beginnings, not eight. Does time imply that projections of rules are violated at every moment?

But if we ignore Parmenides' reference to it at 155e4 as the third discourse—*eti dē to triton legōmen*—and simply interpret this section as a digressive continuation of the second beginning, the critical participant will nevertheless wonder why consideration of the being of time compels this unexpected development in the apparently straightforward method. Again: is *chronos* the reason why the integrity of the method—its projected schema—is undermined and exceeded from the outset of the game?

Is desire for consistency the motivation for ignoring Parmenides' enumeration of a third beginning and viewing the account of the instant as simply a continuation of the second? There is undoubtedly thematic consistency insofar as the instant develops further the problematic of time in which the second beginning culminates. But on these grounds alone we could also call the second beginning nothing but a continuation of the first—if we really wish to be completely consistent—for the second beginning develops further the implications of the problem of time with which the first beginning culminates. This textual inconsistency is unified with the overarching theme of repetition and discontinuity: once again Plato provokes the critical participant to questioning.

Insofar as the account of the instant follows Parmenides' summary of results at 155d–e, it does seem to be what Parmenides says it is, namely a third way of examining the consequences of the one's existence. In this case too, the critical participant will wonder what it is about the problematic relation of time and logos that would lead to the exceeding of Parmenides' projected eightfold schema of the game. Why should consideration of the being of time lead to a discontinuous interjection on the atomic instant?

On any of these interpretations, the attempt to think the existence of the punctual instant is associated with the exceeding of the project Parmenides develops out of Socrates' initial distinction between idea and thing. Parmenides suggested at the outset that Socrates' untrained dis-

tinction between form and thing does not resolve all paradox (e.g.,
135c–136a). To see this, Socrates must reorient his questioning toward the
ideas themselves. Now the question becomes, does Parmenides' reconfiguration of the initial distinction—his troubling play—allow resolution of
the paradoxes it evokes?

Must we simply abandon the coherence of the method and say that
there are really nine (or more) distinct beginnings? This would allow the
third beginning to have a unified existence in its own right, and justify
Parmenides referring to it as such. The form of the dialogue suggests and
yet eludes schematism, and whichever interpretation of structure we select,
the existence of the instant is associated with the undercutting of projected
schemata.

The ironic contrast between the allegedly unproblematic projection
of the hypothetical method and the actual nature of the dialectical activity—that purports to demonstrate this method—frames a moment of *krisis*
or evaluation. Plato tempts the participant in the dialogue with a choice
between an apparently unambiguous but actually inconsistent insistence
on intelligible structure, and an only apparently contradictory but actually thoroughly ambiguous (nonunified) plurality of nonstatements. This
moment reconfigures Socrates' distinction between form and thing: the
krisis of Parmenides' game is that the notion of intelligible presence appears
to resolve ambiguities while in fact it produces inconsistency.

Nonetheless the *Parmenides* is neither systematic nor discontinuous,
and the critical account of the instant will emphatically demonstrate for
Socrates that the being of time eludes representation in the way that the
formal structure of the dialogue does. The text of the *Parmenides* is an analogue for the disclosure of any entity: if the text is viewed as an icon of the
kosmos, this latter must somehow be like a universe of discourse that possesses a unifying form—a wholeness—that eludes systematic representation.
But how do representations of time imply the odd intercontextuality that
Parmenides evokes throughout his discourse? If formality implies transcendence, *eidos* may not be reduced to presence without *aporia*. The dialogue, like the *kosmos*, displays a gestalt that allows neither entirely
consistent unification nor utter disunity.

The theme of repetition and time is introduced in the first few lines
and runs through the entire dialogue. The being of time is interrogated
in Parmenides' game at 140e–141d, and inquiry into *chronos* is again made
explicit at 151e and sustained into 157b—through the remainder of the
second beginning, and through the third beginning—all the way up to the
fourth beginning (157b–159b).

Parmenides exploits the irreducible paradoxes implicit to any positive account of time in order to make Socrates aware of the reductionism implicit to any conceptual representation of being. But because such paradoxes are implicit even to dialectic itself, Parmenides shows Socrates how irony and the *elenchos* may disclose the limitations of other modes of disclosure. As indicated earlier, in the Parmenides poem the goddess uses analogy, irony, and negations to contrast mortal intelligibility with the divine wholeness of *to eon* in the fullness of *alētheia*. The goddess does not give a positive, literal account of either being or truth. The Platonic figure of Parmenides accomplishes something analogous by exceeding, throughout his demonstration, the dialectical method he projects out of Socrates' notion of the separate *eidos*.

This third beginning (155e–157b) is ordinarily interpreted as a straight-faced Platonic theory of motion, or as a synthesis of the first and second beginnings.[1] But unless there is some fundamental inconsistency in asserting on the one hand that the meaning of unity does not change, while on the other hand any particular one entity changes, then a synthesis of the first two beginnings would be entirely unnecessary. The *aporia* Parmenides evokes is the inverse of synthesis; similarly, the inconsistency he reveals is the very inversion of contradiction. Instead of an unintelligible is / is not, Parmenides discloses an unintelligible neither / nor.

If the eightfold hypothetical method of dialectical training were all that is required in order to gain philosophical insight into these doubtful questions, then the third beginning would be extraneous; however the dialectical game exceeds its own structure from the outset. Therefore the problematic of time is not just a corollary or simply another source of further ambiguity. Rather, the motif of time from the initial passages of the *Parmenides* indicates the horizon for developing the doubtful questions relating to the representation of sameness in logos, and the nonpresence at the heart of ideal presence.

Unmixed *Alētheia?*

At 155e, Parmenides suggests they take up the discussion of the one a third time. This third beginning deals with the identity of entities or states that change with time. But because the premises that frame the third beginning are ironical, the critical participant will be open to the possibility of realizing that the account actually deepens the difficulties.

If the one becomes and perishes (156a), it must also follow that when it comes to be many it ceases to be one, and when it comes to be one it ceases to be many. And in coming to be one and many, it must combine and separate. When it becomes like and unlike, it must be made like and unlike. In the same way, when it becomes larger and smaller and equal, it must grow and diminish over time, and come to be equal in time.

But Parmenides argues that, when in moving or changing something comes to rest and stops, or when it begins to move after resting, there must be a moment when it is in no time at all. In order to pass from motion to rest or from rest to motion, an entity must change; yet Parmenides claims that there can be no time in which it exists, but is neither moving nor at rest (156c). The question naturally arises next as to when precisely such change actually occurs. For it can occur neither while the entity is in motion, nor while it is resting, and therefore not in any time at all. There must be this strange placeless thing—the instant—that is not itself in time (156d), for a change of any purely self-identical entity would be possible only if there is a point that is not in time at which the transition occurs instantaneously.

If becoming one thing after having not been that thing implies participation and then not participation in an identical (repeated) sense but at different times, Parmenides' paradox of the instant shows that such repetition of pure identity implies a moment of sheer discontinuity. In this way, Parmenides completes the reduction to absurdity of Socrates' notion of the separate existence of an *eidos* by showing it to imply inconsistency: a singular part of time can only signify in relation to the whole of which it is a part. The problem is that any part—if it exists—is also a whole that is spread out in time. There is no instantaneous part of time; such an instant would disclose nothing, and this nothingness of the part would make the whole nothing.

The instant is an atomic point of time analogous to Euclid's spatial location without dimension; it is a temporal locus that has no temporal dimension. But such a singular atemporal instant cannot unify or synthesize the different senses of "the one" in the first and second beginnings. It is no resolution of this difficulty to assert that motion and rest must be understood to occur together, in different senses, at the same time; for the nontemporal instant is implied by any change that occurs in any self-identical respect. Thus if form is simply what it is, and is not qualified by what it is not, this cannot resolve the difficulty. For the *eidos* cannot allow the instantaneous, consistent identification of deceptive phenomenal images in a moment of formal unification. No disclosure of being would be allowed by this collapsing of toward-itself identity and toward-another indication of existence into a monad of sheer nonpresence.

And the same absurdity would arise if there is no form at all, but only material particles: if a singular atom exists and moves, then it cannot move in time, and the instant in which it moves is entirely discontinuous from every other instant. In short, the unmixed singularity of any being, ideal or real, would imply the discontinuity of every instant of time. Parmenides account implies that when anything changes from motion to rest or from rest to motion, it cannot be in either state. To say that singular parts of any one change—in succession—and that it gradually comes—as a whole—to change, only pushes the problem back, for the same paradox would arise regarding any part. If it exists, any part is spread out in time.

In this way Parmenides' reformulates the intent of Zeno's paradoxical reply to those who deny that the all is one: if the all is a many, change is impossible. If Parmenides' account of the instant is compared to Zeno's paradox of the arrow, then in the change from one location to another, the arrow is neither in motion nor at rest. If time is asserted to be composed of punctual instants of change, then every phase of every phenomenal change would be divided indefinitely into a disjointed multiplicity that would make change completely unintelligible. If both Socrates' conception of the separate existence of the *eidos* and the materialistic reduction of form to presence imply an indefinite multiplicity of discontinuous and unintelligible singularities, how can we avoid the acknowledgement that no being—ideal or real—can exist as singular?

In the first beginning, Parmenides appealed to the principle of non-contradiction in an effort to isolate the meaning of unity in itself. But this singular meaning in itself, abstracted entirely from time and being, was shown to have no meaning: apart from all such signifying differentiations, one is not one (141d-e). This result implies that logic is not atemporal. Because logic implicitly involves the notion of simultaneity, discourse according to itself is implicitly inconsistent; apart from reference to time and being one is not even one. The paradox of the instant shows that simultaneity in itself implies inconsistency.

In the third beginning, by reducing to absurdity efforts to represent the being of time, Parmenides shows Socrates that any assumption whatsoever of singular being is implicitly inconsistent and undercuts the intelligibility of experience. Both the notion of unqualified being and the notion of unqualified becoming make impossible the intelligibility they purport to allow.

The second beginning has been shown to be analogous to the way of is and is not indicated by the goddess in the poem of Parmenides. Like the way of typical mortal discourse, it is equivocal, or two-headed; only

the unifying form offers the hope of sorting out phenomenal ambiguities. But Parmenides now develops a moment of paradox that threatens
any account of formal unification: the third beginning is a way of neither
is nor is not. The indivisible and discontinuous instant is an impossible
axiom: a timeless time-point is a paradox and explanation based on it is
inherently paradoxical.

This extraordinary (*atopon*) thing must occur if change is to be
explained as affecting any singular being (156d). But one (of many) paradoxical implications of his account is that motion and change cannot occur
in time. However, Parmenides has already emphasized that to be is to be
in time (141e-142a); but if this is true, then by his account of the instant
the motions and changes that we engage in and everywhere encounter
could not exist. The movement of thought in the process of dialogue would
also be utterly discontinuous; for Parmenides' account of the instant
involves the claim that change is not in time (156c).

Does Socrates' alleged resolution of Zenonian paradox (at
128e-130a) imply a violation of the law of the excluded middle? To be is
to be in time (141e), but the instant is not in time (156d1 and 156e6).
Therefore the instant cannot exist. At 157a, Parmenides says that the
instant of change neither is nor is not (*kai oute esti tote oute ouk esti*). The
instant divides intelligibility into an indefinite multiplicity of entirely dis-
connected and inassimilable singularities: such unmixed time would not
in any way be unifiable with time as we live it. Neither toward-itself nor
toward-another logos allows the reduction of this *aporia* that informs them
both. If being is, then it is informed by nonpresence at every moment.
Paradoxically, these distinguished moments signify as lived differentiations, but this possibility is their impossibility.

As metaphor, participatory being acknowledges this irreducible difference; being simply cannot be made intelligible if to be intelligible implies
unqualified singularity. Consequently to share or to partake cannot mean
"to assimilate."[2] The account of the instant shows that such assimilation
would be simultaneously and in the same sense dissimulation. Because
the notion of expression of identity in a punctual instant destroys the very
possibility of the intelligibility that it purports to explain; the effort to eliminate all ambiguity multiplies inconsistency.

The Reduction of Teleology

If an immortal could know all the ideas instantaneously in all possible
interrelations, this would still not be *epistēmē*. Parmenides' arguments at

the outset culminated in this claim (at 134e) in order to throw young Socrates into doubt about the possibility of asserting the separate existence of atemporal ideal being in itself, apart from the temporally mediated differentiation of significations. By way of his ironic dialectical game, Parmenides shows Socrates why there is no mastery without slavery, and no unity without plurality: the self-sameness of the ideal is nothing in itself. Therefore, to be a unified moment is to stand out from an indefinite plurality of moments. Even if an entirely atemporal mode of signification were possible, it would be locked in a monadic separation from time and being and therefore, as Parmenides claimed at 134e, it could not possibly be knowledge or account for the limited intelligibility of experience and discourse that it is absurd to deny. Parmenides' account of the instant demonstrates that intelligibility is necessarily finite and that it requires the goal-oriented temporality that informs all modes of *ousia*: the collapsing of the *chōris* of logos in a windowless atomic instant would make any disclosure or truth impossible.

The paradoxical account of the timeless time point is consequently no explanation at all: it is no explanation of change to assert that change cannot happen in time. According to Parmenides' argument, which was the impetus for the second hypothesis, only temporal entities or events can be spoken of meaningfully (141d–142a). Therefore the instant is subject to the same arguments Parmenides voiced at 141d–142a against the singular existence of the one; namely that it does not exist and therefore allows no intelligibility, or opinion, or perception, or even meaningful speech. The account of the atomic instant reduces significant discourse and disclosure itself to nothing because it reduces the opening that is participatory being to an indefinite plurality of discontinuous, singular instants of identity in which no signification of any kind is possible.

Such unmixed *alētheia* cannot be; it would lack the projection and continuity-in-discontinuity of teleological disclosure. But, because the notion of singular existence requires this reduction of teleology, the separate existence of the idea would destroy the possibility of any intelligible signification. Socrates cannot argue that the instant is intelligibility itself, because then logos would be indefinitely many utterly inassimilable monads that neither exist nor do not. Moreover, this conception of form was eliminated at 132b–c. If form is simply identified with thought, this implies an unreasonable regress (132c6–8), as well as the absurdity that either all things are thoughts and thinkers are everywhere, or all things are unthought thoughts (132c9–12).

Both the intelligibility of experience and the fact of change are given and to deny either is absurd. But the conception of existence as singular is implicitly inconsistent. Therefore, the being of time, like that of the form, implies ontological differentiation, rather than dialectical synthesis.

It is not that Socrates' unstable distinction between form and thing must simply be rejected, nor his metaphor of being as participation. On the contrary, both the distinction and the analogical insight are sharpened by Parmenides' demonstration of negative dialectic, to the point that unqualified presence, real or ideal, is rejected. Democritean materialism would imply the same contradictory metaphysics of presence as does Socrates' notion of ideal singularity. The overarching reduction to absurdity maintains its force whether the being asserted to exist in itself is conceived to be *archē*, *eidos*, thought, paradigm, individual, perception, atom, or unqualified becoming. If being were an unimaginably pure flux, it could not be, and change would not *be* change.

The alternative left open to young Socrates is simply to recognize the truth of what Parmenides has by now repeatedly affirmed—that there is no one, or many, or motion, or rest, in itself. The idea in itself cannot exist as singular; to exist means to participate in Parmenides' reconfigured sense: to stand out as unified only in differentiation from an indefinite many. Intelligibility requires the teleological standing out of itself that is transcendence; this otherwise than allows meaningful experience. Such being is participatory in the sense that disclosure in logos is only possible by means of its unintelligible conditions of possibility. Unless the *eidos* is acknowledged to be qualified by what it is not, then no entity can be qualified in any way. This is why, in Parmenides' paradox of the instant, the significance of existence and of all possible disclosure is squeezed out of experience and time and fragmented into an indefinite multiplicity of entirely discontinuous singularities corresponding to every moment of pure becoming. But there could not be any transition into or out of such inassimilable singularities.

The instant, not being in time, would not allow opinion, knowledge, name, or even meaningful speech. Consequently, Parmenides' paradox of the instant does not synthesize, but emphatically undercuts the formal structure of the dialogue and the presence of any being. The instant cannot be said either to be or not to be; but, by the law of the excluded middle, it should either exist or not exist. Parmenides' account of the instant is therefore no resolution; instead it is a multiplication of *chōrismos* and a deepening of *aporia*. *To exaiphnēs* is an odd kind of nonimage; and yet its singular un-existence is implied in the conception of phenomena as images of an undivided intelligibility.

Because Parmenides repeatedly indicates that such unqualified singularities are completely unintelligible, the account of the instant completes the tale: it reduces to absurdity Socrates' attempt to resolve Zeno's paradoxes. But insofar as our very grammar implies this notion of singular being, the truth disclosed in logos is simultaneously a closing over.

Beyond *Aporia?*

The account of the instant shows that if being is one then being cannot be one; if any being—ideal or real—could exist as singular, then being would be an irreducible many. This fragmentation of being into indefinitely many pure monadic singularities would infect the being of time to the point that change could not intelligibly be said to exist. If the disclosure of being in logos is conceived as pure unification, then logos is irreducibly ambiguous / inconsistent. If ambiguity could be universally eliminated, disclosure would be impossible insofar as inconsistency would be multiplied to infinity; and if all inconsistency could be eliminated, disclosure of being would be completely unintelligible flux. But if these imagined possibilities are unintelligible, what is the alternative?

Because the paradox of the instant indicates that the sameness of logos and the differentiations of *chronos* are juxtaposed in every moment of every disclosure, then Plato doesn't attempt to solve the problem of the *chorismos*, he does something more: he seriously considers the paradox. If to be is to be as a whole, nonetheless no whole can ever be made present, either to thought or to perception. And the only way any particular is disclosed is if we know the whole of which it is a part. A child finally learns to recognize the elements of the alphabet when she can repeat the whole, one part at a time. But the whole sign system cannot be repeated instantaneously. The paradox of the instant shows why the particulars in any sign system are also wholes: if it exists, the sign is spread out in time and can only be spoken and recognized part by part, in time: no instantaneous repetition or recognition is possible.

No instant could signify because its sheer apartness would infuse the whole and make any intelligibility completely inconsistent. To interpret the paradoxical third beginning as a synthesis or a resolution is to miss the significance of Parmenides' negative reformulation of Socrates' initial conception of formal existence. The account of the instant is the focal point of the dialogue's many paradoxical moments; one of its implications is that conversion of *psuchē*, in the *Parmenides*, involves much more than simply recognizing the distinction between meaning and entity. It involves the further insight that the distinction may neither be collapsed nor rigorously developed.

It may not be rigorously developed, for the moment of pure separation from time and being in the first beginning implies the unintelligibility of inconsistency: the one could not even be one. But the distinction between ideal and real may not be simply collapsed, because the effort to reduce ideal signification to real presence[3] also implies a moment of unintelligibility. The first two beginnings indicate that universality implies nonparticularity and particularity implies nonuniversality.

What exists manifests as participatory: we may impose reductions on the manifold of being, but these are derivative modes of disclosure. The ironical framing of the account of the instant ensures that its role as *krisis* is obvious to the reflective participant in the dialogue. Far from being an explanation, the paradox of the instant implies a critique of any axiomatic approach to being. The impossibility of signification in a punctual instant implies that linguistic expression of identity toward-itself is possible only by way of indications of otherness, that is, representation of existence. The question in considering the remainder of Parmenides' dialectical demonstration then becomes, does the converse hold true? That is, does indication of significance toward another (representation, or interpretation) occur prelinguistically? If so, then articulations of being are prior to linguistic derivations, and this supplementarity would indicate the horizon for further development of the doubtful questions. This would be consistent with Plato's consideration of goal-oriented human activity—as philosopher, sophist, statesman, lover, friend—as productive developments of the problematic of being / nonbeing, unity/plurality, and the identity and otherness of time.

If Socrates' distinction could be maintained without reconfiguration, then the third beginning would be entirely superfluous and should not occur. But that this is not the case is already implicit in Parmenides' challenging of Socrates prior to the dialectical game (130a–135d). The idea in itself is not foundational for the intelligibility of experience; and yet, if we deny ideal significance in itself, paradoxes of self-reference result. Paradoxically—as the second beginning shows—without the singular sign function, even ambiguity could not be disclosed in logos; even the denial of universality and the privileging of existential singularity presupposes universality.

The development or transcendence that is learning would be impossible to articulate without this identity function of the sign; the very notion of development or progress is impossible without reference to identity, because there would be no entity to change, and no change to occur: only utter discontinuity at every instant. But a positive (synthetic) interpretation of the account of the instant not only implies the complete unintelligibility of change, it also implies the nonexistence of change. These absurdities necessarily result from the effort to collapse the otherwise than of *chōris* into a metaphysics of presence. Because such an effort cannot resolve, but only multiply paradox, the account of the instant completes the reduction to absurdity of the notion that ideal presence is foundational for intelligibility.

What we see by means of the dialectical game is that the structure of the apparently unproblematic eightfold hypothetical method based on Socrates' initial distinction is exceeded from the outset. These two ostensibly distinct modes of discourse interpenetrate in every section of the dialogue. More significantly, the very existence of the third beginning undermines the coherence of the projected method of hypothetical demonstration. The implication is that even if *chōris* could be collapsed, this would allow no disclosure, no signification, and no discourse. Parmenides shows Socrates why the effort to make the idea, in itself, the ground of intelligibility is implicitly nonlogical. Existence is participatory being; this is the finite manifestation and limited intelligibility of changing entities.

It is the insignificance of the atomic instant that shows what is most provocative about Parmenides' dialectical game. Because his demonstration involves numerous appeals to the principle of noncontradiction (and its implicit notion of simultaneity), Parmenides' application of formal schema to phenomena, especially in the second beginning, implies the notion of pure presence in an instant. But by the law of the excluded middle, the instant should either exist or not exist, and yet it could do neither (156e–157b). Consequently, the third beginning shows that when a formal system is applied to phenomena, this resolves some ambiguities, but only at the expense of suspending logical consistency. If logic implies a reduction of being to universalized representations of intelligible presence, nonetheless any representation is implicitly inconsistent.

If any idea had separate existence, this would imply an indefinite multiplicity of pure instants of time that would make the continuity of lived time impossible. Parmenides ironically presents the instant as a strange placeless thing (156c–d), but in demonstrating that this *atopon* can be said neither to exist nor to not exist (157a–b), he is highlighting its unintelligibility.

Parmenides' irony is chorismatic, and therefore isomorphic with the nature of participatory being as it is lived. Discourse implies both intelligible structure and the ongoing exceeding of structure: intelligibility is informed by an unintelligible transcendent dimension. Parmenides' dialectical game shows this by emphasizing that *archai* oppositions such as unity/plurality stand prior to any attempt to clarify them, for they are basic to the very possibility of discursive clarification. The *archai* oppositions inform meaningful disclosure because they are indicative of the symbolic dimension of *psuchē*. But because the linguistic dimension of life arises in this fundamental process of differentiation in indications of existence, all disclosure in logos is necessarily chorismatic.

Is the *Parmenides* literal or figurative? On the most literal interpretation, it is completely contradictory. But negative dialectic discloses antinomies of presence, eliminates positive assertions about being, and clears the way for meta-literal insight. The Platonic moment is the moment of paradox; the crucial point is that Plato's ontological poetry can only be understood as supplementary to negative dialectic.

Because Parmenides ironically exploits these bounds of logos in order to generate the discourse of this dialogue, the text itself is an icon of the *kosmos*. But presence is shown to be defined in relation to what it is not: the nonlogical transcendence of the singular form is a condition of the possibility of logic. Ironic dialectic is an analogue of the identity in opposition that is participation; disclosure implies this differential.

Parmenides refers to the account of the instant as the third (*to triton*) beginning, and this is the only beginning in the dialogue numbered in this way. It is no coincidence that the account of the instant parallels the third (*triton*) of four levels of philosophical insight described in the *Philebus* (12–16). At 12e, Socrates remarks that in itself, no color differs from any other: in respect of being a color, they are all alike. And the same holds true of being a figure. This level of insight corresponds to the discourse according to itself of the *Parmenides*. And yet, Socrates says to Protarchus, if we consider figure according to how some figure compares to other figures, it may be completely opposite to some, but have countless points of difference with others. The experience of any object involves an indefinite diversity of possible relations. This corresponds to the discourse in relation to another of the *Parmenides*. But the ambiguity of experience does not completely undermine intelligibility; some generalizations are still more reliable than others; and no logos would be possible without the notion of identity.

Socrates acknowledges at *Philebus* 15b that it is questionable whether singular being should be said to exist. And yet, in spite of the indefinite plurality of possible changes and predicaments, we cannot think without thinking that it is one singular being that undergoes such changes. Therefore the third moment of insight involves an acknowledgment of the difficulties implied in the assertion that one singular entity changes. This paradoxical moment of insight has to do with identity in change, and Socrates says at 15b–c that the whole seems impossibly to be apart from itself. The philosophical life is mixed, or dialectical, because *euporia* is only possible on this basis: the recognition of paradox in accounts of identity in change leads to the bounds of being and intelligibility. The *Parmenides* shows this insofar as the *archai* oppositions are indicative of existence: any ideal representation of fundamental opposition leads to *aporia* because a representation of being (e.g., the being of time), is a representation of *choris*; that is, a representation of a schism, a pure nonrepresentability.

In the *Philebus*, the fourth level of insight is based on this recognition of paradox and the finitude of intelligibility. Socrates describes this as the wisdom that recognizes the transcendent cause of the combination of limit and unlimit in the development of a single entity. Socrates refers, in describing this life of acceptance, to the recognition that *kosmos* has a transcendent dimension, which he refers to as analogous to spirit (29e ff.). The wisdom that is the acceptance of human finitude involves acknowledgement that the notion of causality transcends intelligibility. Any effort to represent being in itself (e.g., mathematically) is not only figurative, but also implicitly inconsistent.

Because there can be no unqualified explanation of identity in change, the intelligibility of experience points beyond itself to the moment of transcendence. Parmenides shows Socrates that such being is nothing to us; the notion of singular being in itself is completely void of intelligibility. And yet an indefinite plurality of ambiguous prelinguistic associations is also unintelligible. Without the nonliteral reference to being as transcendence, how could identity in change be intelligible? Parmenides' paradox of the instant demonstrates that if unqualified being is said to exist, then it could neither exist nor not exist.

Because this is absurd, Socrates must conclude that any possible disclosure implies the one in many, teleological movement that is participatory being in time. Both the unity of the *psuchē* and the unity of the *kosmos* involve a transcendence that is the beginning, or occasion of finite intelligibility. Transcendence is a standing out of itself that exceeds dialectic. But if this otherwise than is conceived as a positive synthesis, this account undermines the intelligibility it purports to explain.

There is no absolutely signified content to be expressed. It is not simply that tautologies are uninformative; the presumption of simultaneity implies an instantaneous allegedly atemporal intention that undercuts—by its sheer emptiness—the very notion of a discrete moment of disclosure. Parmenides' paradox of the instant completes the reduction to absurdity of representations of being. Because *to hen* and *to apeiron* underlie the numbers, the numbers are inadequate representations of their own conditions of possibility: the very effort to employ them in an unqualified way is nonlogical. The alternative left open is that there are as many forms of time as there are modes of disclosure: in itself, the being of time is nothing. Being is transcendence, and literal discourse fulfills its intelligibility when it acknowledges this figurative moment. Insight arises in the juxtaposition of negative dialectic against the misleading positivism of representations. Philosophical insight involves seeing an image as an image.

Because being exceeds its various dialectically interrelated manifestations, the least inadequate form of disclosure, according to logical criteria, is by way of negative dialectic. But in positive terms, transcendence may only be evoked indirectly. Parmenides' ironic dialectical game supplements the nonliteral accounts in other dialogues (such as the *Philebus*) by reducing literal accounts of being to absurdity. Plato's ontological poetry should be read as the *euporia* that arises in the moment of re-cognition of paradox: any literal account of being invalidates itself.

Being toward the good is disclosed in logos as differentiation of circumstances over against the singularity and nonpresence of an ideal meaning. The *chōris* of this teleology gives rise to the very possibility of disclosure in logos. Because the good is otherwise than beings, teleology involves this striving. Therefore, participation also indicates our being, but the concepts of identity, self, and presence only arise in this movement. This striving is out of the lack that is presence and toward the fullness that is nonpresence.

Time, *Tropos*, and Language

Chōris is not simply a gap between ideal and real entities; difference is as primordial as sameness, both are necessarily disclosed together, even in relation to ideal meanings. If we develop our questioning in the form of expressions of logos directed toward-itself (*Parmenides* 136a–c), then *archai* oppositions will be disclosed, but we will see that taken singly they have no being and therefore allow no intelligibility. But if our discourse is toward-another, then it indicates the ontological differentiation between disclosures. But these are not separate worlds that lie on either side of an unbridgeable gap; they are two inflections of the verb "to be." The many tenses and moods in the discussion of unity/plurality in the *Parmenides* indicate in what way, and to what extent, the discourse of philosophy may meaningfully articulate ontological ambiguities. Parmenides shows that a rigorous separation of meaning and entity cannot be developed; the paradoxes reduce to absurdity the young Socrates' naive notion of ideal presence (133b ff.). Parmenides develops the doubtful questions in relation to the ideas themselves (135e). But the philosophically productive questioning is only possible on the basis of the intelligibility of the ideas (135c), and the focus of such questioning is time.

Brief reflection reveals hidden *aporiai* implied by this ordinary, non-reflective conception, or reduction of the being of time. If we reduce time to a singular instant, we reduce a manifold to an antinomic representation. A monadic and windowless moment of pure presence would allow no *epistēmē* because there would be no possible connection with any other such alleged moment of ideal presence. Relations of ideas may be generated indefinitely in relation to being (143a–145a), but apart from teleological being the formal in itself is a sheer nothing, void of significance. Neither unqualified being nor unqualified becoming can exist, and time considered as a thing in itself is unintelligible. Any attempt to represent *chronos* leads to paradoxes that undercut the intelligibility they purport to facilitate. Such images must be recognized to be images. Parmenides' pivotal third beginning demonstrates for Socrates that the reduction to a representation of the one in many that is being is an invitation to absurdity.

Consequently, Parmenides' reformulation of Socrates' initial separation into a distinction between an orientation toward meaning in itself, as opposed to an orientation toward the relations of difference between entities (135e–136c), is only the beginning of his provocation to thought of Socrates. The evocation in the first two beginnings of ambiguities and paradoxes implicit to this distinction serves to introduce the central problematic regarding the being of time. The paradox of the instant shows that even Parmenides' reformulation of Socrates' initial separation into a distinction between modes of logos is insufficient to avoid impasse.

The impossibility of the rigorous and complete development of the distinction is also indicated in Parmenides' initial response to Socrates, for example at 133c–134e. Parmenides claims that if ideas exist separately, then even an immortal would not have *epistēmē*. Real and ideal relations are disclosed in and through purposive interactions: words are cousin to the deed.[4] If the ordering that is cosmos is disclosed by way of language this cannot mean that disclosure is a human ordering. Parmenides' negative dialectic reveals that what any being is (whether its being is disclosed as ideal or real) intimately involves what it is not. The distinction between the nonempirical and the empirical is undermined insofar as both of these imply the ontological differentiation that is the only absolute (*anhypotheton*) disclosed in Plato's Eleatic dialogues. Its condition cannot be expressed without paradox: being is necessarily relational.

Consequently, even if *alētheia* is accomplished only through logos, nevertheless truth happens beneath human beings. Prelinguistic archaic opposition is disclosed in logos as *chōris*. This differentiation that informs the linguistic dimension of *psuchē* (life) is the boundary of being: it limits thinking but cannot in itself be thought. As a result, both *psuchē* and logos are informed by what they are not.

Because both intelligibility and change are given (and to deny either is absurd), the metaphor of participation in being is not a theory; it simply describes what we are. This is one reason why the question of being is approached in the dialogues by way of inquiry into human existence: as angler, actor, diviner, guardian, brave man, and philosopher.

Reorientation within the Whole

Showing Socrates that the intelligible is not the ground of being is the motivation for the pivotal treatment of time: if ideas existed separately, even an immortal could not have knowledge. Because each of these—unity and being—is forever becoming two and will not stay absolutely unique, the unity of an entity occurs alongside its being, and its being is manifested alongside its unity. But since any part of an existent one is forever becoming two, then in this sense a one which is may be said to manifest the feature of being indefinite in multitude (143a). Anything that is manifests these two, being and unity. But these always implicitly involve a third, difference. Unity may be conceived to be distributed throughout an indefinite and potentially infinite multitude, and to be manifested by way of difference in every part of this multitude (144e). Parmenides has already shown Socrates that if the ideas are separated from being they are unknowable; at this point in his demonstration he shows that if the ideas have being, their interrelations are an indefinite multitude.

This example is typical of Parmenides' reasoning throughout the dialogue. It reveals that the goal of his game (137c–166c) is the same as the goal of his introductory exchange with Socrates (130b–135d). Parmenides' aim throughout the dialogue is to make Socrates aware that the effort to make the *eidos* foundational for knowing ends in *aporia*. Similarly, the attempt to make sense perception foundational in knowing results in entities characterized by an absence of what we can know. The purpose of this Socratic skepticism is to shift the focus of the inquiry away from the criteria of knowing and toward the conditions of the possibility of disclosure (*alētheia*).

Because being is prior to knowing, negative dialectic does not disclose the good as an epistemological foundation. The good as *telos* indicates an ontological difference: at the basis of the self-presence of consciousness is an original difference between eidetic content and the affection it engenders. The striving of interactive existence (participatory being toward the good) at all levels of *psuchē* gives rise to the movement of time: both soul and object are disclosed in and through such interactive striving. But because presence is informed negatively, transcendence is not the development of a human ordering, and being in Plato's dialogues does not merely signify *kosmos*.

The good is not simply an elevation according to the same criteria of significance that are employed by the various modes of disclosure the good informs. Its supplementarity indicates not greater utility, but a different means of evaluation entirely, and a different mode of disclosure. Insofar as it indicates the transcendence implied in (finite) teleological disclosure, good / nongood is a condition of the possibility of intelligibility that in itself may not be disclosed to intelligibility. Because *archai* oppositions are articulations of the axio-ontological differentiation that is basic to discursive clarification itself, they may not be discursively clarified, but only disclosed in a negative or a figurative way.

Orientation (*tropos*) toward various *archai* oppositions discloses being variously. But, Parmenides shows Socrates that although archaic opposition is a condition of the possibility of the formal, the opposition itself is not an idea, even if we mistakenly believe that we may form a conception of it. Unity is only in opposition to plurality; neither the single *archē* nor the single *eidos*, nor the single perception may be discursively clarified. Fundamental oppositions such as this are indicative of the whole of participatory being toward the good. The only way an individual moment can signify is if the whole is re-cognized. But no existent whole is ever present as a whole to either perception or thought. Moreover, the particular—if it exists—is also a whole that is spread out in time.

Because significance involves such contextual juxtaposition, every *eidos* and every act of logos signifies only in relation to this paradoxical wholeness. This holds true even if there is being only where there is the logos of being. Negative dialectic reveals the ideas themselves to be analogous to figures on the wall of the cave: manifestation itself is never manifest. Ideas are only in differentiation from a whole matrix of ideas; in itself the formal signifies nothing. No formal matrix can be present as a whole in an instant; if it signifies anything, the form represents possibilities for repetition of significance. That is, it indicates possibilities of action in a context. Archaic oppositions—as general names for signifying differentiation—are various significations of the whole of embodied, participatory being toward the good.

Because interpretation necessarily implies ontological differentiation as its condition of possibility, we cannot think the *archai* oppositions, much less think beyond them. In itself an *archē* is insignificant, but the differentiation these fundamental oppositions articulate is a condition of the possibility of disclosure itself. Because prelinguistic archaic oppositionality informs disclosure in logos, the idea in itself is also a signpost of the bounds of being. The idea interpreted in relation to other *eidē* and phenomena discloses genus / species divisions—differentiations, not identities—for pure identity is nonlogical.

If the sameness of logos articulates ideal possibilities of repetition, this ideal possibility of repetition signifies only in juxtaposition against presence. The indefinite potential for ideal repetition is a derivative mode of disclosure insofar as being may not be reduced to any representation or system of representations without an illegitimate circularity. Representations would be presupposed to be true in any effort to justify the representations themselves.

The paradox of the instant shows that being (e.g., the being of time) implies differentiation: the sameness of logos cannot make fully present to intelligibility the articulations of participatory being. Because the *archai* oppositions that inform ideal and real disclosure stand prior to any attempt to discursively clarify them, the inquiry into logos and time shows that apart from differentiation, the formal in itself is nothing; one is not even one. Any expression of identity implies differentiation: even logos conceived as the *psuchē* in silent dialogue with itself (*Soph.* 263e; *Theaet.* 189e–190a), still indicates difference and time, because there can be no instant of pure self-presence. The formal requires the materiality of its supplement; there is no context-free knowing. Because the intelligibility of experience implies intercontextuality, the metaphors of *metechein* and *metalambanein* perform what they describe; participatory being is the speaking of *chōris*, the opening where this unstable unification of identity in difference is disclosed.

Is the account of the instant an addendum to the second beginning or a separate hypothesis in its own right? The very existence of the third beginning as a unified division is made problematic by the difficulty of resolving the question of the dialogue's structure. Because Parmenides outlined eight distinct but unified orientations in the hypothetical method (136a–c), if we insist on the coherence of the method, then the excursus on the instant cannot exist as a separate and unified third beginning in its own right; but Parmenides refers to it a third attempt. Similarly, by the law of the excluded middle, the instant must either exist or not exist. But, Parmenides claims that the instant neither exists nor does not exist (156e–157b).

Why does Plato indicate, in these ways, that the instant cannot in any formally consistent way be unified into projected schematisms of hypothetical method? The very structure of the discourse forces an evaluation. Plato tempts the participant in the dialogue with a choice between an apparently unambiguous but actually inconsistent insistence on intelligible structure, and an apparently contradictory but actually thoroughly ambiguous (nonunified) plurality of nonstatements.

Philosophy avoids these extremes of sophistry by an evaluative moment of *krisis*: an insight into the proportionate disproportion that is rationality. Parmenides shows Socrates that any representation of being in itself masks the ontological differentiation that gives it significance. Because of this masking, the ratio of conceptual representation is divisive: such assimilation in logos is dissimulation.

Chapter 6

 келе키

The Fourth and Fifth Beginnings:
The Many

Reorientation

The *Parmenides* is intentionally crafted in a way that resists schematization: this is evident once the distinction between logos toward-itself and toward-another is conceived in even a rudimentary way, because the ironic interpenetration or *allo*-location of these two modes recurs throughout the dialogue. In this way, Parmenides shows Socrates that this distinction may be neither collapsed nor rigorously and completely developed. The absurdity of a simple denial of the distinction is already evident in Parmenides' initial exchanges with Socrates. This type of reductionism implies paradoxes of self-reference: Parmenides suggests that this would be like using discourse to deny the possibility of discourse (135a–c).

And yet his subsequent inquiry into time indicates that disclosure in logos is always aporetic: no whole is ever present in an instant. The notion of pure presence in an instant is logically inconsistent. Without the contrast allowed by will be, based on the retention of was, is would be entirely empty of significance. The existence of any one is signified in logos only by way of this nonpresence at the heart of presence. *To exaiphnēs* is a disjointed and inassimilable monad, subject to all of Parmenides' repeated arguments against such pure singularities (141e–142a; 159d–160b; 164a–b; 165e–166c). Because such singular un-existence involves a suspension of logic, Parmenides states that the instant can neither exist nor not exist (157a).

Does all signification in logos involve this moment of silence, or *alogos*? If any particular signification must involve a whole that is knowable—as a child finally learns to recognize the individual element of the sign system when she can repeat the whole alphabet—nonetheless, because repetition cannot be instantaneous, wholeness as such implies nonpresence. And, if any particular that exists is also a whole that is spread out in time, recognition of any particular element of signification implies the same paradox.

By way of differential allocation of significations throughout, Parmenides both clarifies and obscures: his intentional mimings of sophistry are part of an overall reduction to absurdity of reductionism. Suggestively ambiguous inferences throughout define a mode of *alētheia* by exceeding it. But even the joke reveals a meaningful intention; the humor arises in the odd juxtaposition of significations. Interpretation involves this ongoing differentiation of possibilities of intelligibility. The way of truth is manifold unification in opposition.

In Plato's dialogues the good is invoked poetically from early on, and is said to inform all modes of disclosure and logos. In these well known—but ambiguous—passages, Socrates employs a variety of figurative devices and images made philosophical by the process of discursive reflection in which they arise. If this is philosophical *eikasia*, then the divided line closes round on itself: what seemed to be a less than adequate mode of disclosure in logos appears to be carried up and repeated by the more adequate. And yet the repeated Platonic effort to go back to that which withdraws from knowledge—the beginnings, or *archai*—means that this erotic version of *dialogos* throws into question even the possibility of philosophical dialectic itself. Such intent is hardly naive. Then why the rhetorical tropes?

But there is apparently very little figurative discourse in the *Parmenides*. Instead, Parmenides seems to dismiss Socrates' analogies as failures of argument (as at 131b–c). And yet Parmenides subsequently vindicates meta-literal discourse in that his own dialectical demonstration is ironic and perforated by occasionally humorous pseudo-inferences intended to provoke the less critical participant in the dialogue. Parmenides projects an ostensibly consistent dialectical method that he develops out of Socrates' initial distinction between intelligible presence and the presence of an entity, only to ironically undermine this projected schema from the outset.

The Platonic figure of Parmenides uses the particular—the trope—as part of an effort to show why no property or relation can exist as singular. His *tropos*—his mode or way of *alētheia*—throws itself into question; he repeatedly climbs up a ladder only to kick it away in a moment of paradox.[1] It is thus no coincidence that the subject of the discontinuous third beginning is the paradoxical axiomatics of efforts to represent the being of time. In this way the dialogue partially vindicates metasemantics and yet ironically elicits the limitations of logos.

Many Toward One (157b–159b)

The fourth beginning purports to be an inquiry into what follows for the many toward the one if the one is said to exist. Though the fourth beginning initially appears to be constructive, its ironic mimicry of sophistry is in fact highlighted for the critical participant. Parmenides begins by arguing that since the many others are other than the one, the being of the one is not the being of the others; the others and the one are separate (*chōris*).[2] The others are not completely identical with the one, because if they were they would not be other than the one (157b). Therefore the one and the others are separate. Because Parmenides' initial inference distinguishes other natures from oneness itself, the discourse of this beginning—like the previous three—involves appeals to both of the dialogue's two thematic modes of differentiation in logos, toward-itself and toward-another.

Parmenides draws a distinction at 157b between what is completely one as opposed to what partakes of oneness without being completely one. This signifies the thematic ambiguity of a toward-another orientation. But because oneness entirely according to itself would not even be one (141e), the distinction at 157b may only be interpreted as a difference between a one that is one, and others that partake of oneness but are not completely one. If the first beginning discloses the inconsistency of pure singularity and the third beginning shows why this paradox cannot be resolved, the fourth—like the second—discloses the ambiguity and implicit paradox of toward-another disclosure.

On this interpretation, Parmenides distinction at 157b is consistent with the first beginning, which demonstrates that discourse oriented toward-itself is not simply one mode: even the first beginning implies that only the juxtaposition of different orientations allows significance. The orientation toward-itself that Parmenides briefly indicates in his characterizations of the style of training (135d–136c) is shown—in his demonstration of it—to indicate more than one mode of disclosure in logos.

And according to Parmenides' ambiguous inference at 157b–c, the others (*tois allois*) might be interpreted as referring to some nature taken as defined—an interrelation of *eidē*, or to some actual entity that instantiates these interrelated *eidē*.[3]

Parmenides now infers that these others cannot be said to be completely other than the one. This follows, he claims, from the fact that the others must have parts. For if they did not have parts they would be completely one. But what is other than the one could not be completely one, for then it would be indistinguishable from the one (157c).

In the second beginning a one that exists was said to have parts. The others, Parmenides reasons here, must have parts—otherwise they would be the one. This is consistent with the first beginning: unity has no parts (137d). But the others are others precisely in that they are distinguished by difference from unity itself; in other words, by definition. But definitions are interrelations of *eidē* that are only possible with reference to singularities that are unintelligible in their pure singularity. This fourth beginning then, like the preceding ones, juxtaposes discourse toward-itself and toward-another.

Parmenides continues to appeal to unification as such even though he has demonstrated that persistent inquiry into singularity itself ultimately discloses nothing but inconsistency, and in spite of the fact that such disclosure implies paradox relating to time (157a–b). The implication is that although it is absurd to deny the limited intelligibility of experience, it is also absurd not to recognize that in itself this intelligibility is permeated by unintelligibility.

The reasoning in this fourth beginning is articulated in a way to suggest to Socrates that without ongoing reference to the interrelations of *eidē*, fallacies result. But if appearances are unified and given definition by ongoing reference to singular *eidē*, limited intelligibility is possible. The suggestive difficulty is that Parmenides makes this point by intentionally miming sophistry. But again it is the non-univocal movement of differentiation between identity and otherness that is shown to be the dialogue's way of being and *alētheia*: form itself is only alongside formlessness.

Equivocation would not be possible unless one distinct meaning was used in place of another; an ambiguous inference still depends on the confusion of two *eidē*. But Parmenides also shows Socrates that each of the two meanings that are confused in an equivocation or joke is itself a mixture. Number itself partakes of both one and many, definition and indefiniteness (143a–145a). In the third beginning Parmenides completes the reduction to absurdity of the notion of unmixed being. This fourth beginning does not make the unqualified being of the others thematic because Parmenides has just shown this notion to be contradictory in the third beginning. Parmenides will first indicate again, in this beginning, that *eidē* do allow the possibility for resolving certain kinds of ambiguities. Then in the upcoming fifth beginning he will remind Socrates that inquiry into a single term discloses nothing.

Unification and Formal Wholeness

At 157d, Parmenides introduces an argument to establish the point that parts are parts only in relation to a whole. At first glance, this inference appears to be nothing more than a fallacy, similar to the argument at 145c–d that indicated a sense in which the whole cannot be said to be in the parts. However, like most of the reasoning in this dialogue, this passage proves to be ambiguous, and furthermore, to admit of an interpretation that is not only not fallacious, but that also serves to develop the dialogue's thematic distinction between modes of discourse.

A part is part of a whole and not of some mere plurality, for if something were said to be a part of a plurality in which it is, it would be part of itself, which is impossible, and also a part of the others, since it would be a part of the entire plurality. For if there is one of them of which it is not a part, then it will be a part of all the others except for that one. But, if we proceed in this way (considering the individual members of the plurality one after another) it will not be a part of any one which we examine. Indeed, it could not be a part of any one of the many because it was assumed to be a part of the entire group and not of some one member. But if it is part of no one of all of them, then it could not be part of those of none of which it is a part.

An interpretation according to which this inference is simply sophistry takes it as a fallacy of composition. Parmenides seems to claim that, if a thing is neither a part (nor anything else) in relation to a succession of things considered individually, it cannot be a part of all those things considered collectively. But obviously, just because a part is not a part of any member of a collection, this does not mean the part itself is not a member of the collection.

An alternative interpretation of 157d takes it as illustrating that the notions of part and whole are defined in opposition to each other. A part cannot be a part of a mere plurality but only of a whole of some sort. But plurality as such implies no unity whatsoever. Therefore, plurality, as such, cannot be compared meaningfully to a collection of members because this would introduce the unity of a whole into the notion of plurality itself. Plurality, as such, is not a whole and thus cannot have parts. If plurality were to have parts and be a whole, plurality would have to partake of unity. But plurality itself (by definition), does not have any share of unity. Therefore, a part is part, not of a many, but of a whole.

Immediately following the suggestive inference at 157d is another passage that—even in context—may also be interpreted in at least two ways.

Parmenides begins at 157d–e by claiming that the part is not part of many things or all things, but of some one (*mia*) idea, or one something (*henos tinos*) called whole (*holon*). A nature, as defined has a wholeness and also has 'parts,' in the sense that it is an interrelation of *eidē*. And a thing has parts and is a whole. But, Parmenides next claims that the others than the one must partake *tou holou te kai henos*. This intentionally ambiguous phrase may be interpreted to mean that either the others partake of both unity and wholeness, or that they are features of some one whole.

Parmenides exploits the ambiguity, inferring at 157e that the others than the one must be one complete (*teleion*) whole that has parts. *Anangkē* (necessarily) replies young Aristotle without hesitation. But this conclusion is problematic: it implies that the very act of selecting the others as thematic gives them the wholeness of a coherent logos. But just because the others have a share of unity and wholeness does this imply that they form one complete thing? Parmenides' suggestion of sophistry discloses not only the ambiguity of individual terms, but also the unstable distinction between a thing as defined and the thing in itself.

It is interesting to compare this interpretation of the conclusion at 157e (that the others are one whole) with the beginning of this section of the exercise, just a few lines before this point in the dialogue. At 157c, Parmenides asserted that the others must have a share of unity insofar as they have parts, for if they did not have parts they would be completely one. It is assumed that it would be absurd if what is other than unity were completely one. Therefore, the others must have parts. But if they have parts, they must have a share of wholeness; and if they have a share of wholeness, they must be a completed (*teleion*) whole!

The chain of ironic inference begins with the acknowledgement that it is impossible that the others be completely one, and a few lines later suggests that the others are completely unified. At 157c, Parmenides first employs the notion of having a share of unity in a way that clearly distinguishes this from being completely one. But at 157e, he suggests that since the others have a share of unity and wholeness, they must be a perfect whole.

If this is a joke or provocation, the point of the ambiguity nonetheless suggests that if the others are taken to refer to various *eidē*, the very act of considering them in this way discloses them as a whole. At 157d9–e2, Parmenides says that we call (*kaleō*) something a whole when it partakes in a single form (*mias tinos ideas*), and that it is out of this wholeness that it becomes a complete one (*ex hapantōn hen teleion gegonos*). The implication is that this unification in the act of interpretation gives a wholeness to the plurality under consideration. If unification implies transcendence then it may not be reduced to, or explained by, any possible reference to the sum of its parts. The wholeness of this interpretive act involves both the oneness of the *eidos* in itself and the particularity of the act of interpretation.

But clearly the whole in relation to which the parts are parts is not a mere plurality and is thus neither simply an indefinite many. It is the form that gives unity to the concrete individual thing; it is the idea that unifies the parts and allows them to be one thing, rather than an indefinite plurality. The part is part only in relation to a single form which we call a whole, a unity accomplished, or perfected out of many (157e).

Pluralization and Formal Ambiguity

Parmenides next argues that any distinguishable part must also partake of unity: otherwise, it would not be or be distinguishable. For a part is one thing, distinct from the others. And insofar as a part has only a share of unity, it is other than unity as such. Only unity itself can be unity, although any whole or part must partake of unity in order to be and to be distinguishable (158a).

But things that have a share in the one, Parmenides asserts, are distinguishable from the unity in which they partake. They therefore have a share of difference in relation to the one (158b). Furthermore, Parmenides continues, things distinguishable from unity must be many, for if the things other than the one were neither one nor more than one they would be nothing. Presumably the silent Socrates might recognize at this point another possibility: plurality in itself is other than one and yet has no particular number. This possibility will be the unifying orientation of the next (the fifth) beginning.

Parmenides now anticipates this upcoming orientation, and argues that since the things that have a share of unity (either the unity of a part or of a whole) are many, it follows that just in themselves these things are indefinite multitudes. In anticipating the orientation of the upcoming fifth beginning, Parmenides demonstrates once again that an orientation in logos only "is" by means of ongoing differentiation from other such orientations. Apart from their share in unity, these things are not one, nor do they partake in unity. It is only insofar as they have a share in unity, Parmenides argues, that these things are not a mere multitude (158b–c).

If in reflection, he argues, we take away from such a multitude the least part imaginable, this least part also turns out to be not a part at all, but a multitude. For whenever we consider alone and by itself the nature of the others apart from unity, any view we shall ever have will yield an indefinite multitude (158c). But if any portion of the multitude becomes distinguishable as a part, this one part necessarily has a limit in relation to any other part and to the whole, and the whole has a limit in respect to its parts.

In respect to their own nature, considered apart from the unity in which they partake, the others are a sheer indefiniteness. However, out of the wholeness of the interpretive act, their own unlimited nature is juxtaposed with the defining limit that comes from having a share of unity, and something new arises; they become definite and distinguishable from each other. But their own nature, as abstracted from the way they are experienced and thought, would make them only *apeiron*. So it is that the things other than unity, whether they are considered as wholes or parts, exhibit both definition and indefiniteness (158d).

Because Parmenides ironically imports and exploits distinctions made thematic in other beginnings, the *Parmenides*—as a whole—indicates that *alētheia* in logos involves the disclosure of dialectical differentiations. The fulfillment of reason begins in negatively indicating the limits of dialectic from within dialectic.

Furthermore, Parmenides continues, insofar as they are all unlimited in respect to their own nature as the many, they are each affected in the same way and are therefore alike (158e). And the same is true insofar as they all partake in unity and exhibit limit. But insofar as they display the features of limit and limitlessness, they are qualified by contrary attributes.

Therefore, if we consider entities as exhibiting definition, they are like; and if we consider them insofar as they exhibit the indefinite, we must also affirm them to be like. But, insofar as they display both these contrary characters, then they are unlike, both to themselves and to any others that exhibit the opposing feature. In this sense the others may be said to be both like and unlike themselves and each other (159a). Since the others are such as to be qualified by opposing characters in this way, they may be shown without difficulty to be in one sense the same and in another different, in one sense moving and in another at rest, and so forth.

Parmenides' Synopsis at 159a–b

This fourth beginning (157b–159b), continues to develop the theme of the signifying contrast between modes of disclosure. Although in his summary synopsis Parmenides claims that the others display opposing features, this in itself does not contradict the fifth beginning (159b–160b), in which he will claim that the others than unity display no features at all. This is because in the present beginning Parmenides evokes the others in signifying opposition to unity. But the next beginning is an inquiry into the nature of plurality itself, apart from its dialectical differentiation from the principle of unity. This pure plurality will be shown to be a mere indefinite multitude that displays no features whatsoever. And yet, again, this will be accomplished only by means of both discourse toward-itself and discourse toward-another.

Plurality, according to what belongs to it essentially, is *apeiron*. It is neither one nor many, neither whole nor part. The others, when they are considered in abstraction from the unity that makes them definite and intelligible, are nothing; they are indefiniteness itself. The moment of abstraction in the present beginning, in which the others are considered apart from their participation in unity, anticipates the fifth beginning's thematic evocation of this pure otherness than unity, this *apeiron*.

It is crucial to remember that the one in relation to itself was also said to be *apeiron* (137d10-11). This shows that the notions of the one in itself and plurality in itself are not employed as substantials, but rather are sign functions, or signifying differentials. Pure unification as opposed to pure indefiniteness cannot be the signifying opposition here because both unity in itself and plurality in itself are *apeiron*. Because the one was shown to be *apeiron* when considered in itself, the signifying opposition—if a one exists—is between derivation of expression in itself, and the indication of relations to other natures. This interpretive act of differentiation is more fundamental than expression of identity because it is a condition of possibility for relations of ideas: considered persistently in accordance with its own nature, any unqualified being is nothing; it is pure *apeiron* or indefiniteness. The paradox is that only by way of singular forms of logos can the inconsistency of singularity be disclosed; dialectic is only transcended from within.

Parmenides' game is only intelligible if archaic opposition is interpreted in this way. The prelinguistic articulations of being are already signifying oppositions—not epistemological foundations—and yet the indication of these differentiations is possible only by means of the effacing sameness of repetitions of logos. To say that the formal in itself is nothing, is to say that the conditions of possibility of intelligibility are in themselves not intelligible. Because disclosure in logos is only possible by means of the effacement of its own conditions of possibility, Plato indicates this dramatically by Parmenides' ongoing exceeding of his own method. This intention is evident once we recognize the allocation of the two thematic orientations of logos throughout every section of the dialectical game.

If without qualification all logos must be qualified, this paradoxical moment of necessarily relational differentiation is the reason why philosophical insight is achieved through negative dialectic. The moment of complete unification can neither exist nor not exist. It is only defined in the differential articulations of logos.

This means that mortal logos can either bring itself together in a moment of paradox, or scatter everywhere, in every way, in ordered array. The insight that reveals this paradoxical moment of logos discloses the limitation of orientations that do not. Discourses that are not oriented toward their own limitation seem to be disclosive of being, to the point that to deny this appears simply absurd. But such logos wanders, knowing nothing; it is two-headed and helplessly adrift.

The correctness, apparently constructed in mortal logos, is simply the forgetting of the paradoxical moment such ambiguous disclosure implies. There is no logos that forms a stable bridge between the continent of untrue truth and the island of singular paradox. Any effort involves both. Logos combines incombinables.

The Fifth Beginning (159b–160b): Many Toward Themselves

The fourth beginning presented the others as partaking in unity and displaying opposing features, just as a one which has a share of being was shown to display other features than unity (in the second beginning). But the fifth beginning ostensibly examines the consequences of the one's existence for the many, according simply to themselves. The many others, when considered in opposition to the one (the fourth beginning), exhibited a variety of features in various senses; but the present investigation purports simply to evoke the nature of multiplicity in itself.

However, although the abstract notion of plurality as such is the topic of this inquiry, this idea is referred throughout the fifth beginning to the list of other fundamental oppositions evoked regularly in the dialogue. The implication is, once again, that the pure singularity of any meaning is necessary for thought, although in itself it has no intelligibility. The emptiness of the sign in itself is analogous to a singular nothing (*apeiron*) that becomes significant in the interpretive act—that is, in differentiation from a network of such differentiations—and only then in the context of teleological existence. We see this in the fifth beginning insofar as pure plurality is initially evoked in a negative way by differentiation from the one (159b). It is subsequently disclosed by means of differentiation from part / whole, likeness / unlikeness, same / different, motion / rest, coming to be / ceasing to be, greater, less than, and equal, and by implication, all other such oppositions (160a). The fifth beginning in this way reemphasizes the lesson for young Socrates that any idea signifies only insofar as it is disclosed in and through differentiation.

The Transformation of Significance

Parmenides claims that the others are separate (*chōris*) from the one. The reason he offers to support this claim is that once we have mentioned the one and the others, there is nothing else: we have mentioned everything there is (159b–c). But this toward-itself reasoning ironically echoes a previous toward-another inference at 151a–b.

In the second beginning, the premise (at 151a8–9) that there is nothing else apart from (*chōris*) the one and the others was used to support the claim that the one and the others must be present in one another. But, here at 159c, Parmenides argues that because there is nothing else besides the one and the others, the one and the others must be separate (*chōris*).

The transformation of significance highlights the difference between the toward-another and toward-itself orientations. The inference at 151a–b occurred in the context of the second beginning, a toward-another orientation. Parmenides now claims that the one and the others must be separate and never in the same (*en tautō*) because, in this fifth beginning, he wants to evoke the toward-itself sense of these terms as singular meanings. Parmenides is again demonstrating that a proposition has an entirely different meaning in the context of a different intention; and he is signaling that it is the singular meaning (toward-itself) of what is other than unity that is to be thematic orientation of this fifth beginning.

Next, Parmenides claims that what is most truly one does not have parts (159c). This is a reference back to the one of the first beginning: unity in relation to itself. But, if unity is separate from the others, and does not have parts, then neither unity nor parts of it are in the others. Since unity has been claimed to be both separate from the others and to lack parts, Parmenides now asserts that there is no way the others could partake of unity (159d). Here, once again, Parmenides' intention is to evoke an eidetic sense of pure plurality, a manyness as such.

The others, in the sense in which we are now considering them, are not really even many, for what has no share of unity can be neither one nor many, whole nor part. Since these others are in every way deprived of unity, they have no number whatsoever. Furthermore, they exhibit no single discernible feature, not even likeness or unlikeness. For this reason, they cannot even be said to be unlike unity. Since they are utterly deprived of unity, these others are neither the same nor different, in motion nor at rest, becoming nor perishing, and neither greater than, less than, nor equal. Their utter lack of unity means they cannot be qualified in any way at all, just as the utter lack of plurality made the one in itself exceed intelligibility in the first beginning.

Conceptual Unification and the Divided Line

At 160b, Parmenides gives a brief synopsis of the results of the dialectical game so far. He notes that if a one is, then it may be said to be all things and nothing, both in relation to itself and to the others.

The first five beginnings suggest the image of the divided line. The first beginning disclosed by negative dialectic a unity that was said to be *apeiron*; it is beyond being and intelligibility. The second beginning evoked both ambiguity and the mathematization of what exists (143a–145a). The limited intelligibility allowed by this account, however, was thrown into question by the paradox of the instant in the third beginning (155e–157b). The fourth beginning opposed many other natures to the one, and indicated that the many display a variety of opposing features. But such disclosure (as the third beginning showed) implies that in themselves these others allow no intelligibility, although in differentiation from the principle of unity of which they have a share, they are intelligible in a limited way. Finally, the fifth beginning makes thematic plurality as such, in which entities partake, and indicates that apart from exchange with unity, such being in itself is *apeiron*.

The universe of discourse indicated by these various orientations from archaic opposition is bounded by *apeiron* and permeated by unintelligiblity. The game so far has shown that the intelligibility allowed by toward-itself discourse is revealed only by way of ontological differentiation. Exceeding the divisive ratio that is the juxtaposition of toward-itself and toward-another discourses leads to complete loss of significance.

And yet this *pros* distinction is insufficient to resolve the *aporia* in the disclosure of the being of time, because the two thematic modes or *tropoi* of logos (toward-itself and toward-another) are seen to be ultimately inseparable and yet irreducible. The implication is that the sameness of repetitions of logos is derivative, but that the prelinguistic articulations of being from which logos derives are intelligible only by means of such derivations.

Ironic Dialectic and Teleological Being

The *Parmenides* shows ideas to be disclosive in relation to possibilities of experience, in relation to each other, and in relation to *archai* differentials, general names for opposition that are not comprehensible on the basis of the articulations of significance they themselves allow. Parmenides emphasizes repeatedly that an entity or meaning is manifested along with multiply interrelated others; the derivation of an expression in itself ultimately discloses nothing (142a, 160a, 164a-b, 165e-166b). The unity of disclosure is an organic and finite whole articulated by difference: in relation to particular shifting phenomena, the form is the intelligible unifying sense that makes *epistēmē* possible. But the *Parmenides* shows that it is an entire network of interrelated ideas that signifies. This ideal matrix signifies in its inherent differentiation, and in relation to a moving panorama of phenomena, and always in accordance with fundamental *archai* oppositions.

But Parmenides' game is an ironic demonstration that includes many humorous attempts to provoke his young interlocutor(s). For example, at 149c Parmenides asserts that the things that are other than the one have no share of one or two or of any other number. But at 153a, he claims that the things other than unity, since they are things and not a different thing, must have a share of a number greater than one. Being things other than the one is used first, at 149c, to support the claim that the others have no number whatsoever. Then at 153a, being things other than the one is used to support the statement that the others have a number greater than one. But Parmenides goes on to argue that these others, since they have a number greater than one, must be older than the one, for one comes before any other number (153b).

Because these inferences occur within the second beginning, the thematic distinction between forms of logos is indicated to be insufficient for resolution of the difficulties. It is true that the two thematic forms of disclosure that Parmenides bases on Socrates' initial separation actually interpenetrate at every section of Parmenides' dialectical game. But this simply shows that the apparently straightforward method (and the distinction on which it is based), need to be radically reconfigured.

Generally such losses of focus or ratio in Parmenides' demonstration result from a prior intentional and sophistic shifting of the priority from being to knowing (from nonpresence to presence). Such shifts are repeated again and again, and they are the source of the intentional and provocative suggestion of fallaciousness in the demonstration of dialectical training.

Plato developed the ironic Eleatic contrast between modes of *alētheia*. The linguistic disclosure of phenomenal difference is only along-side the in-formation of intelligible principles: this means that self-sameness and difference are both necessary in discourse about what exists. Another way to approach this very Greek insight is by way of inquiry into discourse: Parmenides shows that representation in itself and indication of otherness are necessarily coimplicatory in logos and may not be rigor-ously distinguished. This again brings us to the Aristotelian problem of the *chōrismos*. The *Parmenides* develops these difficulties with rigor and subtlety. Parmenides first shows Socrates that the ideas cannot exist apart (*chōris*) from beings (130b ff.), and then he demonstrates for the silent Socrates the paradoxes implicit to the notion of ideas as timeless propo-sitions. The *Parmenides* shows that for Plato at this stage of his develop-ment, the otherwise of *chōris* infuses even the ideas themselves: what an idea is implies differentiation or otherness, both from other ideas and from possible experiences.

The dialogue metastasizes the *chōrismos* by reducing to absurdity efforts to represent *chronos*. The indefinite multiplicity of perceptual expe-riences of an entity are unified by a sense, or idea. Existence implies the unification and repetition of a multiplicity of past encounters with enti-ties that are the materiality (contextuality) of instantiated intelligible mean-ing. But Parmenides indicates that the being of time infuses even the relations of ideas that articulate intelligible meaning in itself. The prob-lem of the *chōrismos* is radicalized by the *Parmenides* in that even eidetic dis-course is shown to be articulated by the one in many (teleological) relation that is implied in sense perception.

Chronos is made thematic in the *Parmenides* precisely to underscore the Platonic insight that being has no simple and undifferentiated prin-ciple of explanation: any representation of being is necessarily also a mis-representation. The being of time may not be reduced to the now, or represented as a dimensionless time-point without leading to impasse. The *Parmenides* indicates that neither the presence of beings nor the intelligi-bility of the interrelated ideas is intended by Plato as an answer to the ques-tion of being. The unity of the unifying form itself is hardly seen at all; it is ultimately indefinable. Being is dialogical; it is the participatory being, in accordance with time, of idea and what is presently perceived. The predicament of the *chōrismos* occurs alongside the effort to know any being. If fully meaningful experience is the perceptual presence of a meaning, the tautology implicit here is still a derivative mode of logos. Ironic dialectic reveals this by repeatedly indicating the priority of being over knowing, and of nonpresence over presence. Typically this priority is effected in the dialogues in a negative way; Socrates indicates (often hastily and occasionally fallaciously), the implicit absurdity of some interlocutor's alternative account. What survives these ironic *elenchi?* One common thread that is never cut is the Platonic insight that participatory being toward the good is prior to the tenses and moods of logos that articulate forms of being and modes of *chronos.*

Plato's Socratic Parmenides refers to his own style of training as a game (137b). The predominant tendency in interpretations of the *Parmenides* is to ignore or try to explain away its amphiboly, irony, and pedagogical employment of sophisms. Such interpretations typically attempt to reduce the ambiguous opening that is dialogue to a monological doctrine. Platonic dialogue shows the critical participant why such univocity is finally impossible; therefore even if efforts to reconstruct a univocal Platonic doctrine did not find it necessary to alter the manuscripts, they would still be misguided.

The metaphors of *metalambanō* and *metechein* are significant of the Platonic insight that the manifestation that is being is neither primarily in the mind nor grounded by its position on a line (or grid) intended to represent time (or space-time). The primary unifying event of being occurs insofar as an entity reveals itself in an encounter with a human being. By eliminating various other types of account, Parmenides' demonstration supports the Platonic insight that any being (ideal or real) is a one in many.[4] The central analogies of the *Republic* also indicate this immanent teleology: participatory being toward the good is prior to knowing. A being (*ousia*) is the perceptual presence of meaning; but the erotic dialogue reveals the priority of nonpresence over presence in every disclosure.

The role of the good in knowing means that inquiry is never random. Knowledge is gained in a purposive (teleological) effort to gain information in response to an absence of which we need not even be fully aware. This is precisely what it means to give the priority to thinking about being rather than privileging intelligible presence. Plato avoids relativism insofar as both mind (one aspect of *psuchē*) and object are disclosed alongside one another: neither is cause of the being of the other. It is in relation to another that knowing occurs; being is participatory disclosure. Consequently, it is more accurate to state that for Plato, being determines knowing, rather than the reverse. The framing in advance and the contextuality of intelligibility account for the rhetorical description of knowing as remembering.

But Socrates' poetic depictions of various levels of soul (or life) show that the supplementarity of the good is not conceived by Plato as an intelligible foundation. To indicate, as Socrates does, that the good transcends knowing implies that for Plato the teleological disclosure that is being is never fully present. This in itself would justify the rhetorical employment of imagery, irony, and other tropes in the dialogues. There is no overarching doctrine, no monologic otherworldly discourse that could overcome *chōrismos* and seamlessly unify or synthesize irreducibly different modes of disclosure. Parmenides shows Socrates, by way of reflection on time, why such assimilation (*homoiōsin*) is impossible.

Chapter 7

ᒥᒥᒥ

Denouement: If the One is Not

The One That Is Not: Toward the Others (160b–163b)

The sixth beginning, like the other sections of this dialogue, juxtaposes the two thematic orientations: *pros* itself, as opposed to *pros* others. And as in the other beginnings, in the sixth Parmenides' irony serves a double function. If the suggestion of sophistry perhaps confounds the young Aristotle, at the same time, Parmenides evokes a deeper level of paradox for Socrates. He continues to further differentiate between modes of being and logos, and in the sixth beginning Parmenides reveals typical pitfalls of dialectical differentiation (toward-another) apart from existence: for the sixth beginning begins with the assumption of the one's nonexistence.

Parmenides begins this section of the discussion by noting that when someone utters the phrase if the one is not, we know immediately that this differs (*diapherei*) from the hypothesis if the not-one is not. He asks Aristotle whether these two hypotheses only differ, or whether they are entirely contrary (*pan tounantion*). The young Aristotle agrees (160c), and from this point, at the outset of this beginning, the ambiguities will unroll smoothly.

Parmenides has already repeatedly affirmed that only what shares in being may be spoken of meaningfully. But it is not insignificant that it is in the culmination of toward-itself discourses that Parmenides explicitly denies intelligibility when the subject is considered entirely in abstraction from being. Because this sixth orientation will make thematic the one toward the many (if one does not exist), it is a *pros* the others orientation. In this *tropos*, Parmenides indicates that, in relation to other natures, the one that does not exist admits of intelligibility, but ambiguously. In this way, toward-another disclosure is shown to indicate a mode of being, even on the assumption of the one's nonexistence.

The humorous suggestion of fallaciousness in this reasoning nonetheless confirms that it is the juxtaposition of unifying formality against its others that allows intelligibility. Like the second and fourth beginnings, the sixth shows that certain ambiguities may be resolved by logical rules; that is, by formal criteria of significance. But the sixth beginning acknowledges the paradox of the instant insofar as it evokes a sense in which even the allegedly atemporal rules that allow dialectical differentiation in abstraction from existence are derivative misrepresentations.

On the one hand, if a one is assumed not to exist, some intelligibility is still disclosed by way of formal differentiation. But this means that whether or not the one exists, intelligibility is allowed only by the allocation of differing modes of *alētheia*: conceptual unification in opposition to otherness allows intelligibility insofar as it indicates some mode of being. But if p implies q and not-p implies q, then q is necessarily true. Like the first five beginnings (if one is) the sixth indicates that no term in itself signifies anything: only signifying opposition is disclosive.

On the other hand, in conjunction with the dialogue's sustained thematization of time, the sixth beginning also implies that the allegedly timeless logical rules that resolve certain kinds of ambiguities are also implicitly misrepresentations of being. Parmenides indicates in this sixth beginning that such principles are necessary but not sufficient for disclosure of existence / nonexistence in logos. The sixth beginning indicates both the utility of distinctions with regard to the conceptualization of being as well as the misrepresentation implied by such reductions. The implication is that because being is not simply a thought (132b–c), allegedly atemporal intentions may resolve ambiguity but nonetheless these obscure as they clarify.

The Being of One That Is Not?

Parmenides claims that when we hear phrases like "if largeness does not exist" or "if smallness does not exist," we recognize that in each case it is a different thing that is supposed not to exist (160c). In the same way, when we hear the phrase "if a one does not exist" we recognize that what is said not to exist is something different from other things, and we know what it means (160c). A one taken as not existing is nonetheless something known (*gnōston*), and recognized as differing from the others, whether it is said to exist or not (160c). What is spoken of as not existing is none the less known (*gignōsketai*), and differs from the others (160d). Here, Parmenides' repeated emphasis makes it plain that he is speaking of the one that does not exist in a different way in this beginning than he did at the culmination of the first beginning (141e–142a), where a one in itself was said to allow no meaningful speech if it exists in no way (*oudamōs*).

Parmenides suggests they begin from the beginning (*ex archēs*) and ask if one is not, what must follow (160d). He begins by reemphasizing that if the one is not there is *epistēmē* of it. But in addition, otherness belongs to the nonexistent one itself, in that it is other than each of the others. Even though the one does not exist it nevertheless partakes of other natures, since it is the one, and not something else that is said not to exist. Parmenides is indicating to Socrates that ideas admit of various predications in a way that existences do not. He points out that even if the one does not exist it may be indicated by various pronouns and be the subject of speech in the nominative, dative and genitive (160e–161a). Therefore the nonexistent one necessarily partakes of that (*tou ekeinou*) and what (*ti*) of many other such natures (161a).

Parmenides indicates here that the conceptualizations of logos have a degree of independence from actual presence: even if a one is assumed to not exist, it still displays unlikeness to the others, for it is the one we are supposing not to exist, and not the others. We differentiate it from what it is not one even in the act of denying it existence. In the same way, if this one which we say does not exist has unlikeness toward the others, it must have likeness toward itself. If it had unlikeness toward itself, then our account would not be about the one. Therefore, Parmenides asserts, the one that is not is like itself (161c).

This illustrates the difference between toward-itself and toward-another orientations. If in itself the one has no being whatsoever, then it allows no signifying differentiation *pros* itself. But even if the one is assumed not to exist, then *pros* the many other natures it allows signifying differentiation. This implies that the toward-another orientation indicates existence, but not only one mode of existence. In this sixth beginning, Parmenides discloses another mode of being implicit to the dialectical differentiation of toward-another signification.

Parmenides next claims that the one cannot be said to be equal to the others if it does not exist, because in order to be equal it would have to exist. Yet if it is not equal to the others, he asks, can we not say that they are also not equal to the one? When Aristotle agrees that this follows, Parmenides asks if it is not true that things that are not equal are necessarily unequal (161c).

Again, Parmenides is revealing in this section what *pros allo* orientations do: they indicate existence. Therefore if toward-another differentiations are extended to a one that is not, this disclosure is implicitly paradoxical. Parmenides illustrates this by asserting that the one that is not must have a share of largeness and smallness, since these belong to inequality. This implies that the one that does not exist must have, after all, a share of equality, since equality lies between largeness and smallness, and whatever partakes of these must also admit of equality. Has Parmenides used the claim that the nonexistent one does not have equality as a premise to support the claim that the one does have equality?

At 161c, equality was denied of the one that does not exist, but this very denial of equality was then used to argue that it must be unequal, and this is expressed by the claim that the nonexistent one must have a share of largeness and smallness. But if it has a share of largeness and smallness, the one that does not exist must partake of equality, since equality lies between these (161d). Parmenides is indicating that no positive conception of participation can allow the smooth reduction of all formal oppositions: the distinction between equality and inequality does not reduce to the differentiation between largeness and smallness; the very effort produces *aporia*.

Yet it would seem that the one that does not exist must nonetheless partake of being in some way (161e). For the one that is not must be as we say it is; otherwise, we do not speak truly in speaking of it as we do (161e–162a). Therefore, the one must have a kind of being in order to be nonexistent. If a one is not to exist, then it must have the fact of its being nonexistent in order to secure its nonexistence. What exists, if it is to have complete existence, must have the being implied in being existent as well as the nonbeing implied in not being nonexistent. And what is not, if it is to have complete nonexistence, must have the not-being implied in 'not being existent' and the being implied in being nonexistent. The one that is not, then has both being and nonbeing (162b).

But a thing which is both in a certain condition and is not in that condition must be subject to change or motion. Therefore, a one which has both being and not being must move (162c). But if the sense in which a one is now claimed to have a kind of being is different from the sense in which it was already supposed to have nonbeing, does this justify the inference that a one must change in order to possess both qualifications? This is the kind of inference that served to ironically frame the excursus on the instant.

And yet if a one which is not exists nowhere, clearly it cannot change place. Furthermore, since what is not would never come in contact with the same (*to tauton*), it could not move by revolving in the same location. This inference from the same to the same location makes explicit for Socrates that the discourse of this section of the dialectical game, like the preceding ones, mixes both toward-itself and toward-another qualification. But if a one that is not does not move, does this imply that it is at rest

(162e)? Once more Parmenides indicates that formal oppositions are not univocally reducible one to another by ironically asserting that the nonexistent one both moves and does not move.[1]

But what moves must be said to alter its character and to become other. Therefore, insofar as the one that does not exist moves, it becomes other; but insofar as it does not move, it does not become other. But, if it is to come to be in some new condition, a thing that changes must cease to be in its former condition. So a one that is not comes to be (*gignetai*) and ceases to be (*apollutai*) insofar as it becomes other; but insofar as it does not change, it does neither (163b).

Beneath the game's surface level of provocative irony, Parmenides has developed Socrates' initial separation between idea and thing into a differentiated manifold of various modes of being and truth. If archaic opposition is ontologically prior to any attempt at discursive clarification, negative dialectic can only give immanent clarification to a fundamental opposition such as unity/plurality, by working out the consequences of nonexistence. In this way the sixth beginning indicates that signifying opposition is basic to discursive clarification and may only be disclosed in a negative way: in itself this chorismatic differentiation is nothing. The reductive effort to employ as a term one side of a signifying formal opposition leads to paradox.

This expansion differentiates many senses of being and *alētheia*. Furthermore, this is just the expansion of dialectic into negative dialectic that Parmenides insisted upon at the outset, in characterizing the exercises Socrates should go through if he is ever to win clarity about the forms (135e–136c).

The One That Is Not: Toward Itself (163b–164b)

The sixth beginning indicated why something may not be simply said not to be without qualification. The seventh beginning will also show that if the one is assumed not to be (without qualification) then we cannot speak of it intelligibly. At 163b, Parmenides suggests they go back and ask again what must belong to the one, if it is not. But whereas the last orientation disclosed results of the one's nonexistence toward the others, this time the inquiry ostensibly considers the one that is not entirely according to itself. This means that in this orientation, Parmenides purports to simply exclude those other natures that do not belong to the one.

Parmenides begins by asking a leading question that obscures the differing senses of being, truth, not-being, and falsehood just disclosed.

He asks, "Does saying 'is not' signify (sēmainei) anything else but the absence (apousia) of being from what we say is not?" (163c). Aristotle affirms that "is not" signifies nothing else but absence without qualification, that is, indicates absence singly (haplōs sēmainei). This singular orientation toward absence without any qualification whatsoever (haploustata men oun) characterizes the seventh beginning.

Parmenides points out that what is not in this sense could not have any share of being. But coming to be and ceasing to be anything means getting and losing a share of being in some respect or another. Therefore, Parmenides concludes, a one which is not does not become or cease to be. Consequently it does not suffer any process of alteration, since alteration involves becoming and perishing. And since it does not undergo alteration, it does not move; for movement involves alteration (163d–e).

These inferences are again examples of reasoning that juxtaposes disclosure toward-itself and toward-another. The being, in itself, of these other natures—being, becoming, perishing, alteration, and motion—is shown to be defined only by way of toward-another differentiation one from another. Every section of the dialectical game has implied this. What any nature is toward-itself may only be disclosed by way of toward-another differentiation from other natures. If these contrasts are excluded, no disclosure or being is possible; a nature considered entirely in itself is not.

Since it is nowhere, a one that without qualification is not cannot be at rest in the same place. Therefore, a one which is not is not at rest. Here Parmenides ironically echoes the sixth beginning. There Parmenides ironically claimed that since it is nowhere, a nonexistent one cannot move from one place to another, and is therefore at rest (162c–d). The present toward-itself orientation implies that a one that without qualification is not cannot occupy any place (163e).

Nothing that pertains to an entity pertains to the nature of this one which in itself is not: it has no largeness, smallness, or equality (164a). Indeed, it has no likeness or unlikeness and no sameness or difference. It cannot be discerned as unlike or different from anything. It cannot be said to have any others, since it is unlike and different from nothing. If nothing stands in opposition to it, we cannot even differentiate it as this or that, or in any way whatsoever. Consequently there is no knowledge or opinion or perception of it, nor of anything it has. It cannot be the subject of informative discourse at all (164b).

These conclusions are exactly the same as the conclusions of the first beginning, which also examined a one toward itself (141d–142a). Since whether a one is assumed to exist or not, there is no significant discourse according to it in itself, Parmenides has now demonstrated for Socrates that considered entirely according to itself, that is, without qualification (*haplōs sēmainei*), any *archē*, or *eidos*, or entity, is absolutely nothing. But the next beginning will show that what is formally only absence in fact indicates the fullness of being.

The Many Toward the One That Is Not (164b–165e)

Parmenides next goes on to disclose how the others than unity must be qualified, if unity is not. At 164a, it was said that a nonexistent one toward-itself cannot have others, since it cannot be qualified by unlikeness or difference. But now, at 164b, we are indicating the existence of the very others which do not exist for the one *pros* itself.

This shift from the toward-itself discourse of the seventh beginning to the toward-another disclosure of the eighth beginning signifies the paradoxical differentiation of conceptual unification over against its precognitive conditions of possibility. The eighth beginning evokes the paradox of precognitive disclosure, and shows that unity/plurality cannot be interpreted as merely a conceptual differentiation.

Being itself, like unification, has now been revealed in a variety of modes; for at the culmination of the previous beginning, the many could not even meaningfully be said to be. Similarly, the one in itself proved to be beyond being, even when it was assumed to exist, insofar as to be means to have a share of *chronos*. Furthermore, even a one that is not (toward-another) was said to exhibit a kind of being, insofar as it was still a distinguishable topic for discourse. But this implies that whereas the orientation of logos toward-itself abstracts from time and being, the toward-another orientation in logos indicates existence. The assumption of the one's nonexistence completes the reduction to absurdity of efforts to reduce this archaic differentiation.

Parmenides claims that the many others, if unity does not exist, must still be, since if there were no others, we could not speak of them. And yet we were able to speak of a one that does not exist, both in a limited way in the seventh beginning and somewhat more extensively in the sixth. The difference between the present inquiry and that of the seventh beginning is that in the previous discussion Parmenides was examining the nature of the one toward-itself. The present discussion, however, in the eighth beginning, is evoking the features exhibited by the many others insofar as they exist as individual entities capable of displaying various characters.

But at 164b, in the course of developing a toward-another orientation, it is asserted that the many others must exist, since we are able to
speak of them. And if a one which does not exist may be spoken of, as it
was in the sixth beginning, and if it may display various characters, including even motion, why does it follow that we cannot speak of the others
unless they exist? It would seem that the arguments that were used to support the claim that a one which does not exist still admits of qualification
would also apply to the others in this instance.

Why doesn't Parmenides assert the following? If we claim that the others are not, obviously this claim differs from the claim that the not-others
are not. Does it only differ, or is it not completely opposite—*pan tounantion*—
to say that the others are not and the not-others are not? Furthermore, if
someone were to say that largeness is not, or smallness is not, in each case
he would mean that something different from the others does not exist. And
we know what he means. First of all, then, we mean something knowable,
and next something different from other apparently similar claims, when
we say "the others," whether we add is or is not to these others.

In those cases where an expected parallelism does not occur, as in
the present case, where the one that does not exist still admitted of qualification, but the many that do not exist do not, surely we are meant to ask
ourselves why it did not occur. Similarly, we must question in those cases
where a parallelism occurs unexpectedly, as in the case of the first beginning and the seventh. Although both examined the one toward-itself, the
one that is assumed to exist in the first beginning is said to be beyond qualification, just like the one that is assumed not to exist in the seventh.

This instance is especially interesting insofar as the one's complete
abstraction from being in the first beginning was the basis for the conclusion that a nature considered entirely according to itself would not be;
it could not even be itself. This indicates that the parallelism in the case
of the one may be intended to draw attention to the limitations of any
toward-itself inquiry. If conceptual unification allows disclosure of logical
implications, nonetheless only a shift to figurative discourse indicates that
which transcends intelligibility yet serves as a condition of the possibility
of intelligibility.

Whatever limited truth the claim might have that temporal being is
knowable, does this limited sense justify the further claim that only temporal being is knowable and that it is so only insofar as it is temporal? But
an unqualified many was shown by the third beginning to be completely
unintelligible. The implication is that unity/plurality are significant only
in opposition, and that apart from the embodied contextuality that is

participatory being toward the good, there would be no formality. Unity/plurality does not merely differentiate polar concepts, but also irreducible, archaic differentiation.

If we interpret the eighth beginning as affirming a link between intelligibility and existence—and by implication, a link between existence and unity—then we must also acknowledge the Platonic insight that informed presence is thoroughly permeated by absence.

What Parmenides asserts at 164b 8–10 is *alla men pou dei auta einai: ei gar mēde alla estin, ouk an peri tōn allōn legoito.* "But they must exist: for if they did not exist, there could be no speaking about the others." Does this mean that being, for Plato, is simply the potentiality for discourse? If this is interpreted as confirming a Platonic / Parmenidean link between being and intelligibility, it is also the case that Parmenides has repeatedly shown presence to be informed by absence and ambiguity. The one in itself is not even one. The paradox of the instant shows that logos implies a moment of *alogos.* There is no unity apart from the many, and pluralization cannot be thought. The eighth beginning discloses both the link and the difference between being and the one; if intelligibility involves unification, it also implies differentiation. The *Parmenides* is an aporetic dialogue, and no doctrine can reduce its paradoxes to univocity. Like his *Sophist,* Plato's *Parmenides* shows that *alētheia* involves the contrast of being with being (*Sophist* 257e).

Parmenides argues in the eighth beginning that the others (*ta alla*) must be different (*heteron*), since what is other is said to be different (164b–c). Yet they cannot be other than the one, since it does not exist. But if to be other also means to be different, what is other than the one is different from the one. This holds whether or not the one has a share of being, for in the sixth beginning, where the one was also supposed not to exist, the one was nonetheless discussed in opposition to the others. Indeed, this opposition has been indicated to hold whether or not the one or the others, or both or neither, is assumed to exist. The one is the one in its differentiations from other natures. And the other natures that are not the one cannot be unity in interrelation with itself. Being is shown by the dialectical game to be disclosed by way of juxtapositions of modes of disclosure. Signifying disclosure in logos cannot abstract from such differences; for if the one exists, in itself—apart from time and being—it is not even one.[2]

How is the identity of the one and its negation in the others maintained if unity in itself admits of no intelligibility? Parmenides has shown that wherever the one is there also is being; and that furthermore, wherever being and unity are, there also is difference (143b). This implies that wherever the nature of unity is disclosed, that which is other than unity is also revealed. If this is not the case then the equivalence between otherness and difference, which Parmenides asserts at 164b–c, must be rejected.

We are faced here with a genuine inconsistency if, on the one hand, the equivalence is seriously intended and yet, on the other hand, it is not the case that otherness is disclosed alongside unity. If Parmenides wanted to indicate that unification plays a role more fundamental than that played by what is completely other than unity, why would he assert an identity of otherness and difference? Because difference, and by implication, otherness, were already said to be coimplicatory with unity and being (at 143b), this would imply that unity and plurality are equally fundamental.

This means that either the intelligibility of being is not the whole of being or that nonbeing is in some way accessible after all. In attempting to shed light on this issue, we should keep in mind that in the second beginning, where the coimplicatory status of being, unity, and difference was expressed (143b), we were considering a one that has some share of being. In other words, we were no longer reflecting on the nature or the definition of unification as such, entirely abstracted from time (as at 141d–e), but were considering how unity is disclosed alongside entity.

But in the second beginning this orientation was complicated by the reintroduction of eidetic criteria, and the conceptual unification of being in its enumerability. It is this ambiguous interallocation on the level of *dianoia* that allowed the generation of number.[3] The implication is that being, unity, and difference are juxtaposed in any disclosure. No presence, perception, opinion, knowledge, naming, or even significant speech is possible apart from this archaic opposition. Not-being is not the opposite of being; rather, it is the differentiations between beings.

To Parmenides' assertion at 164c that the others must be other than each other or other than nothing, Aristotle simply responds: *Orthōs*— "Right." But if they are other than each other, they must be other than each other as indefinites, for this is all they are if unity does not exist, since no wholeness can be in them if unity is not. But could such indefinite multitudes really be distinguished from one another? If they have no unity, it is difficult to conceive of them at all, much less to conceive of them as being distinct from one another.

In an Instant, as in a Dream

Parmenides now addresses this precognitive differentiation, or juxtaposition, that articulates existence. Significantly, he argues in this eighth beginning that if the one is not, the others will nevertheless appear (*phainesthai*), and will still admit of *doxa*.

Parmenides claims that if there is no one, there will seem to be an indefinite number of indefinite masses. Moreover, some of them will appear to be even and some odd, but without really being so, since there is no definiteness, and no being, without unity. There will appear to be a smallest among the many, but as in sleep (*hupnō*), this smallest in an instant (*exaiphnēs*) becomes a many which is great in relation to the smallness of the previous multitude. There will be appearances of equality among these indefinite masses, but on closer inspection, such appearances will always turn out to be illusory.

Each mass appears to be limited in relation to the others. Actually, since there is no unity in them, it will be impossible to locate any beginning, middle, or end in them. What appears to be a beginning will always turn out to have something before it. And if something appears at first to be the middle, yet eventually another, more centrally located and smaller point will appear with an even better claim to be the actual middle. But this process might be continued indefinitely, for there is no definiteness if there is no unity.

Just as in a dream (*onar*), when what at first appears real turns out to be mere semblance, so it is with these multitudes that lack unity (164d). Though they may appear at first to be definite and unified, they will always turn out to be merely indefinite multitudes.

This analogical reference to dreaming is another instance of the self-referentially polymorphous discourse that is this aporetic dialogue. That the explication of unification involves ambiguity is indicated by this evocation of precomprehensive articulation. The implication is that unity is not just a feature of objects; but neither is unity simply a transcendental condition of understanding. When the one is presupposed not to exist, and we attempt to speak about other things as they are in themselves, we can only imagine a dreamlike semblance of unified disclosure: there is no unification of apprehension or of the object, but only a free play of differentiation. Insofar as the others are even disclosed, they are always already articulated, for they are differentiations that appear (*phainō*) to have limits and parts.

If unity is not, but these indefinite others are, they will at first appear limited, but then unlimited. They will appear to be both one and many (165c). In a similar way, they may seem at first to be like each other, but on closer inspection each *phantasma* turns out to be different. Like images produced in a painting (*eskiagraphēmena*), they will appear in one way from a distance, but differently on closer inspection. They will at different times appear to be same and different from each other, in contact and not in contact, moved in all manner of ways, and then completely at rest in all respects. They will appear to become and perish, and on the other hand, they will seem not to become or perish. Furthermore, Parmenides concludes, in respect of every possible qualification they will behave in this way, if only plurality is and unity is not.

The eighth beginning serves to develop the themes of the game in two related ways. In the first place, the precognitive articulation of the *phantasma* by reference to dreaming and painting is another manifestation of Platonic philosophical *poiēsis* in an only ostensibly logical dialogue. The openness of this *tropos* makes the *Parmenides* much more than a catalogue or system of categories. Parmenides discloses *aporiai*; he nowhere sets out a doctrine or attempts to schematize many senses of being. On the contrary, every suggested ordering is shown to be incomplete and paradoxical. Such differentiation is indicated by the eighth beginning to be a condition of the possibility even of precognitive phenomenal appearance. When unity is assumed not to exist, the disclosure of existence is nonetheless articulated in a prereflective way. This means that if there is no unification in logos, and no intelligibility, the indication of existence is nonetheless manifested in the form of precognitive articulations.

If the others even appear, they do so in accordance with archaic differentiation, as preconceptual articulations. But insofar as they are taken to be semblances, they are semblances of unity/plurality; this means that in any logos of being, the one is disclosed alongside the many in precognitive *archē*-opposition.

The Many Toward Themselves If One Is Not (165e–166c)

At 165e, Parmenides suggests that they go back to the beginning and state what must follow if the one is not, but the others than unity are. This section proceeds by denying that certain characters belong to the others; it is ostensibly a toward-itself inquiry into the implications for the many of the one's nonexistence.

Clearly if the one is not, the others will not be one. Furthermore, they will not even be many; for if none of them is one thing, then all together they are no-thing. Since no unity is in them, they are neither one nor many. Indeed, they will not even appear to be either one or many; for they can have no connection whatsoever with a one which is not, nor can any element of what is not be present in them, since what is not has no elements. Therefore, no appearance of unity can be in them, for unity is not. Nor can any notion of the unity which is not apply to the others. If there is no one, the others cannot even be imagined to be one, for there can be no *phantasma* of unity if the one is not. But these others cannot even be imagined or conjectured to be many, for a many is unimaginable without a one. If there is no one, the others are neither one nor many, nor can they even be imagined to be one or many (166b). Furthermore, they cannot be or appear to be like or unlike, same or different, in contact or apart, and so forth. If there is no one then, the others in relation to themselves may be said to be nothing at all.

The manyness of the many, toward-itself, is sheer unintelligibility. Without even the dreamlike image of differentiation, the many in themselves are pure nonbeing. Like the other sections of the dialectical demonstration that deny that their subjects possess the qualities in question, this ninth beginning evokes nothingness by eliminating characters that do not belong to the nature of its subject. The process of elimination itself involves notions such as simultaneity, being and nonbeing, and so forth. Such allocations of other natures (besides the subject in question) are not only never eliminated by toward-itself discourse, they are necessary to the process of eliminating those natures that are excluded. Furthermore, apart from these many modes of difference, or relations of otherness, the nature in question shrinks out of being to a mere insignificant gesture, not even a name.

The many in themselves, like the one in itself, prove to be indefinable and not even self-identical. Just as the one in itself allows no intelligibility whatsoever, so the pure otherness of the many in itself is unintelligible; and these results obtain whether or not the one is assumed to exist.

Synopsis

Parmenides summarizes at 166c: if the one is not, nothing is. Moreover, whether the one exists or not, both it and the others, both toward-themselves and toward-another (*pros hauta kai pros allēla*), both are and are not, and both appear (*phainetai*) and do not appear all things in all ways.

The apparently straightforward method demonstrated by Parmenides has thus proved to be anything but univocal. The ironic, ambiguous, and figurative nature of the dialectical game reveals that philosophy is, however, a *meta hodos* in an original sense. Parmenides demonstrates for Socrates that the distinction between meaning and entity is not sufficient for eliminating paradox insofar as the same types of *aporiai* arise on consideration of the ideas themselves.

Parmenides' game develops Socrates' initial distinction between idea and thing into a way of differential *alētheia*: various processes of inquiry with various criteria for the justification of claims. In the game, *to hen* sometimes means unity as displayed, and sometimes as defined. Sometimes it means a particular entity as distinguished from other entities; and, at 153a–b, the one means the number one. And on the assumption that the one does not exist, it is nonetheless differentiated by way of the archaic opposition that informs disclosure in logos. Parmenides' game reveals a corresponding range in the employments of terms for the natures other than oneness.

Like the *Sophist*, the *Parmenides* is an aporetic dialogue that discloses paradox rather than doctrine. The *Parmenides* does not answer the question of being and nonbeing but sharpens the moment of *aporia*. Even if unification is conceived to be intelligibility and being itself, nonetheless the toward-itself orientation in a logos of the one culminates in a nonlogical moment: apart from time and being, the one is not even one. And even if one is not, disclosure involves differentiation (toward-another) of *phantasma*.

The *Parmenides* indicates that the horizon for developing the doubtful questions in relation to the ideas themselves is time. Such reflection reveals that both toward-itself and toward-another orientations are coimplicit in any logos, whether or not the one exists, and consequently the rigorous distinction between these is impossible.

Epilogue: Plato on Time and Difference

Plato situates the *Parmenides* by means of dramatic chronological removes that make thematic the notion of repetition (126a–127d). But if logos implies repetition (the return of the same), and beings are always and everywhere observed to be in a constant process of motion and change (difference), how is meaningful discourse possible? One and the same entity is observed to change and move, to occupy different places at different times. Our interactions in a world of beings always already involve ideas of space, time, and identity. Questions relating to the privileging of sameness in logos and the differentiation of *chronos* are in this way introduced in the dialogue early on by reference to Zeno's paradoxes.

A young and enthusiastic Socrates attempts to resolve Zeno's paradoxes by claiming that there exists an idea in itself of likeness, and another of unlikeness. Socrates asserts that in this way any entity may be said to manifest opposing characters without contradiction (128e–130a). But in the remainder of this dialogue, Parmenides successfully reduces to absurdity the notion that an idea exists separately as the original of which the phenomenon is an image. However, Parmenides' remarks to Socrates, at 135a, show that, at a minimum, forms name the intelligibility of experience and discourse in such a way that to deny this limited intelligibility is absurd. It is the attempt to make a single mode of disclosure foundational that leads to *aporia*.

This is the reason that even if an immortal could know all the ideas instantaneously in all possible interrelations, this would still not be knowledge. Knowing involves unification in opposition; in Parmenides' game intelligibility is immanently disclosed by the juxtapositional nature of teleological (temporal) existence. If modes of temporal manifestation vary depending on the being that one encounters, this does not imply that time is the grounding principle of being and intelligibility. On the contrary, recognizing the priority of being for Plato means that it is the finite manifestation of participatory being toward the good that structures *chōra* and *chronos*, and allows *alētheia* through logos.

As indicated already, one implication of Parmenides' dialectical teaching game is that the real and the ideal are ontologically identified, and yet distinct. But if real, temporal unities are intelligible by means of fundamental differentials, still these *archai* oppositions themselves are not the grounds of being. Considered in themselves they are unintelligible; they are not. Idea and particular manifestation are ontologically unified in that the ground of the possibility of both is identical. This ground is neither the transcendental subject nor the transcendental object. The condition of the possibility of intelligibility and presence is being itself; but participatory being defies conceptualization. Every disclosure of being in logos implies *chōris*. Parmenides shows Socrates that the philosophically interesting separation is not between meaning and entity, but between any being that is disclosed and disclosure itself.

The third beginning (155e–157b) is ordinarily interpreted as a serious Platonic theory of change, or as a synthesis of the first and second beginnings. But Parmenides had already made it clear that the first beginning (137c–142a), deals with the one in relation to itself, and what his arguments there reveal is that he is considering only what is logically implied by the intelligible meaning of unity; the result is that singularly the term *to hen* signifies nothing but a suspension of logic. The second beginning however, ostensibly considers only the one in relation to the multitude of other characters that any unified entity manifests. Therefore, a one that is (an entity) is indicated by the second beginning (142b–155e) to be in one sense moving and in another at rest, in one sense limited and in another unlimited, and so forth. The orientation of the second beginning would apparently not contradict the first, insofar as these two beginnings are distinguishing two different senses of unity. Consequently, a synthesis would be unnecessary.

However Parmenides had also already indicated that only what has a share of time can have a share of being, that is, be an entity (141e). Therefore, since signification in relation to itself attempts to abstract from temporal qualification, such derivation of expression is finally devoid of intelligible meaning. The second beginning ostensibly limits itself to indicating the many correlated qualifications disclosed alongside any entity, although it is in fact permeated by various and even incommensurable ideal relations. This indicates why a perfect synthesis is finally impossible.

The instant cannot stitch together these always already juxtaposed modes of signification, because such a moment of simple and undivided identity makes impossible the intelligibility it ironically purports to explain. The paradox of the instant (155e–157b) is the very undoing, or inversion of synthesis. There would be no signification of any kind in the instant. Without indication toward-another, or representation, there could be no ideal expression in itself: nothing whatsoever would be expressed. This is the reason Parmenides fails to keep discourse toward-itself and toward-another separate in his demonstration for Socrates. He is indicating, by guiding the discussion toward reflection on the being of time, precisely in what way Socrates' initial naive distinction must be reconfigured. The doubtful questions, developed in relation to the ideas themselves by means of reflection on time and representations of identity, show Socrates why the reduction of teleology makes intelligibility not only inexplicable, but impossible.

The articulations in the *Parmenides* of fundamental oppositions implicit in the attempt to represent the being of time makes manifest the incompleteness of logos and the priority of participatory being over foundationalism in knowing. Only the nonhypothetical simple givenness of full ideal presence in an instant would allow the reduction of what is to intelligible presence. But showing Socrates the impossibility of such full ideal presence is the impetus for Parmenides' dialectical game: if ideas were entirely defined in their mutual interrelations, in themselves and apart from participatory being, this would not allow even a god to have *epistēmē* (134c–135a). An instant of unqualified presence, because of its sheer lack of content, would be inassimilable and would undercut the intelligibility it purports to explain.

Parmenides' account of the instant is the pivot of the dialogue; it exposes the weakness of attempts to ground the intelligibility of the *kosmos* in formal principles (and, by implication, material processes). Parmenides demonstrates for Socrates that presence (ideal or real) cannot be foundational for knowing; such an enterprise implies a nonlogical understanding of both intelligibility and time. Not only does the account of the instant imply the suspension of logic in a moment of *alogos*, it also shows that even if the instant were possible, both motion and the limited intelligibility of experience would be impossible. The notion of singular existence implies the fragmentation of time into an indefinite multiplicity of entirely discontinuous and unknowable atemporal singularities that could not in any way be made intelligible. Consequently, the paradoxical account of the instant, like every other section of the dialogue, exceeds its own criteria of significance. Because being, unity, and difference are disclosed only alongside one another, any effort to reduce this disproportionate proportionality to univocity verges into unintelligibility.

Signifying differentiation arises insofar as the *phantasma* of will be, based on the recollection of was, allows is to be disclosed. Because the transcendence that is learning is informed by nonpresence, Socrates says in the *Philebus* that in this moment the whole seems impossibly to be outside of itself (15b). It is this otherwise than (*chōris*) that allows disclosure in logos; consequently it is not only pure unity and pure plurality that the *Parmenides* shows to be ultimately indefinable. The implication is that no being is knowable, taken as something single; it is an entire nexus of ideas in participatory (goal-oriented) temporal being that allows knowing. Every disclosure is defined negatively in relation to what it is not. Even the indefinable *archai* are signifying oppositions, not terms.

But no form of logos, including philosophical discourse, has full access to its own possibilities and limitations, its entire context of significance. The being of every presence is determined by the whole, but the whole is never present. Recognition of this nonpresence at the heart of presence is the transcendence of philosophy. The proportionality of reason involves the insight that being is participatory: ideal expression of identity and indications of otherness are differentiated in all disclosure through logos.

In the *Republic*, Socrates contrasts two ways of thinking. The way up is hypothetical; thinking begins naturally in this manner on the level of practical interaction with entities, and proceeds to technique by way of assumptions that are not really beginnings, but more like stepping stones or springboards. But only on the basis of an insight into the nonhypothetical beginnings of the whole is the way down possible.

The *Parmenides* demonstrates that such beginnings are signifying differentiations or functions that are already interpretive. Beginnings are an irreducible differentiation, rather than a foundation. There is no regress implied here, precisely because archaic opposition signifies a different mode of being from the *tropoi* of logos it informs. The incompleteness of a mode of disclosure is supplemented by origins that complete by contrast. No being or mode of disclosure or *archē* is foundational because of this implicit opposition, or difference.

But significantly, Plato reminds us repeatedly that difference is disclosed in logos only alongside sameness, alterity alongside identity. Because Socratic dialectic both reveals this proportionality and discloses it to be a divisive ratio, such thinking avoids relativism by remembering transcendence. On the one hand, because the only nonhypothetical in Platonic logos is axio-ontological differentiation, Socratic likenesses (e.g., the analogical accounts of the good) are not a reduction of being in itself to presence. Even as early as the *Republic*, the good is said to be otherwise than beings. And on the other hand, Socratic *elenchos* never privileges logos to the extent of denying the moment of *muthos*.

It is a deductive path that leads down from oppositional but informing *archai* functions to various conclusions. In the *Republic*, the way down is said to abstract from present interaction with entities and to go through forms to forms and end in forms (511b3–c2). But the seeing of the implicit differentiation that is involved in all knowing is attained by way of indications of existence, the way up. The way up by interactions with entities and the insight it allows are ontologically prior to the way down to conclusions; expression of identity and formal deduction is derivative, not foundational.

Like the *Parmenides*, the *Theaetetus* makes clear that it is participatory being, the totality of interrelations of different modes of disclosure including but not limited to perception and ideas, that allows meaningful discourse. Philosophical dialogue reveals no simple first elements in knowing that are intelligible in themselves (201e). An apparently simple first element is a mere name except as disclosed alongside other differentials in the finite wholeness that is experience. But Socrates points out that even apparently intelligible composites also manifest this inexplicable wholeness (205d). Modes of being and logos have unity or wholeness in incompleteness. Similarly, in the *Parmenides*, to be is to stand out as a unified individual from a context of multiplicity: what anything is—its unity and wholeness as a particular being—is inexplicable without reference to what it is not.

No mode of *alētheia* is disclosive in itself; unity is organically constituted and is never simply the result of human ordering. Meaning is a one
in many and no particular mode of meaning is foundational. Participatory
being is manifested in human, temporal experience: true accounts are possible only in the field of beings known and perceived (*Theaet.* 194b). But
persistent reflection on time shows that any representation (*mimēsis*) taken
literally implies a reduction of teleology to presence. Philosophy involves
both imagery and the ability to recognize an image as an image.

To conclude, if the *Parmenides* is unambiguous, then it is thoroughly
contradictory and says nothing. But multiplying distinctions indefinitely
to avoid all possible contradiction approaches a limit: there is no unqualified being or unqualified becoming. The alternative left open by the
Parmenides is that ideal possibilities of repetition only signify in relation to
being; ideal expression derived toward-itself yields no intelligibility. Within
these limits, knowing is necessarily goal-oriented and incomplete. By
repeating this loss of focus in both directions, the dialogue indicates the
instability of the ratio that is reason. Human temporal existence implies
the potentiality to remember this *chōris*. Participatory being is this unified
manifold, or opening of identity and difference. The dialogue is an icon
of the cosmos: not a collection of entities (or predications) but an organically interconnected whole, a unification of ambiguous disclosures
informed by signifying oppositions. The formal structure of the *Parmenides*,
like that of any being, is in itself transcendent: it is evoked throughout in
a negative way. If for Plato human being is participatory, nonetheless the
ratio that is rationality is an odd juxtaposition, not a harmonious sharing.
The *Parmenides* discloses this paradox in order to show that the presence
of self-identity is not simple. The dialogue shows that *chōris* is not a problem to be solved; rather it is an essential feature of logos.

Notes

Prologue

1. The key text in which Heidegger formulates this claim is *Platons Lehre von der Wahrheit*, translated as "Plato's Doctrine of Truth," in *Philosophy in the Twentieth Century*, ed. William Barrett and Henry Aiken, vol. 2 (New York: Random House, 1962).

2. Compare Heidegger's comment on the *chōrismos*: "Plato means to say: beings and Being are in different places. Particular beings and Being are differently located" in *What is Called Thinking?* (New York: Harper and Row, 1968), p. 227.

3. Mitchell H. Miller develops an excellent account of Plato's use of mimetic irony to facilitate insight in *Plato's Parmenides: the Conversion of the Soul* (Princeton: Princeton University Press, 1986).

4. Cf. 129a ff.

5. *Parmenides*, 137b3 (Cambridge: Harvard University Press, 2002). For the convenience of the reader, my references to particular lines are from the Loeb Classical Library's bilingual texts of Plato's dialogues. Translations in what follows are my own.

6. Cf. Hegel's observation: "Ancient metaphysics had. . .a higher conception of thinking than is current today. For it based itself on the fact that the knowledge of things obtained through thinking is alone what is really true in them. . .Thus this metaphysics believed that thinking (and its determinations) is not anything alien to the object, but rather is its essential nature. . ." G.W.F. Hegel, *Science of Logic* trans. A.V. Miller, forward by J.N. Findlay (London: George Allen & Unwin, 1969; orig. published 1812–16), introduction, 45. Hegel was correct (but not in the way he intended) when he asserted that some ancient philosophers had a higher conception of thinking. Indeed, Plato's negative dialectic is superior to Hegel's positive version. However, this is precisely because Plato highlights the dimension of nonpresence—or transcendence—that culminates in the seeing-through of the limitations of logos and dialectic itself.

7. For a beautiful account of the conceptual system(s) implicit in the *Parmenides*, see John N. Findlay, *Plato: the Written and Unwritten Doctrines* (New York: Humanities Press, 1974), pp. 229–254. Findlay's scholarship is impressive, but his Plato sounds like Hegel. He interprets the *Parmenides* as a conceptual exer-

cise in dialectic that articulates a system of the whole. The problem is that it is just such constructions that Plato's Socratic Parmenides throws into question. For an account of ancient philosophy as the kind of spiritual exercise I find in the *Parmenides*, see Pierre Hadot, *What is Ancient Philosophy?* (Cambridge: Harvard University Press, 2002).

8. Cf. 134d–e.

9. Cf. *Sophist*, 241d.

10. See *Parmenides*, 152a–e.

11. Language is, as Plato recognized, crucial in isolating the unities in the manifold material presented in and through our interactions with entities. Hans-Georg Gadamer makes this point in *Plato's Dialectical Ethics*, translated by Robert M. Wallace, (New Haven: Yale Univ. Press, 1991). On Plato's conception of the task of dialectic, Gadamer writes: "The natural key to such an investigation is the logos. For the fact that genē can be combined with one another is already evident from the fact that one *says* of all of them that they *are*, which means that they can be combined with being. It also seems clear that not all of them can be combined, indiscriminately, with all of them. What we are left with, then, is that some of them can be combined with one another and others cannot" (p.91). The *Parmenides* indicates how genē *cannot* be said to "combine." That language was a central Platonic concern from early on is evident by reference to such modes of disclosure as *chrēsmos* 'oracular response' (*Apology*, 21c1 ff), *muthologēma* 'mythical narrative' (*Phaedrus*, 229c), *enuption* 'dream' (*Crito*, 44a), *akoē*, or 'hearsay' at *Phaedo* 61d9, and *diapherō*, 'to differ' (*Euthyphro*, 7b3 ff).

12. James R. Mensch develops this point in his interpretation of Husserl's *Logical Investigations*. For example: "in direct perception we grasp an object both as existing and as bearing a definite sense; but in a report of this perception, we transmit, not existence, but the sense of existence. The hearer of our report, in other words, can only ultimately confirm its validity with respect to the object by a perception of his own. . .confirmation occurs not by matching sense *conceived as one thing* with existence *conceived as abstracted from this*, but by grasping *both together*." *The Question of Being in Husserl's "Logical Investigations"* (The Hague: Martinus Nijhoff Publishers, 1981), p. 41.

13. For an excellent account of the interpenetrations of figurative discourse (e.g., the Socratic analogies in the *Republic*) and the conceptual approaches to the ideas (thrown into question in the *Parmenides*), see Mitchell H. Miller, *Plato's Parmenides: the Conversion of the Soul* (Princeton: Princeton Univ. Press, 1986). Miller argues that Parmenides' intellectual gymnastic occasions the conversion of the *psuchē* from becoming to being that the Platonic Socrates calls for at *Republic* 518c ff. But because Plato's Socratic Parmenides playfully exceeds the bounds of conceptuality itself, this conversion might also be expressed as the turning from being (in the sense of the *eidē*) to becoming (i.e., time). For Parmenides not only mimes sophistry, he also evokes the ambiguity and *aporia* that initiates the process of transcendence that is learning.

14. John Sallis shows in *Being and Logos* (Bloomington: Indiana Univ. Press, 1996), that the overarching problematic of later dialogues such as the *Sophist* (as well as the *Cratylus* and the *Theaetetus*) is that of the unity and the plurality of being in time (e.g. pp. 456–459).

15. Gadamer writes: "It is self-evident that the ethics of antiquity was political ethics insofar as it always viewed the individual, his actions and his existence, within the framework of the political community." *Dialogue and Dialectic*, translated by Christopher P. Smith, (New Haven: Yale Univ. Press, 1980), p. 8.

16. Cf. *Cratylus*, 387b8–9

17. This theme of the priority of being is developed very well by James R. Mensch, in his *Knowing and Being: a Postmodern Reversal* (University Park: Pennsylvania State Univ. Press, 1996). Although it doesn't quite do justice to Plato, the book clearly shows the dependence of epistemology on ontology. See e.g., pp. 19–20, and p. 62.

18. Greek *axios* "worthy," and *logos*, "account."

19. A.E. Taylor acknowledged the comic aspect of Parmenides' ironical 'reasoning,' but mistakenly assumed this detracted from the philosophical import of the dialectical game. Thus he claimed that it would be taking Plato's "metaphysical jest" too seriously if one were to examine the arguments of the demonstration in detail. See his *Plato: The Man and His Work* (Cleveland: Meridian Books, 1963), p. 361. But the negative logic of Plato's ironic dialectic is more rigorous than, for example, the *ethos* of geometry: Parmenides shows Socrates that humor and philosophical rigor are not mutually exclusive.

20. See Jonathan Barnes, *Early Greek Philosophy* (London: Penguin Books, 1987), p. 129.

21. Heidegger interprets the organic interconnectedness of Greek thought as symptomatic of an illegitimate prioritizing of practical wisdom: "If, accordingly, φρόνησις is the gravest and most decisive knowledge, then that science which moves within the field of φρόνησις will be the highest. And insofar as no man is alone, insofar as people are together, πολιτική (Nic. Eth. VI, 7, 1141a21) is the highest science. Accordingly, πολιτικὴ ἐπιστήμη is genuine σοφία, and the πολιτικός is the true φιλόσοφος; that is the conception of Plato." *Plato's Sophist*, translated by Richard Rojcewics and Andre' Schuwer, (Bloomington: Indiana Univ. Press, 1997) p. 93. Aside from neglecting Platonic irony and betraying a misguided tendency to reconstruct the philosophy of Plato by reading Aristotle, Heidegger's interpretation also leaves him vulnerable to the rejoinder that failure to seriously consider the dialectical interrelation of knowledge and power (to take one example), might lead to disastrous political misjudgments.

22. On privileging, or deeming worthy, cf. *Republic* 510c8. *Axioun* is from *axios*, "worthy," and is the source of "axiom." It is also worth noting that Socrates uses a form of the same word to describe his efforts, *pragmateuomenoi* (*Rep.* 510c4), that Parmenides uses to describe his troublesome game: *pragmateiōde paidian paizein* (*Parm.* 137b3).

Chapter 1

1. In a note to their translation of the *Parmenides*, Mary Louise Gill and Paul Ryan write: "Like *to hen*, the expression *plethos*, which we render throughout as 'multitude,' is also ambiguous." (Indianapolis, IN: Hackett Publishing, 1996) p. 129, n. 7.

2. Various interpretations of the *Seventh Letter* invoke an unwritten doctrine. One of the best of these interpretations is John N. Findlay's *Plato: the Written and Unwritten Doctrines* (New York: Humanities Press, 1974). But in contrast to Findlay's Hegelian reading of the *Parmenides*, I argue that it is just such a dialectic that Parmenides' game ironically undermines. The unwritten in Plato's thinking is not a doctrine, it is being. Krämer is correct, I believe, in his assertion that Plato's *Seventh Letter* has methodological, rather than substantive meaning (H. J. Krämer, "Aretē bei Platon und Aristoteles. Zum Wesen und zur Geschichte der platonischen Ontologie," *Heidelberger Akademie der Wissenschaften*, 1959, p. 459).

3. Compare the *Sophist* on being as *koinōnein*, "to commune," or "to have intercourse." The Eleatic stranger challenges the notion of the harmonious blending of forms (248a ff.).

4. Martin Heidegger, *Being and Time* (New York: Harper and Row, 1962,), pp.46-49.

5. See the Parmenides poem (B850 ff.), for a parallel. The cosmology of mortals is presented as a verisimilar account: not completely false, but less trustworthy than the way of *alētheia*.

6. Compare "A Dialogue on Value," *The Journal of Speculative Philosophy*, V, no. 1, 1991, pp. 1-24.

7. 128a7-b8.

8. Compare Gadamer, *Plato's Dialectical Ethics*. On p. 119, Gadamer argues that the *aporia* of the *Parmenides* is resolved by a dialectical ethics as is discernible, for example, in the *Philebus*.

9. Compare Heidegger's comments: "for the Greeks an entirely natural interpretation of the meaning of Being was alive, that they read off the meaning of Being from the world as surrounding world. It is a natural and naive interpretation, since this meaning of Being is taken at once (precisely this characterizes naiveté) as the absolute meaning of Being, as Being pure and simple. This shows the Greeks had no explicit consciousness of the natural origin of their concept of Being, hence no insight into the determinate field from which they actually drew the meaning of Being. . ." *Plato's Sophist* (Bloomington: Indiana Univ. Press, 1997), pp. 186-187.

10. Compare E.S. Haldane, *Hegel's 'Lectures On the History of Philosophy,'* (New York: Humanities Press, 1958), Vol. II, pp. 66-67.

11. Viggo Rossvær, *The Laborious Game: a Study of Plato's Parmenides* (Oslo, Norway: Universitetsforlaget, 1983).

12. Robert S. Brumbaugh, *Plato On the One* (New Haven, CT: Yale University Press, 1960).

13. F. M. Cornford acknowledges that ambiguity resolves apparent contradiction, but he ignores Parmenides' miming of sophistry by misleadingly arguing in his *Plato and Parmenides* (London, 1939) that all the arguments in Parmenides' demonstration are valid. Mitchell Miller and R. E. Allen point out the provocative nature of Parmenides' uses of language, and the pedagogical role of the puzzlement induced by it (cf. Allen's *Plato's Parmenides*, rev. ed., New Haven, CT: Yale University Press, 1997). Constance Meinwald's *Plato's Parmenides* (New York: Oxford Univ. Press, 1991) does much to resolve the longstanding scholarly question on the unity of Parmenides' demonstration with the introductory discussion that precedes it; moreover, her interpretation shows the irrelevance of much of the vast literature on the third man argument. Unfortunately, she ignores Parmenides' mimicry of sophistry. Similarly, Robert C. Turnbull, in his *The Parmenides and Plato's Late Philosophy* (Toronto, Canada: Univ. of Toronto Press, 1998), neglects Plato's rhetorical subtlety and instead simply distinguishes between positive, Platonic hypotheses, and negative, Parmenidean ones in Parmenides' dialectical demonstration. The main lines of Turnbull's interpretation reiterate J. N. Findlay's treatment of the dialogue in *Plato: the Written and Unwritten Doctrines*. Findlay's brief but insightful Hegelian interpretation of the dialogue includes a distinction between the positive, expanded hypotheses, and negative, contracted ones.

14. Miller's excellent study acknowledges the pivotal role of the third beginning, and shows how the transcendence of the form is necessary for its immanence (*Plato's Parmenides*, p. 121). Unfortunately, he understands the role of the third beginning on the instant as an appendix that synthesizes the first and second beginnings, even describing the instant as foundational for the temporality of being. But the ironical framing of the third beginning alerts the critical participant that it too is a reduction to absurdity: it is the impossibility of the atomic instant that shows what is most provocative about Parmenides' troubling play. Like Miller, Robert Brumbaugh also recognized time to be a central theme in the *Parmenides*, but Brumbaugh interpreted the section on the instant (155e–157b), as a straightforward Platonic theory of time. See his *Plato on the One: the Hypotheses in the Parmenides* (New Haven, CT: Yale University Press, 1961). This failure to acknowledge irony (and the philosophical role of humor and puns) characterizes virtually all interpretations of the *Parmenides* to date. One exception is A. E. Taylor's *Plato: the Man and his Work* (Cleveland, OH: Meridian Books, 1963). But Taylor interprets the dialogue as an elaborate metaphysical joke.

15. R. E. Allen, in his discussion of Parmenides' demonstration of the divisibility of the one in hypothesis, notes that the argumentation recalls Zeno Fr. 3, and that the assumption in Parmenides' argument of the density of extended magnitudes would have been impossible if Zeno had not known the fact of incom-

mensurability (Allen, *Plato's Parmenides*, rev. ed., p. 29, n. 14). This is consistent with my claim that Plato's *Parmenides* evokes the incompleteness of mathematical representations.

16. The goddess in Parmenides' poem contrasts the signs, or *sēmata* (B8. 2) that characterize the way of being negatively as uncreated, imperishable, unchanging, and not incomplete, with the names used by mortals to describe the manifestation according to various interrelated characters (cf. her use of the adjectival *episēmos* at B19. 3).

17. Gadamer's interpretation of Platonic dialectic casts new light on the significance of Socratic skepticism. Of the impasses in the *Parmenides*, Gadamer writes: "If Plato makes the particular thing's methexis with the Idea into a problem, he is not thereby formulating an unsolved problem of his ontology: he is not posing the problem of individuation; instead, the aporia of this problem is itself meant, indirectly, to make the assumptions of the ontology visible: the fact that in the logos the individual entity is encountered only as an ahyletic *eidos*. The fact that the eidos is always the eidos of an individual thing does not require, for Plato or for Aristotle, an explanation of how the thing becomes individual, but always only—conversely— an interpretation of the claim to being of the eidos" (*Plato's Dialectical Ethics*, p. 96). But this reversal of the entire problematic, along with the fact that Parmenides' dialectical game reveals the ideas to be defined by difference, shows that the troubling play of the *Parmenides* anticipates recent efforts to overcome metaphysics.

18. With the following remarks, cf. Jacob Klein's treatment of *anamnēsis* and *eikasia* in his *A Commentary on Plato's Meno* (Chapel Hill: University of North Carolina Press, 1965) pp. 108–172.

19. On repetition and discontinuity, cf. John Sallis, *Chorology: On Beginning in Plato's Timaeus* (Bloomington: Indiana University Press, 1999).

20. From the Greek *eikones*; cf. *eikasia* likeness.

21. Sextus Empiricus describes the method of *epochē* as follows: "The Skeptic Way is a disposition to oppose phenomena to noumena to one another in any way whatever, with the result that, owing to the equipollence among the things and statements thus opposed, we are brought first to *epochē* and then to *ataraxia* ..." (translated by Benson Mates in *Sextus Empiricus, Outlines of Pyrrhonism* (Oxford: Oxford Univ. Press, 1996). Sextus goes on to describe a way of opposing phenomena to noumena, phenomena to phenomena, noumena to noumena, or *alternando*, phenomena to noumena in order to reveal contradictions that lead to *epochē*. Similarly, Parmenides' dialectical method ostensibly opposes noumena to noumena in the first beginning, noumena to phenomena in the second, and so forth. The difficulty is, of course, that Parmenides violates his own method in a number of provocative ways, and his allegedly dialectical procedure undermines itself by means of reflection on *chronos*.

22. Compare Erazim Kohák: "One hundred Confederate dollars may equal one Confederate war bond, yet that relationship does not give rise to value. Since

both relata are worthless, remaining so in their mutual relation, that relation remains itself devoid of value." ("Why is There Something Good, Not Simply Something? Reflections on the Ontological Status of Value," *The Journal of Speculative Philosophy*, V, no. 1, 1991).

Chapter 2

1. James R. Mensch, *Knowing and Being: A Postmodern reversal* (University Park: Pennsylvania State Univ. Press, 1996), p. 91.

2. On the *arithmos* function of the idea, see Jacob Klein, *Greek Mathematical Thought and the Origin of Algebra*, translated by Eva T. Brann (New York: Dover Publications, 1992).

3. This applies not only to intelligibility in general, but also to the reasonable interpretation of the Platonic dialogue. Most interpretations of the dialogues to date have erred by attempting to explain too much; they discover problems where Plato was evoking mysteries and theories where he offers only reductions to absurdity. One exception to this is Jacob Klein's reading of the *Meno* (cited above). On page 18, Klein points out that "All depends not only on what, but on how, under what circumstances, where, and in what context something is being said. Within the dialogue, the *logos* thus has two functions. One is mimetic, the other argumentative. Their interplay provides the texture into which we, the listeners or reader, have to weave our thread. That is how the drama itself, the 'deed,' the 'work,' the *ergon* of any of the dialogues, which is 'in words' (λογῳ) only, can encompass both, the dialogue's mimetic playfulness and its argumentative seriousness." The overarching theme of the *Parmenides* is that the nature of time makes such interweaving of logos functions inescapable.

4. G. W. F. Hegel recognized negative dialectic to be a feature of Eleatic thought, and also recognized the influence of Heraclitus on Plato. See his *Vorlesungen über die Geschichte der Philosophie*, translated as *Lectures on the History of Philosophy* by E. S. Haldane and Francis H. Simson, Vol. 1 (Lincoln: Univ. of Nebraska Press, 1995). Hegel's interpretation of Zeno's negative dialectic is laid out at pp. 261–278. On page 282, Hegel rightly claims that "Heraclitus may be called Plato's teacher." However, Hegel mistakenly asserts in *Die Philosophie Platons* (Stuttgart, Germany: Verlag Freies Geistesleben, 1962, pp. 60–61) that Plato was not fully aware of the dialectic in his own dialogues. On the contrary, in the *Parmenides* the irony lies in Parmenides' intentional exceeding of the limitations and possibilities of dialectic. The third beginning in the *Parmenides* (155e–157b, on the instant) shows that for Plato, the moment of becoming neither exists nor does not exist. This contrasts with Hegel's positive dialectic, in which the moment of becoming is characterized as both being and nonbeing.

5. Compare *Sophist*, 231b.

6. That the form of the *Parmenides* is ambiguous is immediately apparent when one considers the longstanding scholarly controversy over the status of the

third beginning (155e–157b), because this third beginning cannot be incorporated into the eightfold hypothetical method outlined by Parmenides at
135e–136c. Some interpreters fail even to acknowledge the controversy, and
instead view the third beginning as simply a continuation of the second. But at
155e4 Parmenides begins afresh: *eti dē to triton legōmen*, "Let us speak of it still a
third time."

7. Stanley Rosen, *Plato's Sophist* (New Haven, CT: Yale Univ. Press, 1983)
p. 3.

8. James R. Mensch develops this insight in *Knowing and Being: a Postmodern
Reversal*. However, this text simply repeats the conventional interpretation of
Platonism. Mensch does not consider irony, nor the fact that the poetic accounts
of the good in Plato's dialogues evoke the teleology of acts of human knowing.
But Parmenides' Socratic irony functions analogously to the activity of *Destruktion*
in Heidegger's thinking of being. This gives the dialogue a dimension that is not
represented in positive accounts of Plato's philosophy.

9. At *Theaetetus* 180d7–e1, Socrates alludes to the poem of Parmenides
(cf. Fr. 8), and the characterization of the absolute as unchanging (*akinēton*). Such
negative formulations indicate the limitations of logos: for example, the one in
itself may not be said to be either in motion or at rest. The full disclosure indicated by Parmenides' goddess of *alētheia* is denied to humans. Plato develops
Eleatic thought in the *Parmenides* by repeated emphasis on the nothingness of the
idea in itself.

10. Compare *Republic* 511b–c and 520c–d.

11. As part of his appropriation of certain aspects of Greek thought into
his account of the forgetting of being, Heidegger claims that presence determines
the Greek notion of truth: "If we remember the Greeks were visual, and if we
think of unconcealedness as openness and clearing, then the essential priority
of ἀλήθεια becomes understandable at one stroke. This reference to the basic
characteristic of the open in the essence of ἀλήθεια puts us on the path of the
'most natural' explanation of ἀλήθεια." *Parmenides*, translated by André Schuwer
and Richard Rojcewics, (Bloomington: Indiana Univ. Press, 1992), p. 145.
Heidegger's interpretations of Plato betray a singular inability to recognize and
appreciate irony. On the "visual" Greeks, cf. *Republic* 525a3–5, where Glaucon
notes that sight is aporetic; it presents us with contradictions that are only
resolved by thinking.

12. Kenneth Sayre, in his books *Plato's Late Ontology* (Princeton: Princeton
University Press, 1983) and *Parmenides' Lesson* (Notre Dame, IN: University of
Notre Dame Press, 1996), argues that Plato's thinking took a profoundly
Pythagorean turn in the later dialogues. But Sayre's interpretation relies heavily
on the reports of Aristotle, other scholastic platonists, and some neoplatonists:
namely, those that associated aspects of Plato's thought with Pythagoreanism.
Although Sayre cites Plato's use of nonliteral language as a conspicuous failure of
his "middle-period ontology" (before the development of the so-called "interme-

diate," or "early-late" ontologies), Sayre finds himself compelled to rely on metaphor in giving a Pythagorean account of the *Parmenides*: "But there is no necessity that the numbers or measures in question be mathematical in any strict sense. Among numbers might be temporal moments, which according to *Physics* 219b1–2 are measures of motion. And among measures might be those of moderation, which according to *Statesman* 284B1 accounts for the effectiveness of weaving and statecraft" (*Plato's Late Ontology*, p. 148). The points in the *Parmenides* that Sayre claims to be evidence of Plato's Pythagoreanism in fact support the thesis that Parmenides is ironically satirizing the Pythagoreans.

13. At *Sophist* 249c10–d1, the Stranger attributes the claim that the all does not move (*to pan hestēkos*) to the champions of the one. But the Platonic caricature of the original and greatest of all champions of the one—in the *Parmenides*—discloses a sense in which the one moves, does not move, and is neither in motion nor rest. He shows that no idea, entity, or event (including both unity and motion) is knowable in itself, but only in differentiation.

14. For a full discussion of the distinction, see Constance Meinwald, *Plato's Parmenides* (New York: Oxford University Press, 1991).

15. For a phenomenological description of transcendence, see Martin Heidegger, *The Metaphysical Foundations of Logic* (Bloomington: Indiana Univ. Press, 1984), pp. 166–167.

16. For discussion on the routes, see Jonathan Barnes, *The Presocratic Philosophers* (London: Routledge and Kegan Paul, 1979) vol. 1, pp. 157–165; Mourelatos, *Route of Parmenides*, pp. 47–73, 269–276; and Leonardo Tarán, *Parmenides* (Princeton, NJ: Princeton Univ. Press, 1965) pp. 32–40.

17. Heidegger, "Plato's Doctrine of Truth," in *Philosophy in the Twentieth Century*, p. 263.

18. Cf. *Philebus*, 34b.

19. R.E. Allen does an excellent job of articulating the aporetic structure of the *Parmenides* on the literal level. See his *Plato's Parmenides* (New Haven, CT: Yale Univ. Press, 1997). Allen employs logical discourse just to the point of indicating the limits of logos—but unlike Plato—goes no further. His caustic remarks on the insignificance of Socrates' use of analogy betray an un-Platonic distaste for figurative discourse: "Socrates' analogy of the Day has often been praised for its spirituality: it shows the immaterial nature of Ideas. In fact, it is a mere blunder in argument" (*Plato's Parmenides*, pp. 131–132). Allen follows this with a bifurcation: "if the analogy is consistent, it is not an analogy; and if it is inconsistent, it is not a reply" (p. 132). But he nowhere notes that Parmenides' intentionally sophistical and provocative analogy of the *eidos* to a sail fails insofar as it ignores essential differences: for meaning cannot be cut into pieces in the way that a sail can. Socrates' analogy of the day succeeds insofar as it is figurative and not intended as argument; as a comparison for illustration it is effective in getting its point across—a point Parmenides at 131b–c chooses to ignore. For Parmenides' game also implies that the unity of the *eidos* is analogous to a whole that exceeds the

sum of its parts. But even at the outset, his ironic miming of sophistry in his provocation of Socrates is apparent insofar as in his own poem on *phusis*–to which
Socrates refers at the outset–the goddess of truth made the same point regarding
the unity of what-is (cf. Fr. 8).

20. Compare Klein, *A Commentary on Plato's Meno*, p. 109. The *eidos* is only
apparently severed from time; the teleology of being toward the good involves
both recollection and imagined possibilities of future verification or failure. Like
Klein, James R. Mensch, in *Knowing and Being* (cited above) also evokes the extent
to which apparently nontemporal ideas (such as *mathematika*) are time-laden.

21. The predominant interpretation trivializes Zeno. For a more adequate
reading, see Wallace I. Matson's "Zeno Moves!" in *Before Plato*, ed. by Anthony
Preus (Albany: State University of New York Press, 2001) p.87. Like Paul Tannery
and Giovanni Casertano, Matson recognizes that Parmenides and Zeno were not
arguing that motion is impossible. On the contrary, it is the assumption that what
exists is a plurality of atomic units that leads to this absurd conclusion. In his
Parmenide. Il metodo, la scienza, l'esperienza (Naples, Italy: Loffrede Editore, 1978),
Casertano correctly interprets *to eon* as being, in its unity and plurality. Tannery,
in *Pour l'histoire de la science Hellène* (Paris: Alcan, 2d ed. 1930) mistakenly takes *to
eon* to mean spatiality, but his reading of Parmenides is at least an improvement
over typical treatments among English-speaking philosophers, who generally fail
to appreciate the negative aspect of Eleatic dialectic. One exception to this is
Alexander P.D. Mourelatos; see his *The Route of Parmenides* (New Haven, CT: Yale
Univ. Press, 1970), and "Some Alternatives in Interpreting Parmenides," *The
Monist* 62 (1979) pp. 3-14.

22. Compare *Philebus*, 35a–b.

23. Compare *Phaedo*, (102b–c).

24. *Parmenides*, 141e–142a; 159d–160b; 164a–b; 165e–166c.

Chapter 3

1. Heidegger, "Plato's Doctrine of Truth," p. 265.

2. This result is also noted by Jacques Derrida in *La Voix et le Pheénomeène*,
translated as *Speech and Phenomena and Other Essays on Husserl's Theory of Signs*
(Evanston, IL: Northwestern Univ. Press, 1973). The treatment in this text of
Husserl's struggle to overcome conventional Platonism in his version of phe-
nomenology (see, e.g., p. 53), owes much to the *Parmenides*, for Derrida's deconstruction of Husserl's distinction between expression (cf. disclosure 'toward-itself')
and indication (cf. disclosure toward-another) parallels Parmenides' reduction to
absurdity of Socrates' conception of form.

3. Mensch, *Knowing and Being: a Postmodern Reversal*, p. 5.

4. At 137c4, the Greek is ambiguous; this might also be rendered "if it is
one."

5. Parmenides' argument is: If it is like, then it is affected in the same way, but the one has no share of sameness, therefore it has no share of likeness. Parmenides is apparently demonstrating for Socrates the fallacy of denying the antecedent: he could have simply claimed that if the one is not the same then it is not like, and that if the one is not different then it is not unlike. The essential point is that ontological "differentiation" is not thinkable as the concept of difference.

6. Veronique Fóti has shown in her recent book *Vision's Invisibles* (Albany: State University of New York Press, 2003) how many modern philosophers have abandoned the rigorous level of self-critique implied in this remembering of the transcendent dimension.

7. I use the word "unground" in the sense of Schelling's *Ungrund*. See the *Philosophical Investigations into the Essence of Human Freedom and Related Matters*, which is included in Ernst Behler's collection on the *Philosophy of German Idealism* (New York: Continuum Press, 1987), pp. 276–278.

8. For an account of the dialectical interrelations between *logos* and *ergon* (action, deed), see Gadamer's *Dialogue and Dialectic*, ch. 1: "*Logos* and *Ergon* in Plato's Lysis," pp. 1–20.

9. Miller is correct when he argues that Parmenides' arguments constitute a systematic categorial analysis of the composite one that is "prototypical for (the philosopher) Aristotle's later doctrine" (*Plato's Parmenides*, pp. 95–6. Not only in the *Sophist*, but as early as the *Republic*, there are indications that Plato was considering the implications of teleology (e.g., the role of the good) and *dunameis* (see *Republic*, 477c1 ff.).

10. Perhaps the classic attempt to dispel ambiguity can be found in Gregory Vlastos, "The Third Man Argument in the *Parmenides*," in *Studies in Plato's Metaphysics*, ed. by R. E. Allen (London: Routledge and Kegan Paul, 1967), pp. 241–264.

Chapter 4

1. R.E. Allen, *Plato's Parmenides* (New Haven, CT: Yale Univ. Press, 1997), p. 5, note 5. Allen's point about syntactic amphiboly is a good one; all the more so in that the versions he gives of Parmenides' hypothesis as paraphrased in two different ways by Socrates (at 128a9–128b1 and 128d1) are less ambiguous than the versions in the earliest manuscripts.

2. Robert Brumbaugh, "Notes On the History of Plato's Text: with the *Parmenides* as a Case Study," *Paideia* (Fifth Annual, 1976), pp. 67–79.

3. The introductory passages of the *Parmenides* indicate that in Plato's eyes, although Zeno was a Parmenidean, his negative dialectic did not match the achievement of Parmenides' poetry (see, e.g., 136d–137b). Nevertheless, Parmenides' game both supports Zeno against Socrates' challenge, and indicates a reconfigured notion of participatory being that survives Zenonian paradox.

4. Leonard Brandwood, *The Chronology of Plato's Dialogues* (Cambridge: Cambridge Univ. Press, 1990), p. 251.

5. But W. K. C. Guthrie assigned the *Parmenides* a somewhat earlier date: "he was pretty certainly writing at about the time when Aristotle first came down from Macedonia, aged about 17, to join the Academy." A History of Greek Philosophy, Vol. V (Cambridge: Cambridge Univ. Press, 1978), p. 36. Also cf. Stanley Rosen, *Plato's Sophist: the Drama of Original and Image* (New Haven, CT: Yale University press, 1983).

6. Though not explicitly stated in the *Parmenides*, as it is in the *Sophist*, the principle of noncontradiction is invoked repeatedly. But the third beginning probes the bounds of being and logic by throwing into question the notion of simultaneity.

7. Similarly, being may be said to be divisible only if we imagine it to be something else besides being. Because no presently existing entity exhausts the meaning of the term "being," the transcendent dimension of the meaning of the term reasserts itself. John Palmer's inference that *to hen* in Plato's *Parmenides* simply refers to the physical universe (see Palmer, p. 186) betrays not only his inability to recognize irony, but, more seriously, a failure to think through the dialogue's inquiry into time.

8. Compare 133a–b; 141e–142a.

9. For example, in Parmenides' projected outline of his game at 135d–136c.

10. Cf. Edmund Husserl: "Each truth is an ideal unity with regard to an infinite and unbounded multiplicity of possible true statements having the same form and content," "Prolegomena" *Logische Untersuchungen*, ed. E. Holenstein, Husserlaina XVIII (The Hague: Martinus Nijhoff, 1975), p. 190. However, the reduction to absurdity of efforts to represent the being of time argues against a Husserlian reading of the *Parmenides*. Husserl recognized that the development of a rigorous distinction between the expression of identity in itself as opposed to the mere indication of existence requires the actuality of a punctual now, or instant. But Parmenides' negative dialectic throws into question the existence of such a moment of pure self-identity.

11. R. E. Allen points out, in his analysis of 142b–145a that a dilemma arose for Greek thinkers once the mathematicians proved the infinite divisibility of any line (*Plato's Parmenides*, revised edition, p. 254). For if the parts of the line have no magnitude then the line is not a magnitude. But if the parts have magnitude, the line is not finite. Allen believes the solution of this apparent paradox to be the notion of the potentially infinite, as found, for example, in Aristotle's *Physics*. But unfortunately, Allen argues that the *Parmenides* implies an actual infinite: "if the foregoing analysis of *Parmenides* 142b–145a is correct, the division of unity by being from which the numbers are derived implies an actual infinite" (p. 254), and "the process of division is possible because of the presence of parts" (p. 257). Allen apparently does not recognize that it is Parmenides' ironic application of the term "part" to a form that is the source of the antinomies. But it is precisely

this that allows Parmenides to also 'prove' in these same passages that the one is finite (144e–145a). Rather than proving an actual infinite, Parmenides demonstrates that there is no pure actuality, no is without was and will be. And yet, even in the effort to disclose the role of these nonpresent dimensions of temporality, the is of identity is required. Consequently, the effort to achieve univocity is doomed from the outset: differing logos functions are always necessarily interwoven.

12. For a full treatment of this problematic, see Verity Harte, *Plato on Parts and Wholes: the Metaphysics of Structure* (New York: Oxford University Press, 2002).

13. Miller's treatment of these passages in his *Plato's Parmenides*, shows this beautifully. But Parmenides is not only demonstrating for Socrates ambiguities that might be resolved by appealing to logical distinctions, he is also setting the stage for the upcoming demonstration as to why such efforts to achieve univocity are doomed from the outset. Thus, although the second beginning to some extent reinforces Socrates' appeal to the ideas as the way to resolve paradoxes, the inquiry into time (beginning at 151e) culminates in the third beginning's reduction to absurdity of the notion of absolute identity (155e–157b). The *Parmenides* not only anticipates Aristotle's critique of the 'theory' of ideas; it also shows the incompleteness of any categorial analysis of the existent one.

14. John Palmer, in his *Plato's Reception of Parmenides* (Oxford: Oxford University Press, 1999), mentions this argument in passing (pp. 240–41), in discussing a limitation of Constance Meinwald's interpretation. Palmer then relies on Meinwald's interpretation, but because he is so intent on demonstrating Plato's (and Parmenides') perspectivism, he neglects consideration of the role of irony in the *Parmenides*. Consequently, his interpretation completely misses the significance of the *Parmenides'* third beginning (155e–157b); Palmer simply refers to the section on the instant as "an appendix or corollary" (p. 157, n. 25). But because he ignores the irony of Parmenides' provocative game, Palmer does not realize the extent to which discourse itself is the theme of the *Parmenides*. Palmer does not acknowledge that Meinwald's distinction (which his interpretation employs) is a basis in the dialogue for developing the Platonic insight that all discourse is both toward-itself and toward-another.

15. Socrates' last lines in the dialogue are at 136d3–4, when he asks Zeno to demonstrate Parmenides' style of training in dialectic. Parmenides' demonstration begins at 137c4 and takes up the remainder of the dialogue (to 166c7).

Chapter 5

1. Mitchell Miller's interpretation in *Plato's Parmenides* is particularly effective in its account of the introductory passages of the dialogue. But Miller seems to forget about irony in his treatment of Parmenides' gymnastic. For example, although he acknowledges that Parmenides' logos of the instant is paradoxical (p. 114), Miller also writes, "there will be countless 'instants' in the course of the

thing's existence" (p. 118). On the next page he refers to "the everpresence of the 'instant,'" and describes a thing as "constantly transiting between contrary states" and "constantly passing through the 'instant'" (p. 119). But if the atomic instant is a nonpossibility, a thing cannot pass through it.

2. Compare *homoiousthai* at 156b

3. For example, in Parmenides' sail analogy, and his mimings of sophistry in the second beginning.

4. Jacob Klein uses this couplet from Chaucer's *The Canterbury Tales, The Prologue* as epigraph to his commentary on the *Meno*: "Eek Plato seith, who-so that can him rede, The wordes mote be cosin to the dede" in *A Commentary on Plato's Meno* (Chapel Hill: The University of North Carolina Press, 1965).

Chapter 6

1. On *tropos* (mode, way, manner), cf. Socrates' question about philosophical training at 135d8-9.

2. Parmenides repeats the word *chōris* four times in this initial inference.

3. Compare Plato's *Sophist*: the *megista genē* have contraries but are indefinable. But because man, fire, and water, although definable, have no contraries, the *Parmenides* indicates that insofar as discursive clarification itself is only possible on the basis of indefinables, intelligibility is permeated by the unintelligibility of *chōrismos*.

4. Compare *Sophist*, 259e–260a.

Chapter 7

1. Compare 139a–b. Parmenides' irony is apparent insofar as he has already acknowledged that what is not in motion is not necessarily at rest.

2. Compare *Sophist* 258d7–e3; the Eleatic Stranger makes the same point Parmenides makes at 164c1 ff., that an other is always an other of an other (*heteron heterou*). The Stranger claims that this *archē* of otherness that differentiates all entities is the real nonbeing (258e). The Stranger characterizes his arguments at this point as a trespass (258c) against Parmenides' goddess of *alētheia* (because he and Theaetetus are speaking of what is not). It is interesting to note the correspondence of his conclusions with those of the Platonic Parmenides.

3. This shift occurred within the second beginning, at 143a, with the suggestion of another fresh start, or return to the beginnings.

Bibliography

Ackrill, J. L. 1957. "Plato and the Copula: Sophist 251-259," in *Plato* I. *Metaphysics and Epistemology*, (ed.), G. Vlastos, pp. 210-222.

Allen, R. E. (ed.). 1967. *Studies in Plato's Metaphysics*. London: Routledge and Kegan Paul.

——. 1997. *Plato's Parmenides: Translated with Comment*, 2nd ed. New Haven, CT: Yale University Press.

——. and Furley, D. J. (eds.). 1975. *Studies in Presocratic Philosophy* II: *The Eleatics and Pluralists*. London: Routledge and Kegan Paul.

Barnes, J. 1979. 'Parmenides and the Eleatic One.' *Archiv für Geschichte der Philosophie*, 61:1-21.

——. 1982. *The Presocratic Philosophers*, 2nd ed., The Arguments of the Philosophers. London: Routledge and Kegan Paul.

——. 1987. *Early Greek Philosophy*. London: Penguin Books.

Barrett, W. B. and Aiken, H. (eds.). 1962. *Philosophy in the Twentieth Century*, vol. 2. New York: Random House.

Behler, E. (ed.). 1987. *Philosophy of German Idealism*. New York: Continuum Press.

Bloom, A. 1991. *The Republic of Plato*. New York: Basic Books.

Booth, N. B. 1957. "Were Zeno's Arguments Directed Against the Pythagoreans?" *Phronesis*, 2:90-103.

Brandwood, L. 1976. *A Word Index to Plato*. Leeds, UK: W. S. Maney & Son.

——. 1990. *The Chronology of Plato's Dialogues*. Cambridge: Cambridge University Press.

——. 1992. "Stylometry and Chronology," in R. Kraut (ed.), The Cambridge Companion to Plato (Cambridge: Cambridge University Press): 90-120.

Brumbaugh, R. S. 1961. *Plato on the One: The Hypotheses in the Parmenides*. New Haven, CT: Yale University Press.

Burnet, J. 1930. *Early Greek Philosophy*, 4th ed. London: Black.

——. (ed.). 1997. *Platonis Opera, vol. 2: Parmenides, Philebus, Symposium, Phaedrus, Alcibiades, Hipparchus*. Oxford: Oxford University Press.

Casertano, G. 1978. *Parmenide. Il metodo, la scienza, l'esperienza*. Naples, Italy: Loffrede Editore.

Cherniss, H. 1932. "Parmenides and the *Parmenides* of Plato." *American Journal of Philology*, 53:122-38.

——. 1959. "Plato (1950-1957)," part I. *Lustrum*, 4:5-308.

Cornford, F. M. "Mysticism and Science in the Pythagorean Tradition." *Classical Quartely*, 16:137–50; 17:1–12.

———. 1933. "Parmenides' Two Ways." *Classical Quarterly*, 27:97–111.

———. 1935. *Plato's Theory of Knowledge: The Theatetus and the Sophist of Plato Translated with a Running Commentary.* London: Routledge and Kegan Paul.

———. 1939. *Plato and Parmenides: Parmenides' Way of Truth and Plato's Parmenides Translated with an Introduction and a Running Commentary.* London: Routledge and Kegan Paul.

Curd, P. K. 1989. "Some Problems of Unity in the First Hypothesis of the *Parmenides*." *Southern Journal of Philosophy*, 27:347–59.

———. 1990. "Parmenides 142b5–144e7: the 'Unity is Many' Arguments." *Southern Journal of Philosophy*, 28:19–35.

Derrida, J. 1973. *La Voix et le Phénomène*, translated by D. Allison as *Speech and Phenomena and Other Essays on Husserl's Theory of Signs.* Evanston, IL: Northwestern University Press.

Findlay, J. N. 1974. *Plato: The Written and Unwritten Doctrines.* New York: Humanities Press.

Fine, G. 1978. "Knowledge and Belief in *Republic* V." *Archiv für Geschichte der Philosophie*, 60:121–39.

———. 1990. "Knowledge and Belief in *Republic* V–VII," in Everson, S. (ed.), *Epistemology*, Companions to Ancient Thought, I (Cambridge: Cambridge University Press): 85–115.

Friedländer, P. 1969. *Plato*, translated by Hans Meyerhoff. Princeton, NJ: Princeton University Press.

Furley, D. J. 1973. "Notes on Parmenides," in E. N. Lee, A. P. D. Mourelatos, and R. M. Rorty (eds.), *Exegesis and Argument: Studies in Greek Philosophy Presented to Gregory Vlastos, Phronesis.* supp. vol. I (Assen, Netherlands: Van Gorcum): 1–15.

———. and Allen, R. E. (eds.). 1970. *Studies in Presocratic Philosophy, I: The Beginnings of Philosophy.* London: Routledge and Kegan Paul.

Furth, M. 1968. "Elements of Eleatic Ontology." *Journal of the History of Philosophy*, 6:111–32.

Gadamer, H. G. 1980. *Dialogue and Dialectic: Eight Hermeneutical Studies on Plato.* New Haven, CT: Yale University Press.

———. 1991. *Plato's Dialectical Ethics.* New Haven, CT: Yale University Press.

Gill, M. (with P. Ryan). 1996. *Plato: Parmenides.* Indianapolis, IN: Hackett.

Grube, G. M. A. 1935. *Plato's Thought.* London: Methuen.

Guthrie, W. K. C. 1962. *A History of Greek Philosophy, I: The Earlier Presocratics and the Pythagoreans.* Cambridge: Cambridge University Press.

———. 1965. *A History of Greek Philosophy, II: The Presocratic Tradition from Parmenides to Democritus.* Cambridge: Cambridge University Press.

——. 1975. A History of Greek Philosophy, IV: Plato, the Man and His Dialogues: The Earlier Period. Cambridge: Cambridge University Press.

——. 1978. A History of Greek Philosophy, V: The Later Plato and the Academy. Cambridge: Cambridge University Press.

Haldane, E. S. 1958. Hegel's Lectures on the History of Philosophy. New York: Humanities Press.

Hamlyn, D. W. 1955. "The Communion of Forms and the Development of Plato's Logic." Philosophical Quarterly, 5:289–302.

Hegel, G. W. F. 1962. Die Philosophie Platons. Stuttgart: Verlag Freies Geistesleben.

——. 1995. Vorlesungen über die Geschichte der Philosophie, translated as Lectures on the History of Philosophy by E. S. Haldane and F. Simson. Lincoln: University of Nebraska Press.

Heidegger, M. 1962. Being and Time. New York: Harper and Row.

——. 1962. Platons Lehre von der Wahrheit, translated as "Plato's Doctrine of Truth." Philosophy in the Twentieth Century, Vol. 2, in Barrett, W. and Aiken, H. (eds.). New York: Random House.

——. 1968. What is Called Thinking? New York: Harper and Row.

——. 1984. The Metaphysical Foundations of Logic. Bloomington: Indiana University Press.

——. 1991. The Principle of Reason, translated by Reginald Lilly. Bloomington: Indiana University Press.

——. 1992. Parmenides, translated by A. Schuwer and R. Rojcewics. Bloomington: Indiana University Press.

——. 1997. Plato's Sophist. Bloomington: Indiana University Press.

Husserl, E. 1975. "Prolegomena" Logische Untersuchungen, in Holenstein, E. (ed.) Husserliana XVIII. The Hague: Nijhoff.

Jaeger, W. 1947. The Theology of the Early Greek Philosophers, trans. E. S. Robinson, Gifford Lectures 1936. Oxford: Clarendon Press.

Kahn, C. H. 1969. "The Thesis of Parmenides." Review of Metaphysics, 23:700–24.

——. 1981. "Some Philosophical Uses of 'To Be' in Plato." Phronesis, 26:105–34.

——. 1988. "Being in Parmenides and Plato." La parola del passato, 43:237–61.

Kirk, G. S., Raven, J. E., and Schofield, M. 1983. The Presocratic Philosophers, 2nd ed. Cambridge: Cambridge University Press.

Klein, J. 1992. Greek Mathematical Thought and the Origin of Algebra, translated by E. Brann. New York: Dover Publications.

Krämer, H. J. 1959. "Aretē bei Platon und Aristoteles. Zum Wesen und zur Geschichte der platonischen Ontologie." Heidelberger Akademie der Wissenschaften, p. 459.

——. 1969. "ΕΠΕΚΕΙΝΑ ΤΗΕ ΟΨΣΙΑΣ: Zu Platon, Politeia 509B." Archiv für Geschichte der Philosophie, 51:1–30.

Krüger, G. 1973. Einsicht und Leidenschaft: Das Wesen des platonischen Denkens, 4th ed. Frankfurt: V. Klostermann.

Lachs, J. and Kohák, E. 1991. "A Dialogue on Value." *The Journal of Speculative Philosophy*, Vol. V, no. 1, pp. 1–24.

Lamm, R. C. 1996. *The Humanities in Western Culture*. Boston: McGraw Hill.

Lee, H. D. P. 1936. *Zeno of Elea: A Text, with Translation and Notes*, Cambridge Classical Studies, I. Cambridge: Cambridge University Press.

Matson, W. 2001. "Zeno Moves!" in Preus, A. (ed.), *Essays in Ancient Greek Philosophy* VI: *Before Plato*. Albany: State University of New York Press.

Meinwald, C. 1991. *Plato's Parmenides*. New York: Oxford University Press.

Mensch, J. R. 1996. *Knowing and Being: A Postmodern Reversal*. University Park: Pennsylvania State University Press.

———. 1981. *The Question of Being in Husserl's Logical Investigations*. The Hague, Netherlands: M. Nijhoff.

Miller, M. 1980. *The Philosopher in Plato's Statesman*. The Hague, Netherlands: Nijhoff.

———. 1986. *Plato's Parmenides: The Conversion of the Soul*. Princeton, NJ: Princeton University Press.

Moravscik, J. 1982. "Forms and Dialectic in the Second Half of the *Parmenides*," in M. Schofield and M. C. Nussbaum (eds.), *Language and Logos: Studies in Ancient Greek Philosophy Presented to G. E. L. Owen* (Cambridge: Cambridge University Press): 135–53.

Morrow, G. R., and Dillon, J. 1987. *Proclus' Commentary on Plato's Parmenides*. Princeton, NJ: Princeton University Press.

Mourelatos, A. P. D. 1970. *The Route of Parmenides: A Study of Word, Image and Argument in the Fragments*. New Haven, CT: Yale University Press.

———. 1979. "Some Alternatives in Interpreting Parmenides," in *The Monist* 62:3–14.

———. (ed.). 1993. *The Pre-Socratics: A Collection of Critical Essays*, 2nd ed. Princeton, NJ: Princeton University Press.

Nehamas, A. 1981. "On Parmenides' Three Ways of Inquiry." *Deucalion*, 33–4:97–111.

———. 1981. "Participation and Predication in Plato's Later Thought." *Review of Metaphysics*, 36:343–74.

———. 1999. *Virtues of Authenticity: Essays on Plato and Socrates*. Princeton, NJ: Princeton University Press.

Owen, G. E. L. 1975. "Eleatic Questions," in Allen and Furley (eds.): 48–81.

———. 1966. "Plato and Parmenides on the Timeless Present." *Monist*, 50:317–40.

———. 1971. "Plato on Not-Being," in *Plato* I, G. Vlastos (ed.). New York: Doubleday.

Owens, J. 1974. "The Physical World of Parmenides," in J. R. O'Donnell (ed.), *Essays in Honour of Anton Charles Pegis* (Toronto, Canada: Pontifical Institute of Medieval Studies): 378–95.

———. 1975. "Naming in Parmenides," in J. Mansfield and L. M. de Rijk (eds.), *Kephalaion: Studies in Greek Philosophy and its Continuation Offered to*

Professor C. J. de Vogel, Philosophical Texts and Studies, 23 (Assen: Van Gorcum): 16–25.

Palmer, J. 1999. *Plato's Reception of Parmenides*. Oxford: Oxford University Press.

Peck, A. L. 1952. "Plato and the ΜΕΓΙΣΤΑ ΓΕΝΗ of the Sophist: A Reinterpretation," in *Classical Quarterly*. n.s. 2:32–56.

Priest, G., Routley, R. and Norman, J. (eds.) 1989. *Paraconsistent Logic: Essays on the Inconsistent*. Munich: Philosophia Verlag.

Preus, A. and Anton, A. P. (eds.) 1983. *Essays in Ancient Greek Philosophy II*. Albany: State University of New York Press.

——. (ed.). 2001. *Essays in Ancient Greek Philosophy VI: Before Plato*. Albany: State University of New York Press.

Raven, J. E. 1965. *Plato's Thought in the Making: A Study of the Development of his Metaphysics*. Cambridge: Cambridge University Press.

Robinson, R. 1953. *Plato's Earlier Dialectic*, 2nd ed. Oxford: Clarendon Press.

Robinson, T. M. 1975. "Parmenides on the Real in its Totality." *Monist*, 62:54–60.

Rosen, S. 1983. *Plato's Sophist*. New Haven, CT: Yale University Press.

Ross, W. D. 1951. *Plato's Theory of Ideas*. Oxford: Clarendon Press.

Runciman, W. G. 1962. *Plato's Later Epistemology*, Cambridge Classical Studies. Cambridge: Cambridge University Press.

Ryle, G. 1939. "Plato's Parmenides," in Allen (ed.), 1965: 97–147.

Sallis, J. 1996. *Being and Logos: Reading the Platonic Dialogues*. Bloomington: Indiana University Press.

——. 1999. *Chorology: on beginning in Plato's Timaeus*. Bloomington: Indiana University Press.

Sayre, K. 1978. "Plato's *Parmenides*: Why the Eight Hypotheses Are Not Contradictory." *Phronesis* vol. 23, no. 2:133–150.

——. 1983. *Plato's Late Ontology: A Riddle Resolved*. Princeton, NJ: Princeton University Press.

——. 1996. *Parmenides' Lesson: Translation and Explication of Plato's Parmenides*. Notre Dame: University of Notre Dame Press.

Schelling, F. W. J. 1987. *Philosophical Investigations into the Essence of Human Freedom and Related Matters*, translated by Priscilla Hayden-Roy in *Philosophy of German Idealism*, E. Behler (ed.), New York: Continuum Press.

Schofield, M. 1970. "Did Parmenides Discover Eternity?" *Archiv für Geschichte der Philosophie*, 52:113–35.

——. 1972. "The Dissection of Unity in Plato's *Parmenides*." *Classical Philology*, 67: 102–9.

——. 1974. "Plato on Unity and Sameness." *Classical Quarterly*, n.s. 24:33–45.

——. 1977. "The Antinomies of Plato's *Parmenides*." *Classical Quarterly*, n.s. 71:139–58.

Spangler, G. A. 1979. "Aristotle's Criticism of Parmenides in *Physics* I." *Apeiron*, 13:92–103.

Speiser, A. 1959. *Ein Parmenideskommentar: Studien zur platonischen Dialektik*, 2nd ed. Stuttgart, Germany: Köhler.

Sprague, R. K. 1962. *Plato's Use of Fallacy: A Study of the Euthydemus and Some Other Dialogues*. London: Routledge and Kegan Paul.

Szabó, A. 1955. "Eleatica." Acta Antiqua, 3:67–102.

——. 1992. "La filosofia degli Eleati e il Parmenide di Platone," in V. Vitiello (ed.), *Il 'Parmenide' di Platone*, Laboratorio, 8 (Naples, Italy: Guida): 31–46.

Tannery, P. 1930. *Pour l'histoire de la science Hellène: De Thalès à Empédocle*, 2nd ed. Paris: Alcan.

Tarán, L. 1965. *Parmenides: A Text with Translation, Commentary, and Critical Essays*. Princeton, NJ: Princeton University Press.

Taylor, A. E. 1896–1897. 'On the Interpretation of Plato's *Parmenides*.' *Mind*, 5: 297–326; 483–507; 6:9–39.

——. 1929. *Plato: The Man and His Work*, 3rd ed. London: Methuen.

——. 1934. *The Parmenides of Plato: Translated into English with Introduction and Appendices*. Oxford: Clarendon Press.

Turnbull, R. 1983. "Episteme and Doxa: Some Reflections on Eleatic and Heraclitean Themes in Plato," in and Preus, A. and Anton, A. P. (eds.), *Essays in Ancient Greek Philosophy*, II. Albany: State University of New York Press.

——. 1998. *The Parmenides and Plato's Late Philosophy*. Toronto, Canada: Toronto University Press.

Vlastos, G. 1946. "Parmenides' Theory of Knowledge." *Transactions and Proceedings of the American Philological Association*, 77:66–77.

——. 1965. "The Third Man Argument in the Parmenides," in R. E. Allen (ed.), *Studies in Plato's Metaphysics*. London: Routledge and Kegan Paul.

——. (ed.). 1971. *Plato I. Metaphysics and Epistemology*. New York: Doubleday Anchor.

——. 1973. *Platonic Studies*. Princeton, NJ: Princeton University Press.

White, N. P. 1993. *Plato, Sophist: Translated, with Introduction and Notes*. Indianapolis, IN: Hackett.

Williams, C. J. F. 1981. *What is Existence?* Oxford: Clarendon Press.

Index

◙◙◙

Aeschylus, 14

Agamemnon, 14

aisthēsis (sense perception), 48

aitia (occasion), 24

alētheia (truth; disclosure), 4, 8, 13, 16, 18, 19-20, 21, 28, 30, 31, 35, 38, 44, 48, 51, 53-54, 68, 69, 72, 87, 88, 125, 168; and the allegory of the cave, 23; contrast between modes of, 156, 160; differential, 172; and formal repetition, 26; incommensurability in, 99; in logos, 63-64, 94, 120-21, 150, 173; modes of, 176-77; philosophical, 52; transcendent wholeness of, 50; unmixed, 120, 125-28, 129. *See also* Parmenides, poem of, and the discourse of the goddess (of *alētheia*)

Allen, R. E., 32, 183n. 13, 183-84n. 15, 187-88n. 19; on the actual infinite, 190-91n. 11

alogos (moment of silence), 143, 167, 175

ambiguity, 33, 168, 183n. 13, 191n. 13; of existence, 4; of experience, 134-35; formal, 149-50; in language, 93; ontological, 137; as unity in opposition, 50-51. *See also chronos,* ambiguities relating to

anamnēsis (recollection), 21, 35

anhypotheton (absolute), 138

anomoiou (unlikeness). *See* likeness / unlikeness

Antiphon, 43, 92, 120

apeiron (undefined), 76, 136, 151, 152, 154

apeiron plethos (indefinite multitude), 97

Apollo, 14

Apology (Plato), 21

apophatic dialogue, 9

aporia/aporiai (impasse[s]), 11, 15, 17, 22, 27, 32, 35, 36, 39, 42, 44, 48, 54, 57, 60, 72, 125-26, 139, 154, 173; disclosure of, 170; greatest, 119; hidden, 137; and ideal being, 103; moving beyond, 131-36; of perception, 59

archai (origins), 7, 8, 16, 17, 37, 53, 55, 58-59, 65, 66, 75, 78, 89, 92; *archai* oppositions, 50, 94, 115, 134, 135, 136-37, 138-40, 155; of intelligibility, 93

archē (beginning), 7, 65, 69, 75, 115, 121, 139, 140, 192n. 2

aretē (excellence), 23, 31; of the philosopher, 29

Aristotle (minor interlocutor of Plato's *Parmenides*), 2, 11, 15, 38-39, 98, 102, 103, 110, 113, 148, 159, 169; and reductionism, 104

Aristotle (philosopher), 50, 89, 94, 190n. 5

atomic instant, the, 183n. 7, 191-92n. 1

atopon (extraordinary), 128

Attic tragedy. *See* Greek tragedy

axio-ontological differentiation, 176

being, 21-22, 55, 59, 88, 97, 100, 121, 138-39, 160, 163, 175, 182n. 9, 190n. 7; conceptual representations of, 101; degrees of, 58; as a dialogical relating to the other, 31-36, 156; distinguished from unity, 98, 156, 167, 190-91n. 11; as *energeia*, 41; fragmentation of, 131; instantiation of, 96; intelligibility of, 167-68; as *koinōnein*, 182n.

third man, 54. *See also* Zeno,
paradoxes of
Parmenides, 17, 25-27, 70-72, 74-80,
137-38, 189n. 3; and actuality,
190-91n. 11; counterchallenge to
Socrates, 94-95; dialectical game of
(troubling play of), 1-4, 8, 12, 16, 30,
33-36, 45, 61, 62, 67-68, 72-73, 100,
106-7, 133-34, 173-74, 187-88n. 19;
irony of, 122-25, 162-63, 185n. 4,
191-92n. 1, 192n. 1; on largeness and
smallness, 108-11, 160, 162; laws of in
native Elea, 16; and the sharing
metaphor of meaning and entity, 6;
second synopsis of, 114-17; on
singular intelligibility, 80-84; and
Socrates, 1-10; synopsis at 142a,
85-86; synopsis at 159a-b, 150-52. *See
also* dialectic, negative; logos; one that
is not, the; Parmenides, eightfold
hypothetical method of; Parmenides,
poem of; Socrates
Parmenides, eightfold hypothetical
method of, 8-9, 79; and the first
beginning, 115, 164-65, 166; and
the second beginning, 94-99, 115-16,
121, 123, 127-28, 144, 155, 159, 168,
173-74, 191n. 13; and the third (*to
triton*) beginning, 8, 97, 122-23, 134,
137, 146, 173, 183n. 14, 185n. 4,
185-86n. 6, 191nn. 13-14; and the
fourth beginning (many toward the
one), 145-46, 159; and the fifth
beginning (many toward themselves),
151, 152-53; and the sixth beginning,
159-61, 163-64, 167; and the seventh
beginning, 163-64, 165, 166-67; and
the eighth beginning, 165, 167, 170
Parmenides, poem of, 50-51, 59, 182n. 5;
and the discourse of the goddess (of
aletheia), 51, 125, 184n. 16, 186n. 9,
192n. 2; structure of, 52
Parmenides (Plato), 1-2, 9, 11-12, 21, 22,
26-27, 28-29, 31, 33, 41, 46, 48, 49,
53-55, 60, 65, 86-87, 143-44, 155;
ambiguity of, 55; as analogue for
disclosure of any entity, 124; as an

aporetic dialogue, 167, 169, 172,
187-88n. 19; *chronos* as thematic in,
92, 156-57; and contradictions,
32-33; date of composition, 94, 190n.
5; as literal or figurative, 134-36, 144;
and the metaphor of sharing, 35;
primary aim of, 110-11; structure of,
91-92, 141, 177, 185-86n. 6; synopsis
of questions concerning, 15-18;
unifying theme of, 92-94; unity in,
19-20, 25
participatory being, 30, 35-36, 41,
49-50, 64, 69-70, 74, 87, 107, 140
parts, and the whole, 74-75, 95, 102-3,
104, 147-50 See also *choris* (otherwise
than), as nonidentity; wholeness
Phaedrus (Plato), 15, 20-21, 92
phantasma (phantasm), 169-70, 172, 175
Philebus (Plato), 19, 28, 134-35, 175
philoneikia (contentiousness), 73
philosophy, 29, 43, 45-46, 52, 55, 59-60,
63, 69, 141; as dialogical, 20-21; goal
of, 27; as a *meta hodos*, 171; nature of,
4-5, 16, 18; sign language of, 10-13;
unity of, 41
pistis (trust), 35, 53, 69
Plato, 1, 6, 15, 17, 21, 26-27, 51-53,
92-93, 156-58; conception of the
task of dialectic, 180n. 11; on
individual self-interest, 14;
Pythagorean thinking of, 186-87n. 12;
on time and difference, 172-77. *See
also specifically listed dialogues of*
Platonic dialogue, 4, 13-14, 18, 87, 116,
185n. 3; as erotic, 11
Platonism, 1, 8, 46, 87-89, 188n. 2
pluralization, 166; and formal ambiguity,
149-51
Plutarch, 15
poiēsis (creativity), 9, 13, 16, 20, 29, 66,
86, 88, 93; of imagination, 25;
philosophical, 43, 170; and the power
of dialectic, 51-56
praxis, and disclosure through logos,
116-17
presence, antinomies of, 99-103
projected schema, 114-15